Your heart knows
the way.
Run in that
direction.
— Rumi

SHACKLED

A JOURNEY FROM
POLITICAL IMPRISONMENT TO FREEDOM

To Kim.

With love & gratitude

ADAM SIDDIQ

D1110337

Copyright © 2017 by LINEAGE PUBLISHING, INC.
All rights reserved.

No part of this book may be reproduced in any form or by any electronic or mechanical means, including information storage and retrieval systems, without written permission from the author, except for the use of brief quotations in a book review.

For information about this title or to order other books and/or electronic media, contact the publisher:

LINEAGE PUBLISHING
1320 E. 18th Street,
Los Angeles, CA 90021
www.lineagepublishing.com
info@lineagepublishing.com

ISBN: 978-1-946852-00-7

Printed in the United States of America.

This book is dedicated to everyone who's ever suffered. My family has suffered tremendously, and so many people are suffering today. Despite all the suffering in the world, my mind often goes to a beautiful message from Rumi:

"The wound is the place where the Light enters you."

The body and psyche can break down, but the soul is invincible. We are made of the Light. Let's always remember that and shine brightly. Let's gather together and celebrate that Light which pierces the illusory veil of separateness, waking the world up to a greater, kinder, and unified humanity.

CONTENTS

Adam's Note VII
A Plan For A New Afghanistan 1

PART I 27

One 29

Two 34

Three 38

Four 46

Five 51

Six 55

Seven 57

Eight 62

Nine 67

Ten 71

Eleven 76

Twelve 80

Thirteen 84

Fourteen 90

Fifteen 94

Sixteen 96

Seventeen 104

Eighteen 108

Nineteen 115

Twenty 121

Twenty-One 128

Twenty-Two 133

Twenty-Three...144
Twenty-Four...148
Twenty-Five..150

PART II...**159**
Twenty-Six...161
Twenty-Seven...168
Twenty-Eight..173
Twenty-Nine..180
Thirty..187

PART III...**189**
Thirty-One...191
Thirty-Two...196
Thirty-Three..201
Thirty-Four..218
Thirty-Five...225
Thirty-Six...230

PART IV...**241**
Thirty-Seven..243
Thirty-Eight...246
Thirty-Nine..252
Forty..256
Forty-One..267
Forty-Two..269
Forty-Three...278
Forty-Four...282
Forty-Five..285

Epilogue...288
Gratitude..297

ADAM'S NOTE

I've written this book with the help and on behalf of my grandfather, Khaled Siddiq. This is his life story written from his perspective, in his voice. It is the result of a series of interviews and heartfelt conversations between my grandfather and me. For me personally, the process of writing this book has been a sacred experience.

I first heard my grandpa's story when I was six. I was sitting in our living room one day when my grandparents came to visit. Someone asked my grandpa a question about his past and I learned that when he was six years old, he had been imprisoned. Suddenly, I realized I had no problems in my life. My grandpa talked about his adversity as if it was no big deal. On top of that, he lived with such profound joy and optimism. Observing my grandpa, I realized I had no reason not to live optimistically, no matter what challenges I faced.

That was the last I heard of my grandpa's life in Afghanistan until he published a book in Farsi entitled, "From My Memories." He told me that he'd have it translated in English, and that, when he did, he'd give me the first copy. Every time he visited for the next year, I'd ask him, "Is the book done?"

"Not yet," he'd say. "As soon as it's done, I'll give you the first copy."

Finally, the book was finished, and true to his word, he gave me the first copy. As soon as I could, I dove into it, excited to finally read the fine details of his life story. But soon, all my anticipation fell to shambles at my disappointment in the translation. Not only that, many of the details I had longed to know were missing.

"Baba *jan*, the translator has failed to communicate all the emotion of your life experience. I'd like to write the book with you instead," I told him.

So began the process of drafting *Shackled*. I committed time over the next few years interviewing my grandpa in-depth. It began as a part-time project and soon evolved into a full-time endeavor to the point where I actually moved in with my grandpa and lived with him for nearly a year.

My grandpa's life story deals with a significant amount of tragedy, experiences that bring up raw emotions. To get all the details from him wasn't as easy as asking a few questions. It often took weeks for my grandpa to open up, and I had to learn not only what to ask, but how to ask and when. For example, I learned to avoid asking questions about the sad times in his life at night because then he would have nightmares and difficulty sleeping.

I had my own "unusual" experiences writing the book as well. As strange as it sounds, there were many nights when I couldn't sleep until 4:00 a.m. because I felt the presence of my great-grandfathers and other ancestors in the room with me. This was not a haunting. It energized me. I felt as if they were helping me tell our family's story, and it showed me that, while at first I began writing the book out of a hunger to know my grandpa, I was really writing it for a greater purpose—one that I don't fully understand yet.

Shackled is a true story and I have been greatly honored to have my grandpa's trust to write about something so raw for him. I hope any reader will feel likewise honored to learn the story of my family and the very real challenges and traumas they faced.

My grandfather named me Adam, a name that's uncommon in Farsi but translates to "human." He chose this name, intending that I do my best in life to embody humanity and expand that spirit of humanity with anything I do in my life. *Shackled* is part of that mission.

I hope my grandfather's story brings perspective to any adversity you may be facing in your own life and that it encourages you to add your own humanity to the world. Very simply, I hope it touches your heart.

A NOTE ABOUT THE NAMES

In Afghan culture, it's typical for some people to have a compound name, like Ghulam Siddiq, Ghulam Nabi, Abdul Hamid, Abdul Azim, Abdul Samad, or Mohammad Omar. To ensure the flow of the story, after the initial formal introductions of these names, in some cases I have left only the core family name (Samad, Amid, Habib, Azim, Rahman). In certain cases, like Abdul-Khaliq, where a full first name is not necessarily a compound name, we have left the name as is.

Also, you will see some names ending with the word *"Khan"* or *"jan"*. In Afghan society, *"Khan"* is a term of respect offered to a reputable man whereas *"jan"* is a term of endearment, generally added to the names of family members and close friends. To honor the formality of Afghan culture and to ensure ease of story flow, I have introduced people and showcased their level of importance by addressing them as *"Khan"* or *"jan"* at least once in the storyline.

Lastly, you'll notice some names with a title in front of them, as in the case of *Nayeb-Salar* Ghulam Nabi Khan Charkhi. The title represents their political rank. In terms of Charkhi, that is not my family's surname, but how my family has been known in Afghanistan since the time of my great-great-grandfather, *Sepah-Salar* Ghulam Haidar Khan Charkhi. Therefore, I have introduced these names with political ranks once to give respect to the men while maintaining a better story flow.

A PLAN FOR A NEW AFGHANISTAN

Sepah-Salar (Commander-In-Chief)
Ghulam Haidar Khan Charkhi.

As Afghans, it's in our blood to honor those who came before us. As a young child, I grew up hearing the stories of my lineage and the Pashtun tribe we originate from—Yusufzai[1]. Of all the stories I heard, my favorite ones were about my grandfather, *Sepah-Salar*[2] Ghulam Haidar

---

[1] Translates to "Sons of Yusuf" or "Sons of Joseph". Yusufzai is known as the Great Pashtun tribe in Afghanistan.

[2] Commander-in-Chief.

Khan Charkhi. He grew up in the village of Charkh and later became recognized as a national hero for his bold leadership of the Afghan army and how he led them to victory in the second Anglo-Afghan war of 1878-1880. My grandfather was a man of towering stature, standing six feet seven inches tall with a handsome face, piercing brown eyes, and a long, curly beard that tumbled down past his collarbone. Although there were many stories about his courageous leadership on the battlefield, my favorite story about him was when he unified the province of Kafiristan[3] with the rest of Afghanistan.

It all started in 1895 when King Abdur Rahman Khan became outraged with Kafiristan's rebelliousness and lack of cooperation with the rest of the country. Of all the provinces in Afghanistan, Kafiristan was the only one refusing to embrace Islam as the nation's faith. They were known as nonbelievers for many generations, 1200 years in total, and at the time, they were heavily under British influence. Thus, they despised engaging with the rest of the kingdom. Finally, the King had had enough. In 1895, in his plan to form a centralized government and unified country, he sent my grandfather to restore the Kafiristani's faith in their country. He ordered my grandfather to use force if they refused his proposal. My grandfather accepted the mission, but he had a different strategy in mind.

Ghulam Haidar Khan recruited an army to join him on a mission to unify the country. They set trail on horseback, traveling for days until they finally arrived one morning in the lush green hills of Kafiristan. The Kafiristanis were surprised at their arrival and quickly mounted a defense. My grandfather hopped off his stallion and ordered his men to stand back. He slowly walked towards the Kafiristanis and began to speak, "We do not need to fight," he said. "We only wish to bring peace through Islam. I'll personally and happily build you Islamic schools and mosques, and I'll also recruit some of the best teachers to guide your province through the teachings of the Holy Qur'an. All I ask is that we come to a peaceful resolution."

---

[3] Kafirstan means "the land of the nonbelievers".

Sepah-Salar Ghulam Haidar Khan Charkhi
(first-row, seated second from left) and some troops in Charkh.

The Kafirstanis were clearly against this idea and responded by charging my grandfather's army. His troops stood their ground and quickly neutralized the assault. When the skirmish was over, my grandfather turned to the remaining crowd and mercifully restated his offer, "We do not want to fight you, brothers," he repeated. "We came here to create peace amongst us all, for us to unify as one Afghanistan. All I ask is for us to discuss coming to a peaceful resolution."

A murmur of discussion went through the crowd, and they finally accepted the meeting and after some debate agreed to my grandfather's initial proposal. Ghulam Haidar Khan held to his word. In the coming weeks, he built Islamic schools and mosques, sending teachers from his village in Charkh to educate the people of Kafiristan. The Kafiristanis restored their allegiance to Afghanistan and, after 1200 years of discord, agreed to unification. After hearing the great news, King Abdur Rahman changed the name of the province from Kafiristan to Nuristan[4].

This story is just one example of my grandfather's love and dedication to the people of Afghanistan. He was an inspiration to me. Unfortunately, I

---

[4] Nuristan means "the land of light".

never had the chance to meet him. He died on March 17th, 1898, before the last of the Anglo-Afghan wars. He was honorably buried in a large tomb in Charkh.

The tomb of *Sepah-Salar* Ghulam Haidar Khan Charkhi
in Charkh, Afghanistan.

Ghulam Haidar Khan Charkhi left the world with four sons, each of whom would grow to become some of the most influential men in Afghanistan. Together, these four brothers worked with Prince Amanullah, the grandson of King Abdur Rahman, on a secret mission to create a new Afghanistan.

When Prince Amanullah took the throne as King in 1919, he and the Charkhi brothers knew the country was outdated with its systems, having no democracy, parliament, technological development, standing military, factories, medicine, or bureaucracy. So they took on the task of modernizing the country.

They began by developing international relations with many European nations to upgrade Afghanistan's infrastructure and institutions, and King

Amanullah immediately began implementing his reforms. His first edicts as King were predicated on creating equality for women and freedom for all the people. He abolished slavery and liberated all women from the strict rule of always needing to wear a *chadar*[5], while enforcing rules that prohibited underage marriage and polygamy.

Prior to these rulings, the Kings of Afghanistan were allowed to have as many wives as they wanted. Oftentimes, other provinces and countries would gift a King a *soorati*[6] as a way to secure a connection with royalty. As a result, King Amanullah had many stepmothers, over 300 to be exact. King Amanullah couldn't bear to see his stepmothers suffer in confinement any longer. He couldn't bear to see any Afghan woman suffer so. He had such a loving marriage with his great Queen Soraya that he wanted all women and all the people of Afghanistan to live such a beautiful life. Thus, he freed his stepmothers, giving them the independence to live as they wanted and marry a man they chose.

King Amanullah's mission of modernization began to see immense progress, save one impediment—the English. The British Empire still controlled some provinces in Afghanistan. So, like his father before him, General Ghulam Nabi Khan Charkhi led an army to victory in the final Anglo-Afghan war, resulting in Afghanistan's independence in 1919.

After this long-awaited glorious victory, all of the Charkhi brothers were appointed powerful roles within the King's newly established government. Ghulam Nabi Khan Charkhi became the *Nayeb-Salar*[7], and later on the Deputy Foreign Minister of Afghanistan, and finally the Ambassador to Moscow and Paris. Ghulam Jailani Khan Charkhi became a General, and later the Ambassador to Ankara. Abdul Aziz Khan Charkhi became the Deputy Governor of Kabul and later the Deputy Interior Minister. And my father, Ghulam Siddiq Khan Charkhi, became the General Secretary of the Royal Secretariat, later a representative of the Foreign Minister, and finally the Ambassador to Berlin. On March 3rd, 1926, my father signed an official

---

[5] A headscarf.
[6] A gifted wife.
[7] Deputy to Commander-In-Chief.

friendship treaty with Germany on behalf of Afghanistan.[8]

With their global perspective, King Amanullah and the Charkhi brothers were well on track to create a newer, brighter, evolved Afghanistan.

Nayeb-Salar and Ambassador to Moscow and Paris
Ghulam Nabi Khan Charkhi, 1928.

---

[8] This friendship treaty set the stage for a dear friendship between Afghanistan and Germany. As such, decades later, Germany took great care of the many Afghan refugees displaced throughout the Soviet War with Afghanistan.

Ambassador to Ankara Ghulam Jailani Khan Charkhi, 1928.

Deputy Interior Minister Abdul Aziz Khan Charkhi, 1945.

Ambassador to Berlin Ghulam Siddiq Khan Charkhi, 1945.

His Excellency King Amanullah Khan (center) along with Ghulam Jailani Khan Charkhi (left of King Amanullah Khan), Governor Ali Ahmad Khan Loynab (second from the right) and Mohammad Hasan Khan Ziayi (second from the left) on a tour of Egypt and Turkey in 1927.

His Excellency King Amanullah Khan along with Ghulam Jailani Khan
Charkhi, Ali Ahmad Khan Loynab and Mohammad Hasan Khan Ziayi
on a tour of Egypt and Turkey in 1927.

His Excellency Amanullah Khan (center-left) with Mustafa Kemal
Atatürk (center-right) and Ghulam Jailani Khan Charkhi
(to the left behind, King Amanullah Khan) in 1927.

Ghulam Jailani Khan Charkhi with
one of the high-ranking Turkish officials, 1927.

His Excellency King Amanullah Khan (center) along with
Ambassador to Berlin Ghulam Siddiq Khan Charkhi (second-row, third
from the right), Minister of the Royal Court Mohammad Yaqub Khan
(third-row, second from the right) and Mohammad Hasan Khan Ziayi
(third-row, third from the right) in 1928.

Ghulam Jailani Khan Charkhi (seated left)
with high-raking Turkish officials in 1926.

King Amanullah Khan (right) and Ghulam Siddiq Khan Charkhi (left)
on their European tour in 1928.

King Amanullah Khan (left) and Ghulam Siddiq Khan Charkhi (behind King Amanullah Khan) saluting the people of Berlin in 1928.

King Amanullah Khan (first-row center left) with Queen Soraya (first-row center right) and Ghulam Siddiq Khan Charkhi (second-row center, behind Queen Soraya) on the King's European tour in 1928.

Once Afghanistan was officially an independent country, free from any English rule, it opened the door to international trade, and King Amanullah was determined to seize that opportunity for development. With the powerful relationships developed by the Charkhi brothers, King Amanullah decided to embark on a six-month trip throughout Europe. In 1927, he and his core team, which included my father, went country to country to establish these partnerships.

King Amanullah arranged for a variety of textile, food and industrial factories to be built in Afghanistan. He purchased thousands of military uniforms, weapons, and ammunition in his effort to establish a standing army, and he bought one year's worth of medication for all the hospitals in Afghanistan. He likewise arranged for the construction of laboratories, educational facilities, weather stations, and anything he saw that needed to improve the lives of the people of Afghanistan. The tour was largely a diplomatic success, particularly in the case of Germany, who graciously gifted Afghanistan a number of two-seater airplanes as a token of their friendship.

For King Amanullah and the Charkhi brothers, it seemed like everything was going wonderfully. Unbeknownst to King Amanullah, however, while he and his entourage were in Europe, a conspiracy was developing between the British intelligence and two of Afghanistan's most influential religious leaders, brothers Sadiq and Fazl-Ahmad Mojaddedi. The British Intelligence wanted to reclaim the power they once had over Afghanistan, which primarily meant controlling the country's foreign relations. Meanwhile, the Mojaddedi brothers were strongly opposed to King Amanullah's changes in law, deeming his efforts those of an infidel. They opposed putting a limit on the number of wives a man could have, and they deemed it inconceivable to give women the freedom to choose whether they wanted to wear a *chadar* in public. So the two forces went into business[9] together, creating a plan and employing an illiterate troublemaker from the North as their puppet, Habibullah Kalakani. Kalakani met with the *mullahs* and the British Intelligence agents in the English Embassy to devise his strategy. Shortly afterward, like wildfire,

---

[9] The religious leaders who worked with the British Intelligence were paid to play a role in the conspiracy.

Kalakani recruited tribes from the North in an effort to restore the country to its previous order.

Kalakani led a revolution of anti-Western extremists to overthrow King Amanullah by calling him an apostate and a non-believer for bringing Western ideas into the country. Meanwhile, the British Intelligence pulled strings by paying the religious leaders to influence the masses against the King.

After King Amanullah's return from Europe, Kalakani gathered his troops and led the northern army to Kabul, but on January 14th, 1929, pro-Amanullah forces retaliated in defense of the King's government, sparking a civil war. King Amanullah fled Kabul for Kandahar to regroup, handing the throne to his brother, Enayatullah Khan. Before he left, he gave him the following explanation:

> "Dear brother, I must leave Kabul. The people don't want me here, and I don't want anyone to die because I'm the King. If the people of Afghanistan truly don't want me, I will not be King. I will not see any bloodshed between our fellow countrymen in my name. If they truly want me, they will bring me back. For now, as I leave, I want you to oversee the Kingdom until we find a solution to this chaos."

Enayatullah objected to the move. "Amanullah, I can't accept this," he said. "I'm no King, nor do I wish to be. There must be something else we can do."

"My decision is final. I leave tonight," said King Amanullah.

That night, King Amanullah left Kabul for Kandahar along with Ghulam Siddiq Khan and my uncle, Mohammad Yaqob Khan. Shortly afterwards, Kalakani sent a message to the new King Enayatullah, ordering him to either surrender or prepare for battle. Having no experience as a ruler and no desire for any other people to lose their lives, King Enayatullah surrendered. Kalakani took the throne, sparing Enayatullah's life, exiling him and his family to India.

When news spread about Kalakani's revolt, King Amanullah wrote to Ghulam Nabi Khan, Shuja Alddawlah Khan, and Mohammed Nadir Khan for help. He needed a plan to get rid of Kalakani, or else their plan for an upgraded Afghanistan would be relinquished. My father immediately sent a telegraph to his cousins, Shir-Mohammed Khan and Janbaz Khan. He asked them to recruit local fighters and devise a strategy to overthrow Habibullah and restore order in Afghanistan. Accordingly, Ghulam Jailani Khan left his post as Ambassador to Ankara to assist the planning of the uprising.

Nadir left his post in India and took a train ride to Peshawar[10]. He stopped by the local villages to give passionate, patriotic speeches to the men. "I, along with my companions, need your assistance to join forces and fight against Habibullah, who we all know as *Bache-e-Saqaa[11]*. Once we conquer Kabul, we will restore King Amanullah's monarchy and serve Afghanistan as its commanders and high-ranking officials," he said.

Meanwhile, Nadir corresponded with my father, sending handwritten letters, asking for financial support for the war against Kalakani. Without hesitation, my father personally financed Nadir and his troops. Nadir, in return, wrote letters to my father, updating him with news on the war and thanking him for his financial aid.

The following pages contain two letters Nadir wrote to my father:

---

[10] Peshawar, now a region in Pakistan, was part of Afghanistan at this time.
[11] It means "the son of a water carrier".

Mohammed Nadir Khan's October 16th letter to Ghulam Siddiq Khan Charkhi

16/10/1929

My dear brother Ghulam Siddiq Khan,

I am writing to assure you of a letter I received from Abdul-Hakeem Khan, the commission agent stating:

"Mr. Ghulam Siddiq Khan has sent one thousand pounds from his personal assets to assist you. Please send someone reliable to collect it."

I want to thank you sincerely, and I am sure you know my sincerity to the country, you and the rest of the young compatriots. May God grant us more success. I want to thank you from the bottom of my heart for this gesture of compassion.

A friend in need is a friend indeed.

Dear Brother, although we are entangled in numerous difficulties, there is no point in losing hope. However, the lax morals and deep-seated corruption of the people have multiplied our troubles. If they could feel the pain, they would have cured it without much trouble. No point to explain any further; you know very well what has led these wretched people to treason and heresy—moral corruption and insatiable greed. This is the sole quality of this nation. However, I hope that providence may save this unfortunate country, otherwise,

If someone's luck was woven from a black fabric, even the water of Zamzam[12] may not help bleach it.[13]

We must struggle and be hopeful. In spite of bad health, during the last seven months, our resilience has not faded, and we are still looking forward to the divine mercy. My dear comrade, Janbaz Khan, has been with me for the last seven months and now we are together with all of your relatives. Shah-Mahmood Khan is at the front, and he is in (illegible) now, but Shah-Wali Khan and I are in Jaji, and Mohammad Hashim Khan is in Kaja. Please keep your fingers crossed for us. Herein, I want to sum up this letter by expressing my deep gratitude to you, my dear friend.

Mohammad Nadir

---

[12] A sacred spring in Mecca.
[13] A couplet attributed to Hafiz Shirazi, a famous Persian poet.

Mohammed Nadir Khan's November 16th letter to Ghulam Siddiq Khan Charkhi

16/11/1929

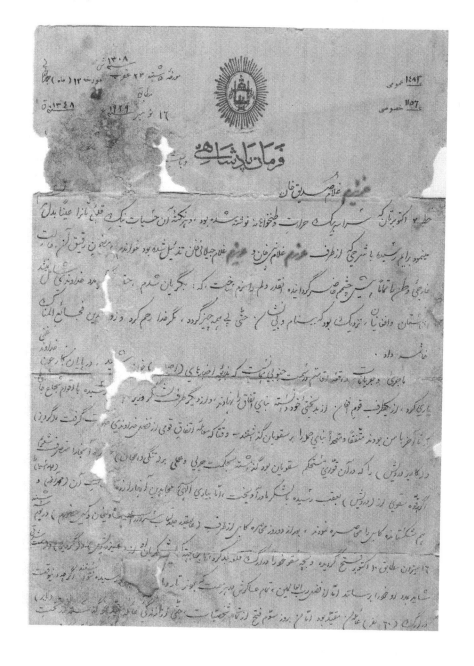

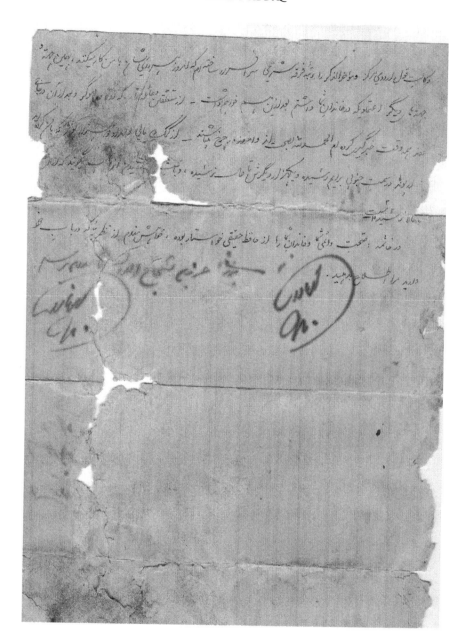

My dear Ghulam Siddiq Khan,

I received your letter from the seventh of October, which was full of patriotic zeal, explaining your good intentions. I read it along with the notes added by dear Ghulam Nabi Khan and Ghulam Jailani Khan. Its tender subject matter concerning the circumstances of our country made me feel so emotional that I burst into tears. Verily, had it not been for the mercy of God, Afghanistan and its people would have been lost in an ocean of nothingness and anonymity; however, thanks to Allah's endless mercy, these excruciating disasters soon came to an end.

The circumstance of the incident in the south is what you might have read in the daily news reports. Eventually, God the Almighty was there to help out. The Pashtun people realized their misery and united, and the troops of the minister, along with the courageous tribes of Jaji, assaulted the Saqavids (forces loyal to Habibullah Kalakani). As soon as the tribal unification treaty was attained with the mercy of God, we conquered Gardiz and Kariz Darvish, where Saqavid forces had their stronghold, and attacked Tangi Waghjan and captured it. Although the Saqavid army had reached beyond Darvish and invaded our forces, with the help of the Mujahideen, we successfully countered and took control of Muhammad Agha and Char Asia and besieged Kabul.

On Tuesday, October 10th, after two days of encirclement, his Excellency, Shah-Wali Khan, my present deputy, conquered Kabul, and *Bache-e-Saqaa* fortified himself in the castle, hoping to receive the backing of his soldiers from Gardiz and Kariz Darvish and the Eastern provinces. However, his troops had been put to rout and could not reform around him. On the third day of the conquest, though sixty members of my family were in captivity inside the castle, I ordered Takht-e-Babur and Bagh Umomi to fire on the walls and inside the castle. After several volleys, the Saqavids' depot and food supplies were set on fire.

At this time, Habibullah proclaimed his willingness to submit; however, having misled the Mujahideen, he fled the castle on

Friday morning, October 13th toward Kuhistan (a mountainous area near Kabul). With the evacuation of the royal castle, Kabul was utterly conquered. I deployed Mujahideen forces to Kuhdamam areas to hunt down Habibullah, and I myself, having entered the city, offered my services for the public. I announced that a national assembly comprised of all representatives of Afghanistan would elect the prospective King. Both dignitaries from Kabul and Mujahideen leaders unanimously entrusted me with this burden; the more I showed hesitation, the more they insisted. So finally, taking into account the increasing insurgencies across the country and the threats posed by Habibullah still being alive, I undertook this heavy responsibility on October 17th, 1929.

I had not fully taken the reins of power when I began receiving pledges of allegiance from every corner of the country. Thanking God for this tremendous good fortune, I focused on the Kuhdamanis (the people of Kuhdaman) who had not yet handed over Habibullah. I ordered the army (led by His Excellency Commander-in-Chief Shah-Mahmood Khan) to attack Kuhdamanis. As soon as Mujahideen troops poured into the region on Saturday, October 23rd, Habibullah and his Viceroy, Syed-Husain, along with his brother Hameedullah, the Vizier, surrendered to the government forces. Among the surrenderers were Malik Muhsin, the Governor, Syed-Muhammad Yawar *jan*, the Minister of the Royal Court, Abdul-Wakeel and Abdul-Ghiath, the Commanders-in-Chief, Muhammad Mahfooz, the Defense Deputy Minister, Mirza Ghulam Qadir, the author, Syed-Hasan, Habibullah's nephew, *Nayeb-Salar* Muhammad Seddiq, the brother of the Deputy Minister of Court, and a number of other political figures. They were arrested and put in the *Arg* prison[14].

While in custody, I promised *Bache-e-Saqaa*, should his execution not be required according to Sharia and the will of the nation, I would waive my personal and family rights and not kill

---

[14] The prison at the Royal Palace where those deemed as most threatening to the ruling regime were placed under high surveillance.

him. Nonetheless, when I discussed the issue with the representatives of the Pashtuns and Hazaras, the council of ministers, and the representatives from Kabul, they all asked for retribution. According to the demands of the national representatives, more than twelve people were handed over, and at 5:05 p.m. on November 3rd, they were executed by firing squad in the moat of the Royal Palace.

With their execution, the seeds of corruption and depravity were uprooted from Afghanistan. There remained nobody to defy the orders of the government. After that, I considered the whole nation, including the Kuhdamanis, as my obedient subjects and did not discriminate against any of them. It is worth mentioning that, while I was besieging Kabul, the Eastern tribes of Mehmendia, Khugiani and Shinwar displayed extraordinary magnanimity by attacking the Saqavids' army and putting them to rout. The case is the same with Kandahar. Today, apart from Herat and Mazer-e-Sharif, which have sent their pledges of allegiance through telegram, the entire Afghanistan has promised allegiance through correspondence, and conditions are improving day-by-day, with the grace of God. Meanwhile, I would like to express my sincere gratitude for your kind words and good wishes regarding my services. I consider you and your brothers the true servants of the country, and I can understand how enamored you are of the soil of this homeland and how you cherish the development of the nation. The effort you and your brothers have put forth, especially my dear Ghulam Nabi Khan, to extricate the country from a pitfall, are indelible in our country's memory. Moreover, anyone who knows that Your Excellency, along with Janbaz Khan and Colonel Shir-Mohammad Khan who partook in struggles and fought courageously on the front lines, can vividly see your spirit of patriotism and fidelity to the nation.

Thus, I have exalted the former to the post of the Central Corps Deputy and the latter to the post of Colonel; they are both cooperating with me now. For this, and a number of other reasons, my trust in your family shall remain as firm as it has ever been. I have often called on your family and kinfolk who were first in Logar and first in Jaji. They are in Logar now and doing quite well, with the grace of God. I also thank you for your financial assistance of two-thousand-pounds. I received £1000 while I was in the South; however, the second part has not arrived yet. In the end, may Allah bless you and your family with everlasting health, and please let me know if you have any special comments.

Give my greetings to dear Shuja Alddawlah Khan

Mohammed Nadir

The letters were warm and welcoming, but Nadir's intentions were not. On October 13th, 1929, Nadir and his army took back the throne from Habibullah Kalakani and executed him in a public hanging. Nadir then appointed himself as King and his brothers as the country's highest-ranking officials.

After he took power, Nadir Shah[15] desperately tried to contact Ghulam Nabi Khan, who was in Ankara, pleading for him to meet with him in Afghanistan. At the time, father of Queen Soraya, Mahmood Tarzi Khan, was in Ankara as well and insisted Ghulam Nabi Khan not go. He told Ghulam Nabi Khan that Nadir was not to be trusted and that he'd likely kill him. After many unanswered requests, Nadir Shah became so desperate that he sent his brother, Shah-Wali, to accompany my uncle on his journey home.

Shah-Wali simply told Ghulam Nabi that he was being called home to discuss the direction of the government now that the civil war was over. When the two arrived in Jalalabad, their last stop before Kabul, a leader from the Mojaddedi family insisted that Ghulam Nabi meet him for *chai* at his home. Ghulam Nabi went while Shah-Wali remained back at the hotel. At the meeting, the Mojaddedi family leader warned Ghulam Nabi not to meet with Nadir Shah, that Nadir was not to be trusted—that he would betray Ghulam Nabi and kill him. He suggested Ghulam Nabi go to Nuristan, where

---

[15] King.

everybody knew his father and all the wonders he had brought to their land. Ghulam Nabi listened, but he didn't follow the man's advice.

When Ghulam Nabi Khan arrived in Kabul, he, Nadir Shah, and other influential men met day after day in the royal Dilkusha Palace and talked about the future of the country. Nadir Shah believed he was entitled to be King since he had gathered the men to overthrow Kalakani. Ghulam Nabi believed the people should have the right to choose their leader, and that they would truly want King Amanullah to reclaim the throne. Though Nadir Shah pressed his case, Ghulam Nabi persisted, arguing that continuing with King Amanullah's mission and nurturing the international relations they had developed were in the best interests of the people of Afghanistan.

Twenty-six days continued like this, back and forth, until Nadir Shah came to the conclusion that my uncle would never side with his agenda. At the end of the twenty-sixth meeting, Nadir Shah asked my uncle to bring his brother, Ghulam Jailani, to the next meeting. The next day, Ghulam Nabi and Ghulam Jailani arrived at the Dilkusha Palace, only to be betrayed. Fearing the influence my uncle had with the people of Kabul, Nadir Shah ordered his soldiers to kill Ghulam Nabi, breaking the oath of peace he had made over the Holy Qur'an. As the soldiers charged him with the stocks and tips of their rifles, Ghulam Nabi stood silent and fearless. He bit down on his hand to hold back even the slightest whisper of pain, a gesture to Nadir Shah that even by taking his life, the new ruler had no power over him or the values he represented. Finally, after a sharp blow to the back of his head and many piercing stabs, Ghulam Nabi died on the floor of the Dilkusha Palace. Ghulam Jailani, however, was spared and sent to the *Arg* prison along with his cousins, Shir-Mohammed and Janbaz.

Nadir Shah ordered his soldiers to bring the corpse of Ghulam Nabi to his family's home. They obeyed, and a number of gunmen wrapped his corpse in a cloak and put it on a stretcher. Then, along with two of Nadir's generals, the soldiers left the palace for my family's home on Andarabi Street on a late, gloomy November afternoon in 1932.

PART I

The city and everyone in it are all unfamiliar.

The mountain, sea, and meadow are all unfamiliar.

There is no more breeze in the alley of old companions.

No more messages from dear ones and the temple square.

No jovial sounds from the town musician.

No nightly songs from the happy birds of the meadow.

There is no more gleeful laughter from the good fellows of the time,

And no more drunkenness or cries from the people of the homeland.

There is no more news of the spring swallow.

Crows occupy the nest of nightingales.

The hue of the moonlight has changed.

The thick mud has drowned the sunlight.

I have become adrift in this unfamiliar territory and have parted from my homeland.

From: **"What happened to Rostam-e-Dastan?"** – Khaled Siddiq

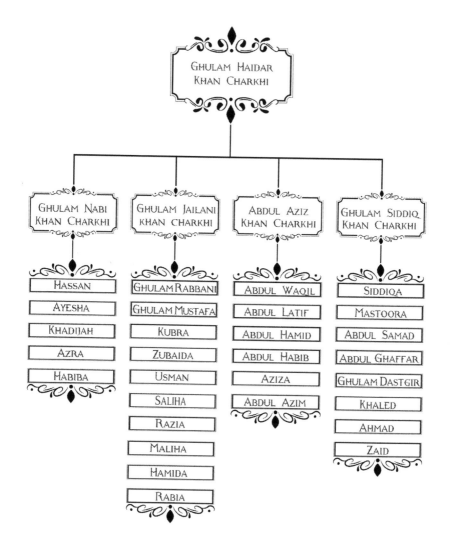

ONE

November 26, 1932

It started out like any other ordinary day in Kabul. At 6:30 a.m., my older sisters woke my brothers and me up for school. Like usual, I rolled over with a big yawn before getting dressed and trundled out to the living room where my mom was preparing breakfast: *naan-e-khusk*[16] with *chai*[17]. After finishing our meal, my mom kissed all of us on our forehead before we left for school. Our cousins were already waiting for us in the center of the *hawili*[18].

In Kabul, the four Charkhi brothers and their families, totaling about fifty people, lived together in a large estate that comprised of a two-story white mansion with a blue-green roof, a huge lush garden, guesthouses, meeting rooms, and a number of one-story, mud-brick homes for their twenty live-in maids, chefs, nannies and assistants.

We lived on Andarabi Street, an area of Kabul near the Royal Palace where the most influential people in the country lived. At this time, my uncles Ghulam Nabi and Ghulam Jailani had been visiting the palace for their political meetings in the *Arg*, while my father and my uncle Aziz both remained in Germany. Because of his hectic schedule as an Ambassador, I had

---

[16] Toasted bread.
[17] Tea.
[18] Courtyard.

no memory of my father, yet I missed him dearly. I could hardly remember the last time I had seen him. I must have been two years old, but even that felt like a dream. In truth, I only knew my father from the stories I heard, and I only knew his face from family pictures.

Among the children of the Charkhi brothers, there were nine girls and twelve boys that were of school age. Each day, as we walked out the gate of our estate, a coach waited to escort the girls to their school, while the boys were accompanied the two blocks to our school by our *lalah*[19], Shahabuddin, an older gentleman with a very long snow-white beard curled down to his chest. That morning, as we walked into class, Shahabuddin walked towards a bench in the school's garden and sat, as he did every day, waiting until we finished our school day so he could walk us back home.

Upon our return from school that afternoon, my family became busy with our usual activities. Most of us children did homework or played in the yard while our mothers discussed the news in a hushed circle. I focused on my arts and crafts assignment of building a model house. My older brother, Dastgir, and cousin, Azim, offered to help. We thought it would be fun to do the project on the roof since we'd have a better view of the mud-brick homes below, our model for the assignment. So we climbed up the ladder with all the supplies and got to work.

Just as I was putting the roof on the miniature house, an eerie sensation came over me like a cool breeze. I looked up and saw the clouds darken, and the wind began to blow with greater force. I knew something was wrong; I could feel it in my gut.

That's when the screams of terror came from below. In shock, I looked over the edge of the roof and saw people emerge and form a circle at the center of the courtyard. I looked at Dastgir and Azim, both of whom had eyes wide with fear. "Come. Let's go," said Dastgir.

We quickly climbed down the roof to discover the cause of all the chaos. As I tried to push my way into the middle of the circle, my mother picked me up and placed my head over her shoulders as she wailed in grief.

---

[19] Watchman.

"What's happening?" I asked.

She stuttered gibberish as she hyperventilated, still squeezing my head tight against her neck as her tears fell onto my forehead.

What's going on? What's happening? Why are you crying? Why is everybody crying? Let me see...

One of my aunts came to comfort my mom, and my mother put me down so that the two of them could embrace in grief and sympathy. I knew this was my chance to see what the commotion was about, so I crawled my way through the adults in front of me, anxiously inching my way forward. I could now make out a figure in the center, but with all the people in the way, it wasn't clear what it was. I kept moving and raced my way forward, only to come upon an unimaginable nightmare.

There in the center of the circle was the brutally beaten dirt-covered corpse of my beloved uncle, Ghulam Nabi Khan. I could hardly breathe as an ocean of tears poured out of my eyes. I grabbed at my suddenly aching heart and buried my face in my other arm as I felt my family's agony reverberate through my entire body. I peeked up once more, hoping it was just a nightmare. It wasn't. Dust covered my uncle's face. His back was bloody, and there was a puncture wound on the back of his head with blood still seeping out.

As I looked around, the grief was overwhelming. I saw my older cousins pound their chests with their fists. I saw my older brothers stand in stunned silence as their tearful faces contorted in pain, and I saw my uncle's wife, Ku Ku *jan*, fainted on the floor with other women and servants by her side. But when I saw Ghulam Nabi Khan's daughter, Habiba, shivering as she replaced the bloody towels under her father's head with new ones, my heart shattered into a million pieces.

After what seemed like an eternity of grief, a group of soldiers entered the *hawili*. They ordered all of the male servants to take Ghulam Nabi's body and prepare it for a proper Islamic burial. When Ku Ku *jan* saw the hole being dug and rushed over to be with the body of her late husband, the soldiers reacted defensively, demanding she stay back. After some time, one of the soldiers left and reappeared with a local *mullah*[20] who led the *Namaze-e-Jena*[21].

Over seventy of us gathered for the funeral. My sisters tried to pray, but they couldn't help but break into sobbing. My eyes were burning, too, but I was certain I had no tears left. My throat ached from wailing so intensely. I stood, hunched over in silent disbelief as the last mounds of dirt were shoveled over my beloved uncle's body. As the funeral came to an end, the soldiers ordered us to stay in our houses until further notice.

Once we were enough distance away from the soldiers, Ku Ku *jan* spoke up angrily, "I heard two of the soldiers speak with some anxiety in their voice," she said. "They want to keep us under strict supervision because they think our chefs will dig up Ghulam Nabi Khan and show him to the city as a martyr. They're afraid of an uprising."

Other than that, we remained quiet throughout the evening—our voices too exhausted from the grief-filled afternoon. But as we were preparing to sleep that night, the entrance door slammed open again, and loud footsteps followed. The soldiers had returned. "All the men must come with us immediately!" they barked.

As my older cousins and our male servants were called forward, my aunts screamed in helpless shock, fearing their sons would meet the same fate as Ghulam Nabi. "Where are you taking them?" Ku Ku *jan* demanded.

"We've been ordered to take them to the *Arg* prison, where their fathers are being held. They are to be held there until further notice. Until then, you must stay on your property at all times," said one soldier. The soldiers then ordered my eldest cousins—Ghulam Mustafa, Ghulam Rabbani, and Abdul Latif—to follow them.

With that, the boys' mothers fell to their knees, wailing in helpless misery. I couldn't bear the sound of their cries. None of us could. But we said our goodbyes, hugging one another, giving what love and encouragement we could. We didn't want to think the thought, but it was on all of our minds. *Will we ever see each other again?* I felt very sad watching my cousins board the back of the lorry. As they sat down, they looked back at us with confused

---

[20] A Muslim educated in Islamic theology and sacred law.
[21] Funeral prayer.

looks through glazed, watery eyes. Then, like a snap of a finger, our elder cousins and all but one of our male servants were taken away. The only servant who remained was Shahabuddin.

Almost immediately after our cousins' departure, seven soldiers entered the *hawili* and stood guard at the entry and exit points.

"What is their purpose?" my mother insisted.

"These men will keep round-the-clock guard. Don't try anything you'll regret," said their leader.

We fell silent, realizing we were trapped in our own home.

As I went to sleep that night, I looked around and saw my sisters trembling with uncertainty. I couldn't fall asleep either. Every time I closed my eyes, I was haunted by the image of my uncle's bloodied corpse, and the piercing wails of my aunt.

TWO

Myself at six years old, during my first year
of political imprisonment—house arrest 1932.

I awoke in a fog, realizing once again the horror of our reality when I saw my sister sobbing in my mother's arms. One by one, each of my siblings and I huddled around our mother, like cubs finding warmth in a harsh winter. I couldn't hold back my tears when my mother's trembling hands reached to take me in a nurturing embrace, and my mother sang a soft lullaby to hush our cries.

Suddenly, there was a loud knocking. I jumped up. It was the soldiers. "Come outside immediately," said one of them. We followed orders and found two well-dressed men waiting for us in the center of the courtyard - Governor Mohammed Omar Khan and Commander Turrahbaz Khan. They demanded all of us boys stand side-by-side in a line.

"Introduce yourselves," said the Commander.

As we all said our names one by one, the Governor and the Commander paced down the line, staring at each of us intensely. They paused in front of the oldest boys, my 12-year-old brother Abdul Samad and my cousin of the same age, Abdul Hamid. The Governor slowly approached each of them, gently stroking their cheeks with the back of his hand. He was checking to see if they had entered puberty. Had he found any stubble on their cheeks, they would've been sent immediately to the adult prison.

"They're clear," said the Governor. "For the time being, you will remain here; however, you must all live in the main house together. The soldiers will be staying in the adjacent houses."

"Will our children be able to continue schooling?" asked Ku Ku *jan.*

The Governor and Commander whispered amongst themselves for a moment. "Yes, but only under the condition that they don't speak about your current situation to anyone, lest you want to add further complications to your lives," said the Commander in a firm voice.

"What about food? Will our servant be able to bring groceries for us?" she asked.

The Commander conferred again with the Governor. "Yes. However, he must receive permission from the soldiers before leaving and abide by your curfew," said the Commander. Shahabuddin nodded to show his obedience. The soldiers paid salutes to the men as they left.

The following day, we tried to return to a routine. Siddiqa and Mastoora woke Samad, Ghaffar, Dastgir and me up. We had breakfast with our mom. She kissed our foreheads as we left for school, though this time with trembling hands. As I looked out at the gate entrance, I felt a haunting emptiness as I acknowledged that my cousins Mustafa, Rabbani, and Abdul-Latif would not be going with us.

As Shahabuddin walked us boys to school, I was flooded with thoughts of my uncle, Ghulam Nabi Khan. I thought about the previous trip he had made home, and how us kids spent every morning having breakfast with him. I remembered his smile and how he picked me up and kissed my forehead. I remembered how, during this most recent trip, after his meetings, when he'd walk into the *hawili*, we kids would stop whatever games we were playing and run to him for hugs. Ghulam Nabi Khan was an incredible source of light, a true father to us all.

One memory of Ghulam Nabi Khan that stuck with me was when I was playing with a cigarette box near the garden. It was a small empty package that had the name "Abdullah" on it. Dastgir saw me playing with it, snatched it out of my hand and threw it up over the roof of one of the servants' mud-brick homes. I started crying loudly. A few minutes later, my uncle drove into the *hawili*. He saw me crying and walked over to me and crouched at eye level.

"Khaled *jan*, what happened?" he asked me with concerned eyes.

"D-d-d-dastgir took my toy box and threw it over the roof!" I said as I tried to control my sobbing.

My uncle called for Khuddadad Khan to come to him.

"I need you to empty out the big cigarette box and bring me the empty package," he told him.

"Certainly, sir," replied Khuddadad Khan, passing me a kind smile before leaving.

"Don't worry, Khaled *jan*, I'll get you an even bigger toy box," my uncle said with a reassuring smile.

My crying had calmed down when Khuddadad returned and handed the box to my uncle. It was now a much larger cigarette box, the kind that contained a dozen cigarette packs, like the one I was initially playing with. It had the brand name "Abdullah" written on it.

"Here you go, Khaled *jan*," said my uncle as he handed me the large empty cigarette box.

In a moment, all my sadness was immediately replaced with joy. I hugged my uncle and ran inside my home to play.

I remained in a trance of reminiscence throughout the school day. It felt so weird to be there under the circumstances. I felt like an outsider. Azim and I dared not speak our thoughts, remembering the Commander's warning. So from time to time, I got lost in thought, daydreaming about my uncles, and wondering where my father was, if he was safe, and when I'd see him again. Then, like waking up from a dream, the school day was over.

I thought about both my uncles and my father every day, but during those early days of house arrest, the one person who came to my mind the most was Ghulam Nabi Khan. It was hard to watch his daughters grieve in the evenings. Fortunately, Ku Ku *jan* was their rock. She'd bring her daughters in together and nurture them with resilient love. Beneath her strength, though, I could see her pain, but that's what made her courageous. She wouldn't let the cruel actions of someone else break her or her family down, and she would employ any means she could to ensure our family was well cared for and had a future.

THREE

Abdul-Khaliq in Kabul, 1930.

In Afghanistan, there is a tribe of people called Hazara. The Hazara people comprised much of the lower class and had faced a great deal of discrimination because of that; however, I came to know many people from this tribe for their big hearts.

One such person was Abdul-Khaliq, the teenage son of my uncle Ghulam Nabi's most trusted man, Khudadad Khan. Khudadad traveled with my uncle almost everywhere, carrying his chest of money. Therefore, Khudadad and his family had lived with us since before I was born, and his son, Abdul-Khaliq, and his younger daughter, Hafiza, were both treated like family.

Abdul-Khaliq was an extraordinary athlete and soccer player. He played striker for his high school soccer team, and I remember watching him practice gymnastics by walking on his hands around the *hawili*. He always entertained us younger children with his joyous displays of athletic ability.

One day when my uncle Ghulam Nabi was in the *hawili*, he saw Abdul-Khaliq and invited him for a walk. As they strolled around the garden, Ghulam Nabi asked Abdul-Khaliq about his studies and his life goals. Abdul-Khaliq felt extremely touched that a man of Ghulam Nabi Khan's influential caliber would spend an hour to mentor him while making other political figures wanting to speak with him wait outside.

During my uncle's funeral, Abdul-Khaliq was on his way home to the *hawili*, utterly oblivious of Ghulam Nabi Khan's death or our imprisonment. He also didn't know that the day my uncle was murdered, his father Khudadad had also been taken away to the *Arg*.

When Abdul Khaliq approached the *hawili* and saw the guards outside, some neighbors warned him that he had to flee immediately to avoid danger. Confused and scared, Abdul-Khaliq ran to one of his friends' homes. He'd shortly find out, as most of Kabul did, that Nadir Shah killed Ghulam Nabi Khan Charkhi. He was encouraged to keep a low profile, and for months, he shuffled between friends' houses to avoid being caught by government officials.

Eventually, the curiosity became too much for him. He had to find out what was going on. So one night, he snuck over to our house, making sure to stay in the shadows where no guards could see him. As he approached the *hawili*, he noticed there weren't any guards watching the back end. It made sense. The wall was 15 feet tall, and they figured nobody would be able to climb it. Abdul-Khaliq spotted a nearby house with a roof slightly higher than our wall. The distance of the jump was several feet, and his target was only one foot wide. Fearlessly, he climbed the house, got on the roof and leaped to the top of the wall. Then, he quickly climbed down, looking out for guards and searching for any of the elders.

My mom noticed Abdul-Khaliq's arrival and secretly got his attention. He nodded and, crouching in the shadows, carefully made his way towards our home. Once he was safely inside, my mom and aunts informed him of the horrific details about all the injustice regarding the death of Ghulam Nabi Khan and the imprisonment of his father, my older cousins, and all the other servants. They made it clear to Abdul-Khaliq that he must stay away or else he'd be taken away as well. Abdul-Khaliq erupted in silent rage.

Hearing about my uncle's execution tore Abdul-Khaliq apart. He insisted he had to help the family somehow. My aunts and mother realized that, like his father before him, Abdul-Khaliq could be invaluable in helping our family stow away their valuables of jewelry, clothes, and other expensive items.

When the guards invaded our home the first day, our mothers did what they could to hide these valuables in secret places around the compound. They stuffed items within cracks and hollow segments in the walls, buried boxes in the garden, and ultimately stowed whatever they could anywhere the guards wouldn't immediately search.

Bi Bi *Khord*[22], my mom's sister-in-law, lived outside the compound. Since she wasn't closely related to Ghulam Nabi Khan, they figured she was in a safe place, outside the radar of Nadir Shah's watchful eyes. Abdul-Khaliq said he could bring the valuables to her. "At least they will be safer there," he said.

Our mothers argued a bit, concerned for the young man's safety, but finally, they agreed to let Abdul-Khaliq take on the task. Abdul-Khaliq knew the risk, and he took it with honor.

Bi Bi *Khord's* house was an hour away by foot. Because the guards were on round-the-clock shifts, Abdul-Khaliq would have to make the pickup and deliveries at night. That night, he took one suitcase of valuables and made his first trip to the safe house. He hid in the shadows, swiftly moving wall-to-wall, bush-to-bush, waiting patiently when necessary to ensure the guards and

---

[22] *Khord* means little. This was the nickname we gave to my mom's sister-in-law.

patrolling police would not spot him. The first trip ended up taking him three hours. He made it just before the crack of dawn.

When Abdul-Khaliq arrived at her home, Bi Bi *Khord* was shocked. She asked him how everybody was doing and was relieved to know we were safe. She told him her husband too had been taken unexpectedly to the *Arg*. Abdul-Khaliq then told her about his new responsibility.

"With all the injustice our families have experienced from this new government, I don't think my house is safe enough to stow these valuables," Bi Bi Khord responded, "but I know a safe place. I will give them to my own trustman. Since he isn't directly affiliated with the family, the Royal Palace wouldn't think of searching him."

Abdul-Khaliq agreed, and Bi Bi *Khord* instructed him to come every fortnight until all the valuables were stowed safely away.

So every two weeks, Abdul-Khaliq moved single parcels of our valuables to Bi Bi *Khord*, who in turn, handed them off to her trustman to store in secret. One day, my aunt gave Abdul-Khaliq a box, not knowing it included a signature gun with Ghulam Nabi Khan's name inscribed on it. Abdul-Khaliq could not resist a gun of such rarity and prestige, so he kept it for himself, telling Ku Ku *jan* he would hold onto it in case he needed it one day. Ku Ku *jan* laughed, taking the young man's words as a joke.

Weeks went by. Abdul-Khaliq continued to deliver our valuables to Bi Bi *Khord*. At the compound, we slipped into our own tolerable routine. Then another tragedy struck…

Did you see how the unjust killing of the butterfly
Did not let the candle live through the night?
- Khaled Siddiq

It was a scorching August day in 1933. I was playing cricket with my cousins outside when, suddenly, two squads of soldiers entered the *hawili*. We stopped the game when we noticed the two groups were carrying something with them. They had two stretchers covered with shawls. I heard a scream from behind me, and a familiar terror shot through my veins. The soldiers lowered the stretchers in the middle of the *hawili*, and all the adults and children crept towards them. There, unmasked, were the corpses of my beloved uncles, Ghulam Jailani Khan and Shir-Mohammad Khan. My uncles' children and wives lost their minds in screams of grief.

The scene ripped open our still fresh wounds and poured salt into them. Wails of agony echoed throughout the day. As we mourned our dead, everyone's faces fell gray, and for the children, whatever was left of our youth disappeared.

After that, the days only grew darker as the flicker of hope we had held onto vanished into a dim light. When Abdul-Khaliq returned for his regular visit, our mothers warned him not to return. "The situation is too dangerous now, and the guards will surely kill you on sight if they find out what you are doing for us!" Ku Ku *jan* told him.

General Ghulam Jailani Khan Charkhi, 1920.

Colonel Shir-Mohammad Khan Charkhi, 1920.

Learning about Ghulam Jailani Khan's death was the last straw for Abdul-Khaliq. He left in an intense rage, and it was the last we would see of him.

Three months after the executions of my uncles, Jailani and Shir-Mohammad, Abdul-Khaliq's high school soccer team won their soccer tournament, and in November of 1933, all the team's players were awarded trophies and invited by the King to a royal ceremony to acknowledge their impressive victory.

Abdul-Khaliq saw this as an opportunity to get revenge. Before they headed to the ceremony, he told his teammates he needed to go to his house quickly and that he'd be back soon. He then borrowed a bike and rode as fast as he could to retrieve the gun of Ghulam Nabi. He hid the gun tightly in his jersey and returned to his teammates. Nobody from the soccer team knew of Abdul-Khaliq's intentions.

The soccer team walked into a room filled with applause, and Nadir Shah stood to congratulate the young men. Abdul-Khaliq was in the second row, eagerly awaiting his encounter with the King. As the team moved closer to Nadir Shah, Abdul-Khaliq snatched the gun from his jersey sleeve and shot Nadir Shah to death.

The whole palace went into shock. All the players scattered, running in all directions. Abdul-Khaliq ran with his arms up to prevent the gun from falling out of his jersey sleeve as he made his way towards the exit with the rest of the team. But, just as they were about to make it out to the main hall, a guard saw Abdul-Khaliq running with his hands in an awkward position and yelled across the palace for the guards to stop the team.

"Who killed the King?!" the guards questioned the teenagers at gunpoint, barking at them like dogs. Finally, Abdul-Khaliq stepped forward, admitting that it was he who had killed Nadir Shah.

With their assassin in hand, the guards took the rest of the team into interrogation rooms. "Were you involved in this treacherous scheme? Answer now or you risk your lives!"

In truth, nobody knew, but that answer was unacceptable for Nadir's brothers and son. In their ruthless need for vengeance, they took eight players from the team, including the principal and vice principal of Abdul-Khaliq's high school, and along with Abdul-Khaliq, his father, and uncle, they were all publicly executed.

Abdul-Khaliq suffered the cruelest and violent death of all. The soldiers forced him to watch his father, uncle, principal, vice principal, and close friends die, telling him that they're all dying because of him. Then, the soldiers broke his feet and legs with blunt weapons. The teenage boy screamed in pain. Then, they tortured him by cutting off his fingers, one by one. Then, they cut off his tongue and his eyes. Finally, they brutally and viciously stabbed him to death with their bayonets. Our family would not learn of these executions until years later.

My cousin and son of Ghulam Jailani Khan, Ghulam Mustafa
(tallest one standing in the center), and Abdul-Khaliq (second from
the right standing in all white uniform) standing with the volleyball
team from their high school in Kabul, Afghanistan, 1930.

FOUR

My brother, Ghulam Dastgir (nine years old),
in our home on Andarabi Street, 1931.

The news of Nadir Shah's assassination reached our family swiftly through Shahabuddin, causing intense anxiety for all of us. Although Abdul-Khaliq had plotted and committed the murder from his own volition without anybody in the family knowing of his intentions, the women of the family were extremely frightful of what orders would come from the

Royal Palace next. Since Abdul-Khaliq was the son of Ghulam Nabi Khan's trusted man, they feared the worst was yet to come.

Unfortunately, they were right...

A few days later, the Governor and the Commander returned to our house with a group of soldiers and female inspectors. They inspected all the women and children one by one and looted anything they could find: jewelry, cash, and any other precious household items.

They then loaded us all into a roofless lorry with only a set of clothes and a blanket for each of us. We were then driven to an old, run-down *hawili* called Sarai Badam. The *hawili* had a narrow, square-shaped-structure, and the yard was only a piece of salt marsh, entirely barren and without a single sign of life.

Along both sides of Sarai Badam were two-story mud-brick houses that looked like nobody had lived in them for years. They lacked ventilation, proper flooring, and anything that would make the place habitable. On the opposite side of the *hawili* were two other mud-brick rooms with a huge wall blocking off any connection to the outside world. That's when we realized it wasn't a home. It was a prison.

We were herded into the dark, damp and cold rooms like animals. There was no electricity and light. Everyone was silent, nursing their own feelings of shock, fear, and anxiety about what would come next.

After a few hours, they brought us a *galim*[23] from our house along with two candlesticks for light. That night, none of us could sleep. Fear, terror, flies, and the piercing cold kept us awake and huddled together.

The next day, the guards gave us some quilts and mattresses taken from our home. Unfortunately, none of it provided us with heat like our *sandali*[24]. The only warmth we found was from the bread our mothers had taken from our home before our departure; however, the food didn't last for long, and soon we were all starving.

---

[23] A checkered, rough carpet.

[24] An Afghan heater. People would sit around the *sandali* with blankets over themselves and their feet underneath as a way to stay warm together during the colder days and months.

We felt deserted in this wasteland. None of the guards came by the next day. The following day, nobody showed up as well. Without any food or water, each day became a fight for survival. The next day, nobody showed up as well. The sting of the freezing wind was taking its toll on our bodies and immune systems. Some of my cousins became feverish; others complained of sore throats and dry mouths.

Our mothers knew, while they could do nothing about food, they had to find some way to quench our thirst. They found an old well in the courtyard of the *hawili* and realized it had not been drained for a very long time. Even though the water was polluted and smelled terrible, they forced us to take some sips in order to save ourselves from dehydration. I struggled to sip the water, while my cousin, Hamid, drank as much as he could and promptly ran outside to vomit.

As my mother was collecting another bucket of water from the well, she pulled up a pair of Uzbeki boots along with some sandals and hats. She realized our new home wasn't just a run-down *hawili* but a place for war prisoners. A haunting sensation ran through her when she understood we had been left here to suffer and die.

My mother walked into the room as if she had just seen a ghost. She told my aunts what she had discovered. They were horrified as well. Ku Ku *jan* suggested we had to get the attention of the guards. "We must soften their hearts with compassion," she said.

For six days, we remained locked inside the *hawili* without anything to eat or drink. The nights were worse than the days. Sleeping on a dirty mattress, curled up in the fetal position, we heard the roaring grumbles and suffered the pain of our aching stomachs. I was so hungry I couldn't even maintain a thought. But my cousin Rabia *jan*, only sixteen months old, was worse off than all of us. She had no milk to drink. Her mother was used to feeding her cow's milk because she was typically not able to produce enough milk of her own. Now, in this Hell, she had no idea how she'd feed her newborn. She dreaded the reality that her daughter might die.

Rabia *jan* wasn't alone. Najia *jan*, my four-month-old cousin who had been born in our house in Andarabi Street during our year of house arrest, was also starving and fighting for her life. Her never-ending shrieks broke our hearts, making the entire family very worried for her fate. In watching my cousin's fight for survival, I understood the ancient Persian saying:

Human beings are more fragile than flowers yet tougher than stones.

Finally, on the seventh day, the gate was unlocked. Two *qabchis*[25], along with two military guards, entered the *hawili*. A divine force must have softened the hearts of the *qabchis* because when my aunt asked if they could bring some cow's milk for her baby, they both left and shortly returned with milk and trays of bread. We children ran towards the trays like wild animals, but our mothers chased after us and ensured we divided the bread equally amongst the families. Without a word, the *qabchis* and the guards left and locked the gate.

Once the bread was divided, we were each given only two pieces to satisfy our starvation. I was too hungry to pace myself. The deep aching growls of my stomach forced me to devour my piece of bread instantly. It was so stale, and my mouth was so dry from dehydration that I almost choked. I took a few gulps of putrid water to wash down the bread. Some of the kids begged for more, but their mothers explained we had to ration the food.

Azim complained the most, "*Madar!* My stomach hurts so much! Please!"

Azim's mother had to muster up every bit of discipline she had to deny him more food. "We must ration the bread Azim *jan*. I'm sorry sweetheart, but you cannot have more," she said while trying to hold back her tears.

After a few more days, the two *qabchis* returned with some sugar, tea, and oil for the hurricane lamps. We learned the two *qabchis* were Mohammad Rahim and Mehr-Ali, both of whom were assigned by the Royal Palace to take care of us and provide hospitality to the squad of troops watching over us. Our mothers complained to the *qabchis* about the cold weather and lack of potable water, begging them to help save the children from dehydration.

After several entreaties from our mothers, the *qabchis* finally brought us some charcoal and cleaned up the well. Along with that, they began bringing a daily ration of two trays of bread and tea and sugar, telling us to make do.

---

[25] Doormen.

A week later, Mamoor Es'haq, the security officer of the Kabul detention center, came to Sarai Badam. He called forth the two oldest boys in the family, my brother Abdul Samad and cousin Abdul Hamid, and ordered them to make a list of all the family members present. They counted 53 people: 36 adults, 12 children, and 5 maids. Mamoor Es'haq also informed them the higher authorities had decided to give everyone a monthly ration of one Afghani[26] for adults and fifty *pul*[27] for each one of us children. Our mothers were very careful with this monthly allotment, using it only for basic necessities like food and warm clothing.

---

[26] The currency of Afghanistan.

[27] One Afghani is subdivided into 100 pul, which were in the form of coins.

FIVE

Bi Bi Mariam (Ku Ku *jan*), Ghulam Nabi Khan Charkhi's wife.
Photo was taken after prison release in 1954.

Days and nights were a monotonous dance with terror. The wind left us shivering, so we remained indoors at all hours in a dark, smoky, filthy environment. During the long winter nights, our mothers would try to lift our mood with soothing words of advice. "Be patient. Everything will work out," they would tell us.

They led prayers, teaching us how to recite verses from the Holy Qur'an. "God will show mercy," they'd say. "Be patient."

One day, Ku Ku *jan* was fed up with this pitiful way of living. She gathered the older boys and girls for an important meeting. With motherly affection, she declared we must end the suffering now, and that from this moment forward, we would make the most of our time, regardless of our situation.

"Now, you senior boys and girls have a big responsibility on your shoulders: you must not let your siblings remain uneducated," she told them.

Together, they came up with a plan for the older siblings to homeschool us younger children with Ku Ku *jan* serving as the school principal. We didn't have pens and paper, so Samad decided to teach us the Farsi alphabet by handing us pebbles to practice with on the dirt ground. This method worked for a while, until we were able to upgrade our writing technology to using charcoal to write on the walls of our rooms.

The days went on in this manner with the older siblings teaching the younger ones, and Ku Ku jan delivering and grading our quizzes and tests. Soon, we were so focused on the joy of learning that we nearly forgot our misery. Every day we felt like we were making progress, which lifted our spirits.

As time went on, our mothers came up with an idea to get us some proper school supplies. When a recently assigned *saqaa*[28], Mehr-Ali, came to bring us potable water, they decided to approach him about smuggling us some paper, reed-pens, and ink in exchange for money from our monthly ration.

Like us, Mehr-Ali was under strict surveillance by a *qabchi*, but our mothers were able to share our problems and convey their request while the *qabchi* was briefly distracted. Just like Abdul-Khaliq, Mehr-Ali came from the Hazara tribe. Despite the risk, he compassionately agreed to do whatever he could to support our education.

The way Mehr-Ali smuggled our materials into the jail was very clever. One *qabchi* always accompanied Mehr-Ali up to the kitchen door, but because the room was so narrow, the qabchi would wait outside, watching vigilantly to make sure he didn't talk to anyone. Our mothers and sisters put

[28] Water carrier.

water containers in the dark corner of the narrow kitchen. While he emptied his water-skin[29], Mehr-Ali took the school materials out from under his shirt and placed them behind the pitcher, pocketing some money our mothers left for him underneath the pitcher before he left.

After the coast was clear and the guards were gone, Ku Ku *jan* went into the kitchen to collect our materials. A few minutes later, she returned with papers, pens, and ink. Joy rushed through the room as kids charged towards her, hugging her with gratitude. Suddenly, life didn't feel like a prison anymore. Life felt like an opportunity to learn every day.

With the help of Mehr-Ali, Ku Ku *jan* turned our educational program into a functioning school. We had fifteen pupils and four teachers, divided into three groups: one with Samad and Hamid, the second with Azra (Ku Ku *jan's* daughter), and the third with Ku Ku *jan* herself. I was in Samad and Hamid's group.

Every morning, we went to Ku Ku *jan's* room to study with our groups until the afternoon. Afterward, we played cricket and hopscotch out in the yard until the evening, when we would return to finish our homework. A profound sense of delight flooded our environment as we children reconnected with the spirit of childhood, warming the hearts of our mothers and lifting the spirits of the group.

Through this system, we quickly learned to read and write Farsi fluently. As we progressed academically, Ku Ku *jan* taught us classes based on lessons from a book called *Panj Kitab*[30].

Panj Kitab was one of the few books our mothers were able to bring to Sarai Badam, along with the Holy Qur'an and *Dalayelukhairat*[31]. We would say the prayer verses together every day. I noticed how it brought a communal spirit among us all, bringing joy to the atmosphere, despite our misfortune.

Throughout this whole time, Mehr-Ali continued to provide us with more books, including the complete poetry works of Khaja Hafiz and Gulistan-e-

---

[29] A receptacle normally made of sheep or cow bladder that is used to hold water. In other words, the old world's version of a canteen.

[30] "Five Books".

[31] An Islamic book with many prayers.

Saadi[32], as well as some other Persian textbooks. He was always cautious with his deliveries. Sometimes when he could feel the *qabchi* watching him closely, he would take the pens, paper, and books back with him and return the next day, or in some cases the next week, before he completed the transfer.

Our mothers also worried that if the guards caught us with our school materials, we would face severe punishment, so they devised a creative solution. At night, it would get frigid, so they used our old homework papers as kindling to start the fire. With this strategy, we were able to stay warm all while disposing of any evidence of our underground school.

This shift in energy, inspired by Ku Ku *jan*, brought joy and purpose back into our lives. When I wasn't studying, I'd be outside building snowmen with some of my brothers and cousins—Dastgir, Ghaffar, Rahman, Hamid, Habib, and Azim. Sometimes we'd play games, like *gudiparaan baazi*[33], hopscotch, and cricket. *Gudiparaan baazi* was my favorite. When the wind would get sharp in the afternoon, many kids in the nearby neighborhood would battle each other with kites. Every so often, when we were lucky, a kite from one of these battles would fall into our *hawili*. We would then run the kite to our mothers, asking if they could thread it with some line.

At first, we had to share, but then Rahman, Azim, and I came up with a solution. We tied some string around two rocks and stood on top of our mud-brick home, taking turns throwing the rocks at nearby hovering kites in our attempts to bring them down. Technically, this was allowed. According to the rules of *gudiparaan baazi*, anybody was allowed to cut down a kite, and there were no limits as to how they could do so. Azim was the most successful with this technique, and soon we had enough kites to battle each other.

For a year, life brightened, until another tragedy struck...

---

[32] The *Gulistan* (Persian for "The Rose Garden") is a landmark of Persian literature, perhaps its single most influential work of prose. Written in 1258 CE, it is one of two major works of the Persian poet Saadi, considered one of the greatest medieval Persian poets.

[33] Kite fighting.

SIX

During the winter months, we grew susceptible to illness and disease. Without support from doctors, our mothers did their best to treat us with herbal remedies.

Due to the extremely poor sanitary conditions in Sarai Badam, three of the children contracted tuberculosis—my dear brother, Samad, and my cousins, Hamid and Habib.

When this news reached the authorities, they ordered Dr. Mir Abdul-Ghani Khan to come to Sarai Badam and treat the boys. Dr. Mir worked as a pharmacist within the Royal Palace. He was a kind man who used whatever means he had at his disposal to help the boys in making a recovery. He even recited verses of the Holy Qur'an, praying for the boys to receive a healing miracle.

Winter and spring passed quickly with a harsh summer blazing on the horizon. The intense heat brought flies, mosquitoes, fleas, and bed bugs. We suffered sore throats, rheumatism, nephritis, influenza, and malaria. Dr. Mir tried to treat all of them, but he only had a limited amount of medicine available to him: pan powder, quinine, salicylate powder, hydrogen peroxide, and a few other tonics.

During these months, Hamid remained confined to his bed with his tuberculosis. Samad and Habib still had the disease as well, but they weren't bed-ridden like Hamid. We all grew worried and feared the end was near for him. On his fourteenth birthday, his brother, Azim, and I went to visit him to give him our good wishes. When we entered the room, we saw his mother sitting by his bedside with a worrisome look on her face. Hamid was in his weakest state yet. He was skinny and pale, and his eyes showed defeat. We did not know how to respond and couldn't help but cry at the desperate scene. As we left the room, Azim looked upwards with tears rolling down his cheek. We prayed for a miracle.

Although I didn't spend much time with Hamid growing up due to our age difference, I looked up to him a lot. He was a strong young man, tall with a chiseled face, thick eyebrows, a sharp nose, and big piercing eyes. Azim, Dastgir and I would often watch him play soccer out by the garden with Samad, Habib, Mustafa, Rabbani, Abdul-Latif, and Abdul-Khaliq. We would marvel at how quick he was and admire his powerful shot. He was also an excellent gymnast, not quite as masterful as Abdul-Khaliq, but the two would train together from time to time.

It wasn't long after his fourteenth birthday that my beloved cousin, Hamid, passed away. His premature death was an awful blow to our family. It scarred us deeply. The shocking reality that we had lost one of our own to tuberculosis made us all gravely concerned about the other two boys with the disease—Samad and Habib. Fortunately, they didn't seem like they were too ill. Sure, they coughed often, and Dr. Mir gave them extra attention, but it didn't appear like the end was near for them. However, my mother and Habib's mother didn't feel the same way. They took every precaution and prayed diligently for their boys to recover.

In the weeks that followed, Hamid's mother, Shiringul[34], had a series of traumatic episodes. Several times, she woke us up in the middle of the night with her helpless, soul-shattering wails. My heart ached for my aunt. Her wails were ingrained in my mind. I learned that the wail of a mother grieving her child is the saddest sound a person can hear.

From then on, we prayed every day for mercy, but it was difficult for us to believe we'd ever see it. Ku Ku *jan* did her best to keep us motivated on our studies by giving us more homework and lessons. Still, I could see there was a part of all of us that felt silently helpless—even the bold Ku Ku *jan*.

---

[34] This was her nickname, which means "sweet flower".

SEVEN

Mahparwar (Shah Bi Bi), Ghulam Jailani Khan's wife
and stepmother of Ghulam Mustafa and Ghulam Rabbani.
Photo was taken after prison release in 1954.

By now, we had been in Sarai Badam for three years. I was nine years old and the days continued in their routine of school, play, and homework. One day, the *qabchi* opened the prison-gate and ushered in another family of seven. The noise of their arrival stirred our curiosity and drew us into the courtyard.

Our eyes and smiles grew with delight! There stood my aunt Bigum, along with her son, three daughters, sister and mother. They were the family of Ghulam Anwar Khan, my father's cousin. I had grown up playing with my cousins at family gatherings, and it was a pleasant surprise to reconnect with them. Our mothers rushed over to welcome the new guests with long, affectionate embraces, and we gladly obeyed the orders of the *qabchi* to vacate a few rooms to make space for them.

While us kids reunited, playing hopscotch, our mothers helped the new arrivals settle into their new homes. As the evening approached, we all huddled together for a meal. In the silence, our mothers' anticipation and curiosity grew, longing for news of our other family members.

Before Anwar's family turned up in Sarai Badam, Mohammad Is'haq, the government official who brought our monthly ration, had hinted on multiple occasions that some of our family members in the *Arg* prison were still alive. Every time we heard the news, we felt comforted and it brought our hopes up that maybe one day we would all reunite.

With the arrival of family from outside, this was the chance for our mothers to confirm that good news. Unable to hold it any longer, my mother finally asked my aunt, "What happened to the rest of the family?"

A fearful silence fell over the room.

My aunt began to cry as she told us the horrific news. "After Abdul-Khaliq killed Nadir Shah, he and everyone closely connected to him were sentenced to a public execution. They were dragged out in shackles and chains, forced to step on the platform as guards tied nooses around their necks. Then, those poor innocent people were kicked off the deck, one by one. Afterwards, they were all buried in a mass grave. No respect. Dumped away like trash."

A loud gasp followed. We all looked at each other, shocked, saddened, heartbroken, fearful, and in disbelief. Finally, Ku Ku *jan* asked the question we all wanted to know. "Who else, Bigum *jan*?"

There was a long pause as Bigum ushered the strength to maintain her composure. "Khuddadad, his uncle, the principal and vice principal from his school, eight of his friends from the soccer team and school, and our dear

Mustafa, Rabbani, and Abdul-Latif," she said, sobbing heavily.

My heart sank to my stomach upon hearing the names of my dear cousins. Our mothers began screaming the names of Mustafa, Rabbani, and Abdul-Latif with intense grief. All of us as a whole cried as the familiar searing pain of loss burned into our hearts. The women embraced my aunts who had lost their sons. My aunts collapsed in shock from their grief, going unconscious on the floor. The old wounds of our family had once again been ripped open. The suffering was unbearable. I sobbed until I wore out, eventually passing out on my mother's lap.

I woke up in silence the next day. None of us kids wanted to play, and none of the adults spoke. Nobody had any appetite. Our eyes were puffy from crying and our voices hoarse from wailing. We huddled helplessly in the dark, broken of spirit.

My dear cousins, I wish I had spent more time with you. I wish I could've learned from you. May you all rest in peace.

Ghulam Mustafa Charkhi, 1930.

Ghulam Rabbani Charkhi, 1930.

Abdul-Latif Charki, 1930.

From left to right: Is'haq, Abdul-Khaliq, and Abdullah, 1933.

Abdul-Khaliq (first-row right) and his fellows Mahmoud Khan (first-row left) and I'shaq (second-row right) behind Abdul Khaliq.
Photo taken minutes prior to their executions, November 1933.

EIGHT

My brother, Abdul Ghaffar.
Photo was taken after prison release, 1948.

The days and nights passed dreadfully, until one day Ku Ku *jan* gathered us together for some encouragement.

"Children! We must be patient with the will of Allah," she advised. "It is time to restart your lessons and leave the rest to Allah."

We knew her words were right and agreed we should return to our lessons.

Ku Ku *jan* asked Mehr-Ali for support providing extra textbooks and materials for the new students joining our group, and he kindly agreed to the request.

But before we could resume our lessons at full pace, an unfortunate incident happened. Three nights after Ku Ku *jan's* talk, soldiers barged into our room, questioning us, demanding to know why we were indoors all the time. Ku Ku *jan* spoke on our behalf, telling them we were grief-stricken by the news of the execution of our teenage relatives. "Our spirits have been crushed," she explained. "We've spent most of the days grieving." The guards believed her, all but one.

"You only learned this news recently, but it's been quiet here for months," he said. "What are you hiding?"

Ku Ku *jan* restated that life there was miserable, and reminded him that we had also lost another child to tuberculosis. "We have nothing to hide," she said. "We have nothing."

"Nonsense. During the first months here, the kids were playing outside every day. For the past year, though, I've seen much less activity... Guards! Search everywhere. Something is going on."

The guards ransacked the place, flipping mattresses and throwing pillows, blankets, and carpets across the room. Finally, underneath a rug near the corner of the room, they discovered the pens and papers.

"You are not allowed to have these!" the guard barked. "How did you get them?"

"We brought them with us," Ku Ku *jan* lied.

"Well, I'll be confiscating them. You are not allowed to run a school in this prison. You were brought here for punishment, and you must languish here until further notice."

We children were heartbroken, but after the guards left, Ku Ku *jan* reassured us not to worry. "We'll have to be more secretive with how we compose our routine. For now, I'll ask Mehr-Ali to bring us more supplies. Don't worry kids. Everything will work out fine, so long as we trust in Allah."

Not long after that incident, Commander Turrahbaz came with two other officers. He called all the boys to step forth and stand before him. He checked each one of us thoroughly as he had in our home, then he separated a few of the older boys from the group. "These boys have reached puberty and are morally no longer suitable to be amongst the women. They shall be sent to the men's prison," the Commander stated.

The teenagers were my brothers, Samad, Ghaffar, and Dastgir, along with my cousins, Yahya and Ubaidullah. They were all ordered to go to Dehmazang prison, except for Yahya, who would be taken to the *Arg* where he would join his father, Janbaz Khan. Our mothers were immediately stricken with panic at the thought of losing any more of their sons.

The Commander tried to console them. "There is no need to worry about your children's fate. No harm will come to them. They are merely being relocated," he said.

Our mothers were understandably skeptical. How could they believe anything that came from these officials? All the news they had ever heard since the beginning of our horrific ordeal had been dreadful.

The Commander paused for a moment, looking to see if there was anything he could do to comfort our mothers. "I would invite you to come as well just so you can feel assured they are simply being relocated, but it is a men's prison with strict regulations. What I can do is take two of the younger boys with us so they can see where their older siblings are going. After all, their word is worth more to you than mine," the Commander suggested. He then glanced over at Azim and I. My stomach dropped.

My mother spoke up. "What about the kids? How do we know they will return? How do we know we won't soon see the corpses of our children thrown on the floor in front of us?"

"Trust me. My only intent is to assure you your boys will be safe. I am only here to relocate the older boys as I have been ordered."

My mother gulped down her anxiety and accepted his suggestion.

"We must leave now. It's getting dark," he said.

Our mothers spent a few minutes in tears, hugging and kissing their oldest sons goodbye. They understood the gravity of the moment. They had no clue of how, when or if they would ever reunite with their children.

"Be safe my son," my mother whispered as she kissed my forehead. It did little to console me. I was in a trance, unable to comprehend what was happening.

The gate out of Sarai Badam opened. Several guards escorted us outside and onto a large, open, dust-covered lorry. I clambered onto the back with Azim. I suddenly realized this was the first time I would be seeing the outside world in years, and though anxious, my heart brimmed with excitement. As we pulled away, I looked back at Sarai Badam and realized how small our prison appeared from the outside.

As we drove through the streets of Kabul in the late afternoon, I was completely disoriented. I had no idea where I was or what time it was. All of my senses were scrambled as I looked out at the vaguely familiar roads passing by. Motion sickness hit me, and everything blurred. I couldn't tell what direction we were driving in, whether we were moving backward or forward. I gripped the side of the truck with both my hands, clenching my stomach as I tried to minimize the dizziness.

Suddenly, the vehicle stopped. Another guard approached the back of the lorry to see what it was carrying. He spoke with our driver before allowing us through the gate. Soon after, the truck came to a second abrupt stop. The guards ordered us to get out and follow them with our brothers and cousins. Azim and I walked behind them, stunned by the size of the prison before us. *They must be able to fit thousands of people in here!* Our older siblings were taken into a room to have their official documents transferred to the jail while we waited outside.

As I looked down the long, dark, empty hallways, a chill went down my spine. The silence was eerily loud. What haunted me more was a sense of death. I felt like there was no way out of this place, and that people would stay here until they died. I started worrying for my brothers and cousins.

Minutes later, my brothers and cousins returned from the room as official inmates of Dehmazang. Then, two soldiers called us forth and guided the older boys to their new home with us following behind. As we passed a few corridors, I noticed over one thousand men standing in a line, shackled from their ankles to their necks.

How can anyone live like this? I thought. *Why would someone do this to his fellow man?*

Finally, we came to a small, dark, cold cell. This cell would be our brothers' new home. Today was the first time in my life I had seen shackles on people, and to see my brothers shackled destroyed me. *They've done nothing wrong. Why are you chaining them up like they're something dangerous?* My grief then turned to worry. *What if they chain Azim and me now?* The guard must have noticed by apprehension.

"Now you see your brothers are safe," the guard said to us. "You'll tell your mothers. We must leave now."

We hugged our older siblings goodbye. Though we knew there was no certainty we would ever see each other again, we did our best to quell our emotions in front of the guards.

"God is always with you," said Samad when I went to hug him.

The guards then separated us and closed the gate. "We must hurry now," they said.

Azim and I were silent the whole drive back, hoping someday soon we could reunite with our brothers. It was nightfall when we returned, but our mothers were up, waiting anxiously. As we entered the *hawili,* they rushed over to us, thanking God for our safe return and eager to hear the news. We told them their sons were safe and all living together in the jail. They sighed with relief and thanked God for His mercy.

When we woke up the next morning, there was a feeling of emptiness in Sarai Badam. The energy of our older brothers was now missing. The silence of the space laid bare our old wounds. It was as if our whole family understood at the same moment the uncertainty of our family ever being together again.

"With my teachers gone, who will teach us?" I asked Ku Ku *jan.*

"*Bachem*[35], I will carry on the lectures for now. We must do our best to adapt to these new circumstances."

Ku Ku *jan* was right of course, and despite the emptiness that we felt in our hearts, we pressed on with our studies.

---

[35] Dear child.

NINE

It seemed like just another typical visit when Dr. Mir came and examined all of us again. One by one, he asked us our symptoms and listened with compassion, prescribing remedies and giving condolences for our losses.

But this time, just before he was about to leave, he turned to my mother and said, "The other day I met with Prime Minister Mohammed Hashim Khan. I told him that Sarai Badam was not large enough for all the people it accommodates. I mentioned that the whole environment is contaminated with germs. I told him how being in Sarai Badam has infected almost all of the prisoners and even led to the death of a young boy. I asked him if you all could be moved to a more spacious *hawili*. His Highness agreed, so soon you should have a better place, *Inshallah*[36]."

"*Inshallah,*" my mother replied.

A few days went by. We prayed, hoping for Dr. Mir's request to come true until one night after dark, the *qabchi* abruptly woke us up. "You must gather all your belongings quickly," he said. "There are men here to transport you elsewhere."

We jumped up and walked outside to find two military lorries with two officers, three *qabchis*, and a squad of prison guards waiting for us. "Don't worry about bringing everything," one officer said. "You just need your basic belongings."

"Where are we going?" my mother asked.

---

[36] God-willing.

"To another prison: Sarai Ali Khan."

Our mothers quickly gathered our clothes, hiding books and school materials in the rags whenever the guards looked away. Then, the *qabchis* ushered us onto the lorries before we took off. I was worried I might get sick again, so I clenched onto the side of the truck with both hands. But this time, I was okay. I looked up and saw a bright full moon illuminating the clear night sky. As we neared Sarai Ali Khan, I noticed the Kabul River beaming under the moonlight. "Look! Look!" I told my cousins. We looked out the lorry with excitement and marveled at nature's beauty.

Shortly afterwards, we arrived in front of a large gate. The lorry came to an abrupt stop and one guard stepped out to unlock the gate. I was surprised to see electric lights. I hadn't seen any in years. Something once so ordinary was now a profound blessing. Mesmerized, I stared at the flies and mosquitos clinking against the glass light covers.

Other than electricity, Sarai Ali Khan wasn't much different than Sarai Badam. We moved into one-story rooms, which encircled three of the four surrounding walls of the *hawili*. The fourth wall had a large gate separating us from a smaller *hawili* where three *qabchis* and seven guards lived together. We went to sleep feeling a little more optimistic, and the next morning, we re-established our routine.

In the mornings, our mothers made bread dough and gave it to the *qabchi*. He would take it to a baker and return after an hour with large pieces of *naan*, keeping a few pieces of bread for the other *qabchis* and himself. We ate *naan* with *chai*, and afterwards, Ku Ku *jan* and Azra taught us literature throughout the afternoon. We then would take a break for lunch, often eating some combination of *naan* with eggplant, potatoes, turnips, and carrots. After lunch, we had another class session, usually taking quizzes in the afternoon. After class finished, we would spend the rest of the day playing in the *hawili*. Fortunately, we still had our kites and were able to continue playing *gudiparaan baazi*. When the night came, we went into our homes and had dinner, eating more *naan* and vegetables. Sometimes, though, we were lucky enough to afford some lamb.

We adjusted to our new environment within a week, all of us but Habib.

His tuberculosis had been worsening since the death of his older brother, Hamid, and since we moved to Sarai Ali Khan, it had grown more severe.

One day, as we were preparing to go to Ku Ku *jan's* room for class, Habib's mom burst out of her home, screaming in tears and collapsing on the ground in front of us.

"He's gone!" she screamed. "My son is gone!"

Everyone rushed out to attend to her. Soon after, Azim and Aziza appeared, tearfully wailing like their mother. We then knew the awful truth. Habib had finally succumbed to his illness. He was only twelve.

I went to comfort my cousin.

"This life is like living in a nightmare," Azim said to me through tears. "What's the purpose of living this way? How can they let us suffer like this? It doesn't matter. They don't care. And today I've lost my last surviving brother."

I felt heartbroken. I didn't know what to say. I couldn't comprehend Azim's grief. I hugged him as we cried, mourning the terrible loss of our beloved Habib.

"That's not true, brother. You still have me," I responded.

But Azim was right. His family had already lost their oldest son by execution and now three other sons to tuberculosis: Hamid, Habib, and Waqil, who died one year before our house imprisonment. Azim was now the only remaining boy in his family.

My thoughts turned to my own family. *First Hamid, now Habib? What's going to happen to Samad?* I couldn't bear the thought of losing my older brother.

Our screams and wails of grief eventually alerted the guards. The gate unlocked and they ran into the *hawili*. After learning about my cousin's death, one *qabchi* left to summon a *mullah*.

When the *mullah* arrived, he ordered the qabchis to wash Habib's body and prepare it for a proper Islamic burial. My heart was constrained by grief as I watched the qabchis wrap Habib's body in the customary shawl before placing it on a stretcher. The *mullah* led us through a funeral prayer in the center of the *hawili*. Tears muddied the dirt floor beneath our feet, and the cries of the broken hearts of my family reverberated through my chest. At last, the guards took our cousin away to be buried. Habib's mom grabbed onto the stretcher, crying as she looked at her son's lifeless face. "Why God? Why?" she cried. The other mothers ran to comfort her.

"Where are you taking him?" she cried.

"To a burial ground, don't worry," said a guard. As they left, all fifty of us embraced, devastated by yet another tragic loss. As I looked back at the guards taking my cousin away, a haunting truth hit my gut. *We'll never know where to find his grave.*

TEN

My sister, Siddiqa. Photo taken after release, 1947.

My cousin, Ubaidullah, Ghulam Anwar Khan's son.
Photo taken after release, 1947.

Throughout the following weeks, torment seeped in from all corners: the vermin of the night, the isolation of the day, the grief of our lost loved ones, the fear of what would happen next, the persistent nightmares. The only thing we could do was busy ourselves with our studies. That, at least, would shine a light on our darkness.

Ku Ku *jan* and Azra continued to lead our classes, and I was lucky enough to get some extra classes with my cousin, Habiba. Oh, how I loved listening to her speak French during our morning lessons. That beautiful language and its unique phonetics were music to my ears.

Three years passed like this until a new surprise greeted us. It happened during the *Eid*[37] holiday. I was playing cricket outside with my cousins when we heard the gate open. I stopped and turned my attention to the entrance when I saw Ubaidullah walking towards us. My eyes filled with delight at the

---

[37] Eid is a Muslim holiday that follows Ramadan.

sight of his smiling face.

We hadn't seen Ubaidullah in years since he left with my older brothers for Dehmazang. My cousins and I raced toward him like two galloping colts, taunting each other about who'd reach him first. Our mothers heard our roars of joy and rushed outside. When Ubaidullah's mother saw her son, tears of gratitude flowed down her cheeks as she ran towards him, holding her long dress above her ankles so she wouldn't trip.

Ubaidullah's sister followed her mother as the two kept crying, "*Chesm roshani*[38]."

"How did you get here?!" his mother exclaimed.

"Father sent a petition to the Kabul police headquarters, asking if I could visit you all during the *Eid* festivities. With God's grace, they approved his request."

With trepidation, my mother finally asked, "How is everyone in Dehmazang?"

"We're doing fine. I'm concerned about Samad, though. Some days he doesn't do so well. He coughs a lot. He went to the prison hospital before, but it seemed like whatever treatment they gave him didn't last."

"I miss him so much. Ubaidullah *jan*, please look after him. Please ask the doctors if there's any more they can do." She went on just like any worried mother would. I understood her concern. Hearing my brother's condition had flooded me with anxiety too.

"Of course, *Khala*[39] *jan*. We're all doing our best and praying for him. I'll see what else the doctors can do. How are you all?"

Everyone fell silent.

"Our dear Habib passed away," said Siddiqa.

Ubaidullah looked shocked. Habib was like a younger brother to him. He held his hand over his heart as tears streamed down his face. Now he understood our concern. Habib had tuberculosis, just like Samad. He went over to hug Azim, Aziza, and their mother. The whole group shared a renewed moment of grief.

"No more talk of tragedies," Habib's mother interrupted. "We've suffered

---

[38] Refers to the sparkle in one's eyes when they are filled with joy.
[39] Aunt or auntie.

enough. Let's focus on the positive while you're here. What has life been like in Dehmazang?"

"We've all been focused on our studies. We're lucky to have some of the most accredited scholars in the country living in our neighboring cells. Our lessons have been great and challenging."

"You shouldn't worry about us," Ubaidullah continued. "The only thing that worries us is the lack of communication. The only news we ever hear of your wellbeing is from that soldier you send over with our clothes."

At Ubaidullah's comment, inspiration struck my sister, Siddiqa. Every week, the guards brought the dirty laundry of our older siblings from Dehmazang to Sarai Ali Khan for our mothers to wash, dry and fold. Siddiqa saw this as an opportunity for a genius solution.

"Ubaidullah *jan*, I have an idea that can solve this problem. Follow me." Siddiqa eagerly told us to come into the house, and we followed with curiosity.

"Now, please listen carefully and make sure to let my older brothers know of this as well," she said, holding up a cloth for Ubaidallah to see. "I'll write a letter on a piece of clean white linen and embed it somewhere between the surface layer and the undercoat of the *buqchah*[40]. With cloth, there won't be any physical paper that could make any sort of rustling sound to alarm the prison guards when they inspect the parcels. When you receive the laundry, all you need to do is open the marginal stitches of the *buqchah*, read the letter, and then reply in the same manner."

We were captivated as she walked us through the process, showing us how to sew the cloth in a stealthy way. Then Siddiqa closely watched Ubaidullah, making sure he knew how to sew the letter properly. Our excitement brimmed as we realized we now had a means of communication that could work under the radar of the guards.

"I'll send the first letter," she said. "I'll also sew an extra piece of linen so you can write back. Ok?"

Ubaidullah agreed. As funny as it seemed, Ubaidullah was so excited that

---

[40] a piece of double-ply cloth that served as a wrapper for a bundle of clothes.

he almost couldn't wait to go back to Dehmazang just to receive the letter. A few hours passed by with delight until, near dusk, the guards called Ubaidullah back. We said our goodbyes, acknowledging there was no guarantee of another visit anytime soon. Normally such a realization would have brought us all to tears, but this goodbye was different somehow. With our new communication system, we now had hope, a way to make the separation more bearable.

When the laundry came next time, Siddiqa sewed our letter in with an extra piece of cloth like she had promised. Eight days passed until we received our first letter in return. It was a true Godsend.

Aside from our daily lessons, our family bond was the only thing that helped us move through our suffering, and with letters now going back and forth every week, we had a way to maintain and strengthen that bond.

Most of the time, the letters carried only recent news and check-ups to make sure everyone was okay, but in truth we didn't need a long letter. Just being able to read one word from them on a piece of cloth was enough for us to feel certain that they were okay and for us to feel that we were still united as a family.

Sometimes I'd see the guards ruffling through the clothes parcels. I'd chuckle inside, knowing how blind they were to our secret. In some small way, we had finally beat the system. Our newfound joy continued for the next few weeks, until I received the worst letter of my life.

ELEVEN

It was mid-morning when the *qabchi* delivered my brothers' dirty laundry that day. My mother had grown to love these deliveries. She brought the pile of clothes to our room with a smile on her face, dumped it on the carpet, and eagerly began searching through them to find our weekly note. I kneeled down next to her anticipating the news.

A flicker of light sparked in my mother's eyes. "I found it!" she said before opening the message and excitedly scanning the words. Suddenly, she became still and breathless until, unconscious, her head thudded against the floor. My heart thrummed with fear. "Mother, Mother! What's going on?" I said, shaking her. "Please wake up!"

Siddiqa grabbed the note from our mother's hand, and a similar look of horror came over her face. She fell to the ground, her face on the floor, sobbing with sudden grief. I picked up the note to read it myself:

> I'm sorry that I have such terrible news to bring. Our dear Samad died three days ago. He died prematurely in the Dehmazang clinic due to malnutrition and lack of proper medicine. God bless his soul.

I felt the weight of a boulder in my chest as I went to hug Siddiqa and attend to our mother. My other sister Mastoora quickly joined, concerned about the situation. "What's wrong?" she asked. In tears, I pointed to the note. She read it, and then dropped to her knees and sobbed heavily with Siddiqa and me as our mother slowly regained consciousness. When she saw us crying, she held us in her nurturing arms while we grieved our terrible loss.

The sounds of our agony called the rest of the family into our house. We told them the horrible news, embracing one another as we grieved together in a shared experience of suffering.

At just seventeen, Samad was the oldest boy to die of tuberculosis yet. I hadn't seen him since the day I left him with my other brothers and cousins at Dehmazang. We asked the *qabchi* if we could have a funeral service for him, but we were denied. "It is not in our power," the *qabchi* said.

"Why do you deny me the right to see my child's face one last time?" my mother cried.

"We cannot do anything about it," the *qabchi* replied coldly.

It was impossible for us to accept we would never see Samad's face again. It was even more tragic to know we'd never know of his gravesite. My older brother, my hero and teacher, had vanished into thin air.

The next morning, Ku Ku *jan* brought us all together for an important meeting. "This is the third child we've lost to tuberculosis since living in these prisons. It's obvious that these putrid, damp, disease-infested places are causing our health to deteriorate. We must do what we can to improve our living environment; otherwise, I fear more of us will succumb to illness."

"We can tell the *qabchis*. We were able to soften their hearts to bring us food and milk, and even clean the wells back in Sarai Badam," my mother suggested.

Our mothers agreed. They walked towards the gate to gain the attention of one *qabchi*. The man walked over indifferently.

"What do you want?" he asked.

"Please sir, we need your help! We've lost another child to tuberculosis. He died in Dehmazang after he contracted it back in Sarai Badam because of the poor sanitary conditions of the jail there. There must be something you can do to help improve our environment here. Otherwise, this disease will continue to run rampant! More of us may die!"

"That is not my job. There's nothing I can do about it."

"There must be—,"

"There is nothing. Now go back to your room!"

Rudely silenced, our mothers walked back with their heads hung low. "We must not give up. If this *qabchi* chooses to be heartless, we will speak to someone else," said Ku Ku *jan*.

Dr. Mir continued to make his bi-monthly visits. He told us our diseases and symptoms were related to rheumatism. "This should help ease the symptoms," he said holding up the same medicine he always brought, salicylate. It was all we had, and he was the only one with a genuine desire to help us, so we trusted him.

Ku Ku *jan* took the opportunity to beg Dr. Mir for help with improving our environment. She told him about the three boys we'd lost to tuberculosis, and Dr. Mir, being a compassionate man, promised he'd do whatever he could. "I'll bring this to the attention of the Prime Minister," he said.

Dr. Mir made many requests, but he never heard back. A few months passed until we saw him bring something new with him on one of his visits.

"This is pain powder," he said. "It should help ease the suffering for those of you who have pain in your limbs."

I took a handful of pain powder and swallowed it down with water. The taste was horribly bitter. I waited for twenty minutes, expecting it to get rid of my pain. Twenty minutes later, my arms, legs and back still ached. Thirty minutes passed. An hour. Nothing.

The story was the same for everybody else. The harsh truth was that no matter what medication we were given, our health symptoms would continue to escalate in this sickening place.

Ku Ku *jan* would not let us surrender to our poor living conditions. She continued to plead with the *qabchis* and guards to do something about the dampness that seeped in from the floors and walls of the mud-brick homes. The *qabchis* were like a broken record, coldly restating it was not their concern. Despite the constant rejection, Ku Ku *jan* never gave up.

As time went on, our health continued to deteriorate. On Dr. Mir's next visit, he was shocked to see how ill we had become. He called the *qabchi* over and said, "You go to the citadel every month to receive your salary, don't you? As far as I know, you will see His Majesty in person to present your monthly report of the prisoners. Could you please inform His Majesty that the prisoners' health keeps deteriorating because of the miserable conditions here in Sarai Ali Khan? And please ask him for his approval to change these rooms. I have personally shared the issue with the Prime Minister but have never heard back."

A month later, the *qabchi* finally brought a mason to have the rooms renovated. Unfortunately, the task was not done correctly or with any care. I watched as the man dug out the dirt and mud from the rooms and built a new raised floor only one meter above the dirt floor. The new wooden floors initially got rid of the humidity, but it was not long before the stinking dampness rose up from the mud-bricks of the walls and from beneath the wooden slats. Our daily life became an endurance test for our already weakened immune systems.

Some of us feared the older women, our caretakers, wouldn't make it much longer. Our mothers feared for us children. Everyone worried about everyone else. Studying with Ku Ku *jan* every day was the only thing that kept me motivated through these tough times. Always determined, Ku Ku *jan* asked the *qabchi* to bring the worker back, but she was coldly ignored. "You are wasting your time old lady," the *qabchi* laughed.

There was no hope. Our suffering in that filthy, pest-infested environment would continue for another year.

TWELVE

Light snow marked the start of winter in 1939. My family and I huddled in our room, with our backs on the ground; our feet nestled under the *sandali*, our bodies covered with the few blankets and rags we had to stay warm.

We heard four loud knocks on the door, and my sister got up to open it. It was a soldier. "We need all the teenage boys to step out right now," he said.

My mother began to fret.

"It's ok," I said, hugging her to reassure her.

As I walked out the room, I saw Azim and Rahman standing in front of a squad of soldiers and a brigadier. "You boys have grown up now," said the brigadier. "The authorities think it is no longer morally befitting for you to be amongst the ladies. Therefore, I've been ordered to take you to Dehmazang prison. You have one more week to stay with your mothers and sisters and to say your farewells."

Behind us, our mothers and sisters began to cry. We all realized that, unless we were freed someday, this was going to be the end of our time together as a family.

The week passed by in the blink of an eye. Throughout the week, I reflected on all the suffering we had experienced over the past eight years. The events played in my mind in flashbacks. The arrival of the bloodied corpse of Ghulam Nabi Khan. The killings of Ghulam Jailani Khan and Shir-Mohammad Khan not even one year later. The intense hunger and cold. The constant struggle to survive. The untimely deaths of my cousins, Hamid and Habib, and my brother, Samad.

Although we had endured trauma, being together had made it much more bearable. I felt a tremendous amount of gratitude toward Ku Ku *jan*. Had it not been for her, I would surely have been illiterate, but her school had changed my life. Through her courageous leadership and loving encouragement, I learned I could make progress in my studies despite my environment. I knew I'd miss her, just as I would I miss my mom and my sisters.

My departure threw me into a state of ambivalence. I felt sad about leaving the women in my family, but I was excited to be joining my older brothers. I couldn't wait to be with them, to tell them all that I had learned, and to see what I could learn from them. Mostly, I felt a sense of pride. Being admitted to the adult prison meant I was now a man. Just thinking of it made me long to see my father. Though I barely knew him, I missed him terribly. I wondered where he was and what he was doing. I wondered what he would have thought if he could see me now. *Would he be proud of the man I have become?*

When the brigadier arrived with his soldiers, our mothers and sisters wept as we exchanged our final goodbyes. They kissed our foreheads and prayed for our health. When I went to kiss my mother's hands goodbye, she fainted. "*Madar!*" I cried. Before I could help her, the brigadier grabbed my arm and ushered me outside to the waiting lorry. I looked back with tears pouring down my face. The last sight I saw before leaving Sarai Ali Khan was my mother unconscious on the ground with my sisters crying beside her. With a lump in my throat, I swallowed the hard truth: there was no guarantee we'd ever see each other again.

Azim, Rahman and I stepped into the lorry with our belongings. The soldiers sat beside us, staring at us intensely. I could already feel something different about the way they looked at the three of us. It was demeaning. *Perhaps this is how soldiers treat adult inmates.*

A frigid wind stung my face as we drove through vaguely familiar streets. I didn't realize how long it had been since I'd seen the outside world. I pondered what life was like outside the prison walls, but my mind went blank. I couldn't even imagine it. The only free people I'd seen in the past eight years had been soldiers and *qabchis* with the occasional visit of a commander or official.

After a fifteen-minute drive, we reached a massive building with an iron gate. *This must be the Arg*, I thought. My legs sunk like a heavy anchor as I realized this was where my uncle Ghulam Jailani Khan, my older cousins, and Abdul-Khaliq had all been held captive prior to their executions. A haunting chill rattled my spine.

The vehicle stopped. The brigadier came to the rear and ordered my cousin Rahman to get out. This would be the first time in years Rahman would be able to see his father, Janbaz Khan. I felt a slight tinge of envy at the thought of their happy reunion. I wished I could see my father. We bade Rahman farewell before two soldiers ushered him inside. After fifteen minutes, the soldiers returned. The engine rumbled to life and we left towards Dehmazang.

Another fifteen more minutes, the lorry stopped at the familiar Dehmazang gate. The driver honked the horn a few times before the truck proceeded slowly through another large gate. We were escorted off the lorry into the main corridor of the prison. "Wait here," said the brigadier. He returned shortly afterward with the warden, a well-dressed gentleman in a nice grey suit.

"You are officially under the supervision of the warden and must abide by the regulations of this jail," said the brigadier. He then left to board the lorry. The warden told an imposing man standing nearby to lead us to our brothers' room. The man obeyed and called for two other prisoners to carry our sleeping pads, blankets, and pillows.

"Follow me," he said.

The man led us down the same dark, mysterious hall from our first visit here. We approached another gate, guarded by two armed soldiers. The man exchanged a glance with the guards, who then let us through. We entered another compound. This one was much darker, and it reeked of urine, mildew, body odor and smoke. I didn't dare think about what else.

As I looked into the cells, intense, black eyes stared back at me brimming with rage. As I looked at these filthy men with their long, scruffy, grey beards and ragged clothes, fear overwhelmed me, but I knew I couldn't let them see me as weak. I straightened my shoulders and looked straight ahead.

After that, the prison began to feel more like a maze as we turned down one hallway after another. Finally, the man stopped in front of a room. He knocked on the door three times. I wasn't sure what to expect. All I hoped was I wouldn't be in a cell with those scary looking men. Then the door opened, and I locked eyes with my brothers. A flood of joy and gratitude rushed through me as we embraced one another.

"This is your new cell," the man said, interrupting our reunion. "Here are your beds. I will check on you later to get you situated." The other two prisoners gave us our bedding and then left together.

I didn't care what the man said. I didn't even feel like I was in prison. I was overjoyed at seeing my brothers.

"It's great that you came here," said Ghaffar.

"Yes. Who is that man who brought us here?" I asked.

"He's one of the senior inmates now working as a *deh-bashi*[41]. He's in charge of watching over a number of us and giving updates about us to the warden," said Ghaffar.

"And what about the scary looking men in the other hall?" I asked.

"Those are real criminals. Don't worry. They can't harm you," he said.

Suddenly, some other visitors came from their cells. "We heard a lot of excitement," said my uncle, Anwar Khan. Ubaidullah was with him, along with Mir Enyatullah Khan and some other family and friends who I hadn't seen in over eight years. Our special reunion overflowed with love and gratitude. We celebrated with warm embraces and stories until late.

As everyone began making their way back to their cells before bed, Anwar Khan turned to me with a smile and said, "You know you are a man now."

I felt a rush of emotion in my chest. My eyes began to water. I nodded with pride and thought about my father and how it would feel to hear those words from him. I wished I could see him, and that he could see me. But I pushed the emotions down with a deep exhale. I was a man now, and I was determined to make my father proud by making the most of my time in Dehmazang.

---

[41] Watchman.

THIRTEEN

When I awoke the next morning, I took in my new surroundings. The cell was a lot smaller than I thought. The entire room was about nine square meters with two tiny windows in the back, secured with iron bars. There was a *sandali* table in the middle of the room, surrounded by our mattresses. *So, this is my new home*, I thought.

My brothers stirred awake, and when they noticed there was nobody else around to disturb our privacy, we started talking about all the events that had taken place at Sarai Badam and Sarai Ali Khan. My brothers listened to my news and shared their own stories about life in prison.

"Here, all the prisoners have to work. They have to do different jobs from dawn to dusk in exchange for a loaf of bread in the evening. These jobs are mainly breaking stones, molding bricks, carrying building material with a wheelbarrow, and occasionally baking. Thanks to some compassionate prisoners working in the bakery, they've been smuggling bread to us every day since we first got here. They know who we are and they encourage us to focus on our studies instead of physical labor."

"Dehmazang consists of three blocks: *Mahbas-e-Umumi*[42], *Qala-e-Jadid*[43], and *Taemir-e-Jadid*[44]. The first two prison blocks were already built before we arrived here. The third one was under renovation, and recently it was reopened.

---

[42] The Main Prison.
[43] The New Fort.
[44] The New Block.

There's one notoriously known corridor in *Qala-e-Jadid*: *Makhsoos*[45]. These prisoners live in solitude and are strictly monitored to ensure they don't build any relationships or have contact with anybody else," said Ghaffar.

"Aside from the pollution and the reek coming from the *chilim*[46], Dehmazang doesn't seem much different than Sarai Ali Khan," I said.

Dastgir was quick to correct me. "Unfortunately, here in Dehmazang, the guards are crueler," he said. "They may address you with derogatory comments, and in those situations, you must be obedient and respectful. This is not the place to speak your mind. Those who do get whippings."

"Also," Dastgir continued, "there are two wardens in charge of Dehmazang: Duran Khan and Mr. Abdul-Khaliq Khan. Duran has a sadistic personality. He orders brutal whippings, solitary confinement, and other forms of torture upon the prisoners, often when they've done nothing wrong. Mr. Abdul-Khaliq, on the other hand, is a professional and a gentleman. Hopefully you'll never have to meet Duran, but if you do, keep your mouth shut. Quiet your thoughts if you can. Duran is ruthless and will seek any opportunity to break prisoners down. I've seen it with my own eyes."

"He's whipped you?" I anxiously asked.

"No. Not me. But he has beaten and tortured many others here."

Hearing all this crushed my spirits and made me wonder why human beings would inflict so much pain upon one another. Dastgir noticed my expression and sought to reassure me. "The good news about this place is we're surrounded by scholars. If you enjoyed classes in Sarai Badam and Sarai Ali Khan, you'll feel like you have struck gold here," he said. "We learned Arabic from Mir Enyatullah Khan."

Dastgir was referring to our distant uncle—a quiet, grounded, peaceful man, very into reading.

My brother showed me an Arabic textbook of his titled *Sarfi Bahaye*. "We'll teach you Arabic with this. I'll teach you how to read, write and speak German as well."

---

[45] The special corridor.
[46] Water pipe. Most of the criminals at Dehmazang were smokers, some of whom were addicted to *chars*, a type of hashish.

German! My father had been the Ambassador to Germany. How proud he would be if I could speak German and Arabic fluently with him. I felt even more motivated to get started on my studies.

Over the course of the next week, my brothers introduced us to many other inmates. One of them was Tahir Besmel. He instantly became a great friend of mine. He was 30 years old with thick, curly black hair and ever-present eyes. "This is the man who taught me German," Dastgir told me.

"Your brother has been my most excellent student," said Tahir.

"How do you know German so well?" I asked.

"About twelve years ago, King Amanullah Khan sponsored a few dozen other colleagues of mine and myself to study in European Universities," he explained. "He believed one of the best investments he could make in the country was in the higher education of the younger generation. Thanks to his generosity, I was sent to study at a German University."

Tahir went on and told me the joys of his life in Germany and how I must visit there someday. But fury showed in his eyes when he spoke about the state of our own country upon his return. Tahir told me how deeply disappointed he was by the corruption of the government and the outrage he felt when Nadir Shah betrayed King Amanullah, and how he decided to do something about it. With his degree in hand, he assembled a group of thirty scholars to meet at Coffee Delbar[47], a local coffee shop owned by an Afghan Sikh[48] man who was also Pro-Amanullah. These scholars and the owner met regularly to discuss plans to bring Amanullah's initiatives back into action. Somehow, the Intelligence Office caught wind of this think tank and sent an undercover agent into the shop. The agent infiltrated the Pro-Amanullah meeting that day and reported back to the Intelligence Office. Later that same day, everyone at the meeting, including the coffee shop owner was jailed at Dehmazang. Tahir introduced me to his colleagues and even the coffee shop owner, all of whom I thoroughly enjoyed meeting.

My first week in the men's prison progressed rapidly. Dastgir was right. The education I received was much more rigorous compared to what I had

---

[47] Sweetheart.
[48] A follower of Sikhism.

experienced at Sarai Ali Khan. When at the end of the week, the *deh-bashi* entered our room and asked my brothers politely if he could chain Azim and me, I almost forgot I had gone the whole week unshackled. I had been so overjoyed with all the time I'd spent with my brothers that I almost forgot I was still a prisoner.

"It was my duty and responsibility to shackle your brothers the first day, but I didn't want to interfere with your joyful reunion," said the *deh-bashi*. "If you two are seen unshackled by the warden, he'll punish me with 500 lashes." We thanked the *deh-bashi* for his generosity and followed him down the hall.

The *deh-bashi* took us to another man who was waiting for us with chains, two sets of shackles, a hammer and some nails. The man started with me. "Stand here," he said. "Put this on." He handed me a leather harness connected to a circular piece of iron at the bottom with two iron rods extending downwards. He then put a thick, cold iron shackle around my right ankle and began hammering one of the iron rods along the side of it and shut it with a nail. The shackle was so tight around my ankle that the iron cut into my skin. I tried my best to keep my composure as the man began closing the shackle around my left ankle. After my ankles were shackled, he put a leather belt around my neck, which had chains hanging off of it. He locked the chains to the circular piece of iron on my waist.

Looking down at the shackles around my feet, I was haunted by disbelief. *How can a King believe that I'm such a threat? How can a government perceive me as a criminal? What have I done?*

"Next," he said. It was Azim's turn. I stared in horror, watching the iron shut around Azim's ankles. I could now see the reality that there wasn't a set date for our freedom. Of course, my family and I have known this for years, but feeling the tightly closed iron shackles around my ankles caused me to greater understand the horrific reality of our situation.

"You're all done now. Return to your cells," the man said.

The *deh-bashi* walked us back, and I saw blood trickle onto my feet as I shuffled awkwardly to our cell. When I saw my brothers, I was in shock. "How do you sleep with this? How do you sit?" I asked. The entire set up was constraining; I struggled to even sit on the floor. I never thought sitting could be such a luxury until that moment. My brothers crackled with laughter as they watched me, then Dastgir helped me up.

"You don't always need to have the belt around your neck. You only need to keep it on during the afternoon prisoner count," he said as he helped me remove the leather belt. Although the chains attached to the belt were still connected to the harness, I felt less constrained. "If you want to sit down, you need to pull the harness buckle slightly outwards to give some distance from the metal rods and your legs. This will allow you to gently lower yourself without losing your balance."

I tried to do as my brother instructed, but I fell on my back again. We all laughed. It made the situation lighter. Dastgir helped me stand up and I tried again. Finally, I did it correctly. "My ankles are bleeding," I told my brothers. "Is that normal?"

"Yes, for the first few days. Don't worry, though. Your skin will toughen up," Ghaffar said.

He was right. For the next several days, our ankles kept bleeding. Eventually, the bleeding stopped, and the shackles seemed to irritate our feet less. But the pain of the shackles wasn't our only problem…

One night while we were all asleep, Azim's entire body began twitching uncontrollably. I looked at him and saw that his jaw was locked shut. He was making a buzzing noise. My brothers and I jumped out of bed, fearful and unsure of what was happening to our cousin. We held him still as drool dripped from his mouth and his eyes rolled back. "Has he ever done this before?" Dastgir asked me.

"No, I've never seen anybody do this before," I said feeling worried. We didn't know what to do. Azim was not responding to us. After 20 minutes of watching over him, he started to rock back and forth slowly until he finally fell sound asleep.

The next morning when we woke up, Azim asked us, "Did I have a seizure last night?"

We were speechless. "How did you know?" I asked.

"I cut my tongue. Sometimes that happens when I have a seizure. I hope I didn't disturb you all during your sleep."

"How long have you had this condition?"

"Since Hamid died."

A gloomy silence fell over the room. As much as we had suffered, we knew Azim had suffered more.

My cousin, Abdul Azim.
Photo was taken after release, 1947.

FOURTEEN

As the days wore on, I met more political prisoners. Each of them shared their personal stories about the events leading to their incarceration. Mohammed Aziz Tukhi was one man who shared a story I could not forget. He was Abdul-Khaliq's classmate, as well as friends with Abdullah and I'shaq. He told us how they had all been tortured by brutal methods like *qin-u-fana*[49], whipping, oil-burning and sleep deprivation.

"The soldiers beat and tortured us mercilessly, accusing us of being part of Abdul-Khaliq's plot to assassinate Nadir Shah. We did nothing! We knew nothing of it! But that didn't matter. That didn't stop them from whipping us or crushing our bones with metal rods."

Some of the other inmates who were transferred to Dehmazang from the *Arg* prison told me that they had seen the executions of my uncles Jailani Khan and Shir-Mohammed Khan. Some of them even witnessed the executions of my cousins and the gruesome killing of Abdul-Khaliq.

"It was terrible, absolutely terrible and heartbreaking," one of them said. "My mind is forever scarred. And the worst scene of all was watching what the soldiers did to Abdul-Khaliq. It was utterly inhumane…the soldiers acted like they were ripping up a ragdoll with their weapons."

They also spoke about the sweeping terror and fear imposed by the power hungry Prime Minister Hashim, who now had supreme rule over the court

---

[49] A torture technique that involves placing metal rods between fingers and crushing the fingers against them, as well as using the rods to crush the legs and shins.

and absolute authority to order anybody's execution at the snap of his finger. As they recounted the horrific acts of the Prime Minister, they would vigilantly survey the area around us to ensure no eavesdropping guards were in sight. I knew they risked brutal punishment for speaking out in this fashion, but they spoke so quietly, their own shadows would barely be able to hear them.

They told me how soldiers dragged them out of their homes and dumped them into Dehmazang without any documentation or records regarding their arrest. When they tried to reason with the guards, the guards told them that questioning decisions by authorities could lead to more severe punishment. All they could do was quietly accept the injustice lest they wanted to be whipped unconscious. To make matters worse, they weren't given any information about the length of their sentence. Their fate was up in the air, like a tossed coin that would never land. This made us all grow more pessimistic about someday regaining our own freedom. Perhaps we have all been left there to suffer until we eventually die after living a meaningless life. As far as we knew, we were the ghosts of the country—invisible and forgotten.

How could human beings be so violent and stonehearted? I thought. *How could they impose torture, suffering, and murder on their fellow human beings without any hesitation? Are their hearts asleep? How can they even sleep soundly at night knowing what they've done?*

The suffering of the political prisoners went beyond the walls of Dehmazang. Some of these men had worked as government officials in their previous lives. They had monthly salaries that supported their entire family. After they were dumped into Dehmazang, their salaries were cut off, and their families and children were now suffering in extreme poverty.

Still, these imprisoned fathers did their best to support their families. I would often see them knitting and sewing tablecloths, jackets, shawls, socks, and gloves to sell for a few Afghani, which they turned around and sent to their families so they wouldn't go hungry. Abdul Hadi Dawi was one of these fathers. He was a scholar and one of the pioneers who fought for our constitution and democracy. After Nadir Shah took the reins of power, he was suddenly laid off from his government job and taken into the *Arg* and later transferred to Dehmazang. Out of curiosity, I asked him if his family ever told him what life was like in the outside world.

He began speaking with a distant look in his eyes, "After years of imprisonment, I was finally allowed to have my family members visit me. My jail mates were eager for the visit, too. They wished to hear of my family's health and news from outside. Unfortunately, there was no news I could give them. I had to tell them my family was not much better off than we were."

He then cited this line of poetry:

"The east wind peered into the nightingale's nest and said:
'I find the prisoner's household in trouble.'"

Others told me about their experiences with Commander Turrahbaz and the physical and verbal abuse he'd inflicted on them and other prisoners.

"You don't want to get on this man's bad side," they said. "He can be absolutely heartless."

During the afternoons, many prisoners gathered around the loudspeaker in the prison yard to listen to the latest national news. Occasionally the radio station would also play music. The radio was on for two hours per day, but my brothers and I wouldn't spend much time there, instead choosing to focus on our studies.

As late afternoon approached, the *deh-bashi* and two other soldiers would walk down a long line of shackled prisoners, conducting a head count. The inmates were not allowed to leave the prison yards during this time. If there was an error during the count, which happened about once a week, the whole process was repeated twice or even thrice until we heard the megaphone say, "One thousand, four hundred and fifty-four. You can all return to your wards now."

After the announcement, we were allowed to have a short break before returning to our cells. A long line of a few hundred men would form in front of the restroom. Others went to the corridor where we were allowed to use a small brass charcoal burner to make tea, using water from a small stream flowing through several *hawilis* outside Dehmazang and into our ward—the same stream we used for drinking water, washing clothes and taking baths. After this short break, my brothers and I went to Tahir's room for our afternoon lesson.

Every evening, a news program played through the loudspeakers in the neighboring *hawili*. The only way we could listen to it was if we climbed onto our high windowsills and carefully listened outside. Naim Besmel, Tahir's cousin, typically volunteered for the task. We'd help lift him up to the cement ledge, and once he was seated, he would grab onto the iron bars for stability and position his head so he could listen while the rest of us waited in silence. After nearly an hour, Naim lowered himself from the windowsill and began reciting the news. We listened intently as he informed us about national events and the ongoing World War.

At night when we slept, troops of mosquitos, fleas and other bugs entered our cell to attack us. Before I went to sleep each night, I thought about my family and sent them my prayers. These thoughts often turned to my father. I wished I could see him. I felt depressed that I couldn't remember his face and voice. I'd dream of the hundreds of conversations we'd have together in Farsi, Arabic, and German, and I'd pretend to hear him tell me, "I'm proud of you, son."

When I'd wake up the next morning, my focus would be sharp and clear: I wanted to progress in my language studies so I could speak with my father and make him proud.

FIFTEEN

Two years went by before political prisoners were allowed to have *mulaqat*[50] from their relatives. Typically, these visiting days happened every Friday. The *paiwazes*[51] gathered outside the main gate, eager to see their confined relatives. Inmates were then guided near the main gate where the only thing between them and their relatives, between prison and freedom, was a one and a half meter wall.

Paiwazes who managed to come earlier in the morning were able to get a better glimpse of their imprisoned loved ones. Otherwise, it was so overcrowded that those who arrived late had trouble communicating with everyone trying to talk over one another.

Meanwhile, a *deh-bashi* along with several soldiers vigilantly supervised the gathering from both sides of the barrier. If anybody did or said anything contrary to the jail's regulations, they would shout, "Time up! Time up!" So for the most part, everyone behaved. Still, there were always *paiwazes* who would try to get a few extra minutes with their loved ones. Soldiers from both sides would then separate the parties, pushing them away from the wall before the inmates were herded back inside.

Female *paiwazes* were allowed to come inside the jail complex wearing a *chadar*[52]. I often saw them sitting with their male relatives, who gave up their

---

[50] Visit.
[51] Visitors.
[52] Head-covering cloth.

seats and squatted against the walls. Some of the inmates would look for a more comfortable place to meet their female relatives, taking bed sheets and cloaks to make a tent-like shelter where they could talk to their relatives with some privacy and peace of mind.

When men somehow missed their Friday *mulaqat*, they became so enraged they cursed the oppressive Prime Minister and King's names out loud, wishing for their downfall. If the soldiers heard these prisoners, they would punish them brutally with whippings in plain sight. Sometimes they were even sent to solitary confinement, deprived of their *mulaqat* privilege for weeks until countless requests were made to the superintendent from both the inmate and their *paiwazes*. Then, only under certain conditions and with more supervision than usual, were they permitted to have a *mulaqat* with their family members.

My brothers and I were curious if we'd have any visitors. During one of the *mulaqat* days, we walked outside, searching for familiar faces on the other side of the wall. To our disappointment, there was nobody. I asked Mir Enyatullah why we didn't have any visitors. "Khaled *jan*, your relatives are all imprisoned, and for those who aren't, they would languish in prison alongside us if they came anywhere near us. The ruling regime would imprison anyone who got close to the Charkhis."

Sadly, I heard this from other inmates as well. Family friends were afraid of reaching out to us because they knew if they did, they would soon be on the other side of the wall with us. Knowing this reality crushed my morale. The only thing that made me hopeful was the weekly laundry notes we still received from our mothers and sisters. Our mothers continued to give us nurturing advice, reminding us to be patient and to trust in God that everything would work out for us eventually. Although it was hard to believe the message, their heartfelt encouragement gave us the will to persevere.

SIXTEEN

Farooq *Telegrafi*, 1925.

The majority of political prisoners had been languishing in prison for many years without any certainty of an eventual release. Consequently, some of them occasionally made a "release plea", asking their free relatives during a *mulaqat* day, usually during the *Eid* holiday or Independence Day, to send the following message to the Prime Minister:

We are not guilty of any crime and have been in prison for so long. Our family members are living without their fathers and guardians. They have neither food nor shelter. Thus, we beseech Your Highness, on the occasion of these holy and sacred days, to show some leniency and mercy by setting us free. After all, we have had our share of pain and suffering during these long years of incarceration.

The Prime Minister usually delivered the same response:

Captivity and freedom are not my concern. Instead of wasting your time writing me petitions, you would do better beseeching God's mercy to soften my heart to let you be free.

Based on their dossiers, political prisoners were normally categorized as *basha*[53] and *baz*[54]. Both of these terms came from birds found in Afghanistan. *Basha* indicated a lifetime imprisonment, whereas *baz* meant an occasional review of the dossiers. All executions and life sentences were enforced without any investigation or trial during the dictatorships of Nadir Shah, his son and heir to the throne, Zahir Shah, and his successor, Prime Minister Mohammed Hashim Khan. The fates of all these lives were up to these men alone. Unfortunately, there was no reasoning nor justice.

The poet Ferdowsi says:

When you plant a tree that does not bear good fruit, even if you water it with the waters of heaven, when the fruit comes, it will still be bitter and inedible; Same as if you leave the eggs of a crow under a peacock, after the peacock's work is done, the eggs still yield crows.

Witnessing these entreaties and refusals showed me the radical injustice that had befallen Afghanistan. A king or leader of a nation is expected to have a farsighted vision, exhibiting justice and divine attributes. After all, a king is

[53] Sparrowhawk. Rhymes with the Persian verb "basha", which means "let it be".
[54] Falcon. Rhymes with the Persian verb "baz", which means "again" or "later on".

given the title of *zill-u-allah*.[55] They are supposed to be the agent of Allah on Earth and represent the Almighty among His people. In Islamic countries, this is a position of high responsibility, but these power hungry people consistently misused the Holy title as they persecuted and purged the educated and sincerely patriotic. In order to satisfy their beastly whims, these rulers took away their citizen's human rights, even depriving their children (like me) of an education.

An honest and patriotic leader is not afraid of an enlightened and intelligent citizenry. Instead of feeling inferior and threatened by geniuses, they stand by them and make great use of their minds for the sake of the country's development and progress. Unfortunately, the ruling regime took a different path.

One frosty, winter night, about four hundred people were herded into the prison with their hands in chains and fetters. They were dressed in *chapan* and *gupicha*[56], wearing wellington boots and a particular type of belt around their waist typical of people from *Pardarya*. We learned they were suspected supporters of Ibrahim Big[57]. Within a matter of weeks, they all mysteriously disappeared. We realized later that the entire group had been killed and buried in a mass grave without any funeral, slaughtered in the dead of night.

Afterwards, gossip spread rampantly between the inmates that the Defense Minister Shah-Mahmood had made his way to the Qatghan province to end an insurgency of pro-Ibrahim Big rebels. Upon arrival, he ordered the massacre of a large number of civilians. Local residents described "a minaret of human skulls." Following this massacre, Shah-Mahmood detained many other civilians and sent them to Kabul where they were likewise executed and buried in a mass grave.

One day, responding to this injustice, one of the political prisoners wrote a petition in English and courageously handed it to a United Nations delegate who happened to be visiting the political prisoners in our section. The

---

[55] Shadow of God.

[56] Coarse, quilted cotton clothes.

[57] Ibrahim Big led troops from Turkmenistan to fight for their country's freedom against Russia. Zahir Shah and his family were supportive of Russia, and thus saw Ibrahim Big as an enemy.

prisoner was Mohammed Omar Khan, and he was one of the scholars who pursued his University education in Germany.

In his petition, Mohammed Omar Khan mentioned he had been detained without any investigation or trial, subjected to cruel torture from the warden, and ultimately left without any certainty about how long he would be in prison. The UN delegate enclosed the petition in a detailed report of his observations he presented to the Prime Minister. He expected the Prime Minister would be a responsible person who considered such grievances and honorably treated his political prisoners according to international standards. The next day Mohammed Omar Khan was sentenced to six months of solitary confinement along with whippings and other forms of torture.

That was not the only injustice we heard about. Another fellow prisoner, Farooq *Telegrafi*[58], who had decided to make his own release plea, told us the story of how he had been detained:

"During the revolution, when war was raging between the forces of *Bache-e-Saqaa* Habibullah Kalakani and the pro-Amanullah Khan militants in Southern Afghanistan, there were rumors in Kabul and the surrounding areas that His Majesty Amanullah Khan was returning to reclaim his Kingdom. From the suburbs of Kabul, we could hear the bangs of artillery just outside the city.

"I was busy working in the telegraph office along with my colleagues, wiring orders from the ruling government to the concerned authorities when the door abruptly opened, and in came a tall, handsome man dressed in dusty war clothes with a rifle and cartridge belt hanging from his shoulder.

"'Congratulations brothers! Victory! Victory!' he shouted in extreme excitement. 'I have an urgent message to send to Rome[59]. Could you give me a pen and piece of paper please?'

"We immediately put a pen and sheet of paper on the desk, and the man wrote the following wire:

---

[58] Telegraph operator.
[59] At the time, King Amanullah was in Rome with his family for their safety.

CONGRATULATIONS YOUR MAJESTY! KABUL HAS BEEN CONQUERED.

"The feeling of happiness and jubilation was so intense among all of us at hearing of the end of the war that we burst into tears and embraced each other with joy. We immediately wired his telegraph to Rome and courteously asked him his name and anything he could tell us about the conquest of Kabul. He replied, 'I am Shir-Mohammed from the Charkh district in Logar. I am the first officer to reach Kabul after *Saqavid's* breakdown in Waghjan pass. I came here to wire this telegraph to King Amanullah Khan. Other commanders including Nadir Khan and Shah-Wali Khan are right behind me and should reach Kabul within minutes.'

"With that, he left the office.

"Because of this happy and exciting news, my colleagues and I did not want to stay in the office any longer. We headed to the center of Kabul to see what would happen next. Long afterwards, I came to know that the handsome young officer was the same Shir-Mohammed Khan who was one of the well-known gallant soldiers and cousins of Ghulam Nabi Khan Charkhi.

"From that moment, all of us eagerly awaited King Amanullah's return and the restoration of his Kingdom in Kabul. However, our hopes were dashed when the pendulum of power shifted to Nadir Shah. After that, Hashim became Prime Minister and Shah-Wali was named Marshal and 'Conqueror of Kabul.' As you know, this was extremely unexpected for our people.

"When we heard that Ghulam Nabi Khan had been invited to Kabul to iron out the differences within the Kingdom, we were hopeful, and it reinforced our expectations of the return of Amanullah Khan. However, all our optimism was dashed again when, only a month later, Nadir Shah killed Ghulam Nabi Khan and Colonel Shir-Mohammed Khan, the exuberant man we met that day in the office, was sent to the *Arg* along with Ghulam Jailani Khan and some of his other cousins.

"Then there was the day when we heard that Nadir Shah had executed Colonel Shir-Mohammed Khan and General Ghulam Jailani Khan. With these executions and mass imprisonment, a pall fell over Kabul. Everyone was in a state of anxiety and terror, not knowing what the ruling regime had in store for its people, whether they would be dumped in prison or executed at the snap of a finger. During this dark period, my colleagues and I were detained and put in prison on the charges of having wired Shir-Mohammed Khan's telegram to His Majesty Amanullah Khan. In jail, we were told that our punishment was changed from execution to lifetime imprisonment."

Much of Farooq *Telegrafi's* story was familiar to me. I remembered what my uncle, Anwar Khan, had told me about these events during my first week in Dehmazang. Nadir had come to Logar[60] with Shah-Wali and had been accommodated in a part of my family's ancestral compound in the Charkh district. Janbaz and Shir-Mohammed were living in Charkh at the time protecting the women and children who had been displaced by the *Saqavids*, and Nadir Khan and his brothers shared their plans and war strategy with my uncles, stating their intent to restore Amanullah Khan to his throne. Nadir Khan's passionate and patriotic speeches inspired many to fight and being loyal officers of Amanullah Khan's government, my uncles believed in Nadir and supported his plans.

My uncles used their influence to gather people from southern Jaji, Mangal, Chakhansor and other areas for their mission to reclaim Kabul. Every day, from morning to evening, people would gather and discuss the liberation of Kabul. Each time these people gathered, they would end their meetings zealously vowing to cooperate in this righteous cause and praying for the mercy and help of Allah.

A month later when all the people were ready, Colonel Shir-Mohammed led the operation and fought courageously, defeating the Saqavid forces in

---

[60] A province in Afghanistan located in the eastern part of the country.

their final battle at Tanga-e-Waghjan. As soon as Kabul fell into the hands of the pro-Amanullah Khan forces, Nadir took power and announced himself King of Afghanistan. He assigned the most important positions of government to his brothers, making Hashim the Prime Minister, Shah-Mahmood the Minister of *Harbia*[61], and Shah-Wali the Marshall. During the war, Nadir had appointed Janbaz Khan as Corps Commander and Shir-Mohammed Khan as a Colonel. Shortly after Nadir's betrayal, though, the former was sentenced to life in prison, and the latter was sentenced to death for wiring the telegraph to Amanullah Khan.

Hearing Farooq's story stirred rage in all of us as we were reminded of the injustice that had happened to our family and the disrespect and cruelty experienced by those who had made release pleas. Still, many prisoners persisted in pleading for their freedom.

On one unbearably hot summer day during World War II, many of the prisoners who were fed up with our insect-ridden living conditions met to discuss their ideas for finally attaining freedom. They decided to write an emotional letter to the Prime Minister with the intention to soften his heart to compassion, assigning the task of drafting the letter to Saduddin Baha because he was the best writer in the group.

Mr. Baha drafted the following letter:

To Your Highness, Prime Minister! We are writing to draw your attention to the fact that our files are lying untouched in the office of the warden as if it was inscribed on the skin of a frog and tossed onto the road. We look forward to your response.

When the other inmates read Mr. Baha's draft, they were shocked. "Mr. Baha! If the Prime Minister reads this letter, his heart will not soften. This letter will only provoke him to subject us to further torture and endless Hell!"

Mr. Baha said that he was no longer hopeful about being released. He felt it was unnecessary to write anything that begged for the mercy of such a cruel

---

[61] War.

warlord who disguised himself as a national leader. He also mentioned that it would be better to wait until the war was over when the United Nations would have to adopt new worldwide measures regarding political prisoners.

Prisoners listened to the news on a daily basis, hungering for updates indicating the end of the war. My brothers and I listened as well, but we knew it wasn't enough to hope for some light at the end of the tunnel. Ultimately, we had to bring such light to ourselves, so while others waited for news, we put all of our focus on our studies.

SEVENTEEN

Eid arrived, making the atmosphere of Kabul alive with celebration. Gifts were exchanged, feasts were prepared, and the people of Kabul were in high spirits, except for us prisoners.

Since most of the guards were sent to Chaman Huzuri[62] for the King's parade, only a few guards remained to watch over Dehmazang. Out of fear, these guards imposed more restrictions on us than normal. So while people were celebrating until the late hours of night, we were to remain silent in our cells.

During *Eid*, I contracted a fever that came with intense chest pains and gave me difficulty breathing, especially at night. It was a challenge just to fall asleep. My throat was on fire, and my chest felt as if needles were stabbing into me. I'd wake up in the middle of the night from recurring nightmares, reliving the horrific images of seeing the dead bodies of my beloved uncles and cousins. To distract myself from my suffering, I stared out the window of my cell at the bright full moon until I grew so tired that the pain couldn't keep me awake any longer. One evening, as I was struggling to rest, my cell door swung upon and in came the *deh-bashi* with two guards.

"Chain inspection! Anyone who is not fettered must come forth."

With my illness, I had written permission from the doctor to remain unchained. That did not deter the intruders.

"You," the *deh-bashi* pointed at me. "Come with us."

---

[62] A park in Kabul where many major holidays and festivals were celebrated.

The three men walked me down the hallway and into the adjacent corridor. There, several chained prisoners were waiting for us with hammers and shackles. I lined up behind the few dozen other men, and as my turn approached, I tried to make light of the situation. I imagined I was being given a pair of chains as my *Eid* gift[63]. This eased my mind a bit, only until I once again felt the cold iron pressed skin-tight around my wrists and ankles.

The sounds of chains clinking against one another followed me on my walk back to my cell. I heard especially angry grunts from one inmate behind me. I looked back and saw him approach his cell. Just before opening the door, he paused, scanning the area around him as if he wanted to make sure there weren't any guards nearby. Then, he exploded with fury, "My God! Is this an Islamic or non-Islamic country?"

"Who said that?" yelled a voice.

I quickly scurried into another corridor, peering back to see what was going to happen. Five men appeared from the other side of the hall—four guards and one man who seemed to be their leader. Although I hadn't seen him before, I knew in my gut that it was the wicked warden, Duran. My heart sank.

"Fetch that pest!" Duran ordered the guards.

Like hunting dogs, they aggressively dragged the inmate in front of the warden.

"Now, what were you saying?" asked Duran.

The prisoner was trembling like an earthquake. "I did not s-s-say anything, S-sir, I was just pl-pl-pleading with my Lord."

"Liar! I heard you calling us infidels. If you confess, I might forgive you. Otherwise, I'm going to whip you so fucking hard, you'll be lucky if you can stand on your two feet one month from now."

Trembling even more, the inmate stuttered, "I h-have not called y-you an infidel, Sir. I h-have only asked m-my God if I'm in an Islamic or non-Islamic country s-s-since we're not allowed to p-participate in *Eid*."

An inferno rose in Duran's eyes. His face tensed as he yelled, "Guards, hold this infidel steady and whip him as hard as you can."

---

[63] During *Eid*, it's typical for people to receive gifts, especially from elders.

I squinted in agony as I witnessed two guards whipping the man. The lashes were so brutal his shirt was torn to pieces, sending streams of blood crawling down his back.

The poor man screamed in agony, pleading for mercy, "I'm sorry! Please forgive me! I haven't done anything wrong! Oh please, Sir! For God's sake! Please, Sir! I repent my foolish words!"

An evil joy came to Duran's face.

"Whip him harder! Harder!" Duran shouted.

The prisoner's blood-curdling screams rang in my ears. Eventually, the yelling stopped, and he fell to the floor, unconscious. A painful silence tore through the hall. The warden stared emotionlessly at the bloodied body for what seemed like an eternity. Then, he smiled.

Like a dead man awakening from the grave, the prisoner slowly regained consciousness. A few times, he struggled to stand up, only to fall flat again on his face. The guards laughed. Finally, two guards grabbed his arms, pulled him up to his feet, and ushered him into his cell. I waited until Duran and the guards were out of sight before I casually and silently walked back to my own cell.

When I finally returned, my brothers gave me anxious looks, perhaps because I had been absent for so long.

"What happened?" they asked.

Still shivering from the shock, I related the horrifying event I had just witnessed.

"Did they do anything to you?" Ghaffar asked me, checking me for injury.

"No," I replied. "They never saw me. I was hiding in the shadows."

My brothers exhaled with relief. "Thank God they didn't see you. Duran is capable of much worse," said Dastgir.

I tried to sleep and forget about the incident. Unfortunately, the images of the beating haunted my dreams. I suffered horrible chills the whole night. Every time I closed my eyes to sleep, the nightmarish scene would play through my mind again. I was shocked that a human being could find joy in inflicting so much pain upon his fellow man. The image continued to haunt me throughout the next few weeks. I prayed it would be the last time I would see such violence.

When another hot summer arrived, *deh-bashis* were ordered to maintain higher surveillance to ensure all prisoners were working during the daytime. Aside from my brothers and I, a few other prisoners had chosen to skip work during those hot summer days. One of them was Khaja Mohammed, a former attendant for my uncle, who slept in our cell.

One day, a *deh-bashi* went cell to cell to make sure everybody was working. When he came to our cell, he noticed Khaja there. The *deh-bashi* was fine with us not working since we were teenagers focused on our studies, but he informed Khaja that he was not exempt from labor. Khaja gently refused, stating he didn't want to work nor did he want a loaf of bread.

"I shall only serve these four young men," he said to the *deh-bashi* as he opened his hand towards us.

"Who are they?" the *deh-bashi* asked suspiciously.

"They are my masters," replied Khaja with respect and sincerity.

"Ok then. Let us go to the warden so you can tell him yourself. I don't have the authority to exempt you for this reason."

Khaja followed him. An hour later, when he came back, he was holding his face with the end of his turban. His face was bloodied and swollen, and his mustache was missing.

"Those bastards beat me black and blue," he said quietly. "When I repeated the same words to Duran, he exploded with anger and ordered the guards to beat me as hard as they could. 'Snatch the mustache off of this shameless bug,' he yelled. 'Let him know what it means to disobey orders!'

"I did my best not to submit to those beasts. I held my ground as long as I could. But the beating was so brutal that I collapsed to the floor, where they punched me a few more times, laughing at me and calling me worthless scum. They had to make sure they crushed my morale before letting me go."

Unfortunately, Khaja wasn't alone. His beating was just one of the many oppressive acts of Duran and his soldiers. With him in charge, cruelty became natural and expected.

The prospect of one day experiencing such a beating gave me great fear. Despite the darkness, I continued to focus on the one thing that brought me light: learning.

EIGHTEEN

O ne summer day in 1943, I was out in the prison yard with my brothers studying German when, suddenly, a bunch of commotion arose about the arrival of a new political prisoner. Many of the other inmates began chattering about how the man had been checked into *Makhsoos*[64], "the special corridor", the night before. Those in *Makhsoos* were deemed the most troublesome prisoners, so they remained in solitary confinement and their break times were spent in a separate, highly supervised area of the prison.

What could this man have done to be put under such intense scrutiny? I wondered.

The man was Sheikh Bahlool, a scholar from Iran. We didn't know much about him at first, but six months later, some of the other prisoners managed to talk to him for a few minutes. They met him by the outdoor gate separating the political prisoners from those in solitary confinement. After their conversation, gossip spread throughout the corridors about who he was and the reason for his imprisonment.

"When the Iranian King, Reza Shah, issued a decree under which Iranian women were ordered to remove their *hijab*," explained one of the inmates. "Sheikh Bahlool, along with many other clerics, criticized the royal command at the Goharshad Mosque in Mashhad and tried to instigate people against the edict. When Reza Shah learned what the people were saying about him at

---

[64] A section of Dehmazang prison where the most high-risk inmates were sent into solitary confinement.

Goharshad, he ordered his security forces to open fire on the Mosque. Many civilians were mercilessly gunned down. Shocked by the tragedy, Sheikh Bahlool fled to Afghanistan where he was immediately detained for not having proper documentation, and now he's been transferred here to Dehmazang prison."

The inmates remarked about Sheikh Bahlool's extraordinary level of intelligence.

"This man is a genius!" one said. "His memory is extraordinary. He can recite the world's greatest textbooks, and he is known to have memorized thousands of poems! Supposedly he memorized the entire Qur'an when he was only eight years old! You must meet him when you get a chance."

A month later I had that chance. While many of us were out in the yard, a squad of guards announced that we could finally share the same yard space as those from the "special corridor." I watched closely as 35 isolated souls were escorted outside to commune with the rest of us.

One of the men beckoned to one of the inmates who had spoken to us about the new prisoner. The man was short, dark-skinned and had a thin grey beard, and he quickly became the center of attention.

"I think that is Sheikh Bahlool," I whispered to my brothers. We walked towards the growing circle of people and stood in awe alongside the others as Sheik Bahlool enthusiastically and elegantly recited dozens of poems from two of the greatest Sufi poets, Rumi and Hafez. One verse he said profoundly touched me.

"'I said, 'What about my eyes?' He said, 'Keep them on the road.' I said, 'What about my passion?' He said, 'Keep it burning.' I said, 'What about my heart?' He said, 'Tell me what you hold inside it?' I said, 'Pain and sorrow.' He said, 'Stay with it. The wound is the place where the Light enters you.'"

Hearing that last sentence, I began to wonder if there was a greater meaning to all this—a greater purpose. Suddenly, I found myself grappling with contradictory thoughts. *There is no higher purpose to my entire family being imprisoned. There is no higher purpose to my brother and cousins dying prematurely, or my uncles and older cousins being executed. The ruling regime is corrupt, inhumane, tyrannical, and misusing power. We're the unfortunate ones.* But then,

I'd hear another voice. *Perhaps, because of this grand suffering and pain, I know the resilience of the soul. I know the importance of kindness and love. I know that no matter what happens in life, I always have the choice to make the most of my situation.* This internal dialogue played out in my head, like two kites battling each other in *gudiparaan baazi*. At my core, though, I knew Rumi's words were true.

After Sheikh Bahlool finished his recitations, the audience applauded him. Then, he spoke about a magnificent opportunity:

"I wish to bring you the knowledge and wisdom I've gained over the years. Everybody is welcome to join me for classes every day. Tomorrow I will hold a lecture right here on advanced Arabic literature. In order for me to teach every one of you at my best, I will need to teach you in smaller groups: one group at ten a.m., another at noon and the last at two p.m. Make sure to bring notebooks and pens if you have them."

I was overwhelmed with excitement. Arabic was my favorite subject, and I wanted to master it. I walked up to Sheikh Bahlool and introduced myself, thanking him for the extraordinary opportunity.

"I would be honored to have you as my teacher," I said.

"I would be honored to have you as my student," he replied with a smile.

I shook Sheikh Bahlool's hand with the utmost respect and returned to my cell excited for what the next day would bring.

The next day, my brothers and I met with Sheikh Bahlool at ten a.m. "Today we will focus on the principles of Arabic literature," he told us.

For two hours, he recited advanced lessons purely from memory. I was astonished. *How could a man have such a powerful mind?* He made sure to quiz us every hour, and anytime we had questions, he always answered them with profound attention to detail. I was inspired to see that despite his current disguise as a prisoner, this man was a scholar of soaring intellect.

Through his wisdom, Sheikh Bahlool brought light to the space around him, and I was so motivated to achieve his level of intelligence that I stayed for extra classes. Sometimes I stayed so late that we were allowed to speak one-on-one until the guards ordered us all to return to our cells for the daily count. This one-on-one time was precious. Even though I was in jail, Sheikh Bahlool made me feel like I was at a prestigious University.

One day during a one-on-one class, Sheikh Bahlool gave me a small task.
"I want you to read this letter aloud to me."

"Certainly," I replied.

"Dear mother," I read, "I'm fine. There is no need to worry. I know you haven't seen me in over a year, and I'm writing to let you know that I'm in a prison in Kabul, but I am happy. In fact, I'm very happy. I have 17 students that I'm teaching here. Whether I'm in prison or outside in a beautiful house, what matters most is that I'm teaching people, and I have found that gift here."

I realized why Sheikh Bahlool wanted me to read the letter aloud. He wanted to show me that happiness isn't dependant on where you are, but with what you make of life. I was impressed by Sheikh Bahlool's optimism. I couldn't help but feel good about life at that moment. I think everyone felt that way around him.

During the first few weeks of class, each class had approximately six students. Sheikh Bahlool wanted us to make progress quickly, so he pushed us through a rigorous curriculum of more and more advanced lessons. Unfortunately, most people couldn't keep up. One by one, people dropped out. Eventually, only three students remained: Dastgir, Attah Muhammad (Abdul-Khaliq's cousin), and myself.

At that point, Sheikh Bahlool suggested it would be better for each of us to spend one-on-one time with him. That way, we could individually progress with our mastery of Arabic literature, as well as philosophy and metaphysics. We took turns with our teacher, one of us going at ten a.m., the other at noon, and the last at two p.m. At nights, Sheikh Bahlool would write his own poetry and prepare coursework for us. His dedication to teaching was truly remarkable.

Beyond his intellect, Sheikh Bahlool had a soft heart for all living beings. One day during our class time, a sparrow injured itself when it fell to the ground near us. Sheikh Bahlool paused the lesson and walked over to the suffering bird. He picked it up, noted the sparrow's wing was broken, and hid it in the loose-hanging sleeve of his *perahan*[65]. That night, he nurtured the sparrow, giving it food, water and a place to rest in his cell. He kept this routine for the next few weeks until the bird regained its strength to fly. This particular incident didn't just happen once. Only a few weeks later, another sparrow fell, and Sheikh Bahlool once again provided a place for the bird to rest and recover.

After a while, the sparrows began visiting Sheikh Bahlool every day. They would chirp and land on his shoulder and hand, trusting him with their life. Never had I seen a man have such a profound connection with nature before.

Anybody who spent some time with Sheikh Bahlool knew his heart was full of love, and his mission was to contribute to others. For his monthly prisoner salary, Sheikh Bahlool received 210 Afghani. He kept 60 Afghani for himself to pay his daily meal expenses and then distributed the other 150 Afghani to the prisoners who were working like slaves to support their penniless families.

Sheikh Bahlool never spoke of his charity, though. I found it out through the other prisoners. One time before class, a teary-eyed man came up and thanked him. "*Tashakhur, besyar tashakhur*[66]. You are an angel," he said. Sheikh Bahlool responded with a humble smile and handshake.

"What was that about?" I asked.

"Nothing, just a small favor," he replied. "Let us continue with our studies."

People continued to speak about Sheikh Bahlool's wisdom. Finally, word got out through the guards to one of the wardens, Mr. Abdul-Khaliq. He was an educated and generous man who was in charge of supervising the construction of handicrafts by the criminal prisoners in exchange for their daily loaf of bread.

One guard told Mr. Abdul-Khaliq there was a political prisoner named Sheikh Bahlool who was a respected scholar and had a mind like a human encyclopedia. This intrigued Mr. Abdul-Khaliq, and he immediately called Sheikh Bahlool to his office. Upon meeting Sheikh Bahlool, he was indeed astonished by his intellect. He asked Sheikh Bahlool if he could come to his room and teach him regularly as well.

---

[65] A long-sleeve Afghan shirt.
[66] Thank you, many thanks.

Sheikh Bahlool was more than happy to agree. Thus, Mr. Abdul-Khaliq began taking private classes from him every day, inviting Sheikh Bahlool to come to his office every afternoon. Mr. Abdul-Khaliq was so enthusiastic about what he was learning that he told the Commander of the Kabul police headquarters about Sheikh Bahlool. Soon enough, the Commander became Sheikh Bahlool's newest student, receiving lessons from him every Wednesday.

The days kept getting brighter. One afternoon, a photographer from the United Nations came to document political prisoners. I was in the prison yard when I noticed him and acted quickly on the opportunity. I bribed the photographer with 10 Afghani if he could take a picture of my brother, Sheikh Bahlool and I. The photographer scanned the area, making sure no guards were watching him. He agreed. We stood up next to our teacher with a proud pose. Seconds later, the photographer's Polaroid camera flashed, and he handed me a blank photograph and told me to wait for the image to appear. When I saw three figures begin to develop from the still wet paper, I hid the picture to keep it safe.

My brother Ghulam Dastgir (left), Sheikh Bahlool (center),
and myself (right) in Dehmazang prison, 1945.

That night when we went back to our room, my brothers and I looked at the picture and laughed with joy at our extraordinary good luck. We had not had a photograph in thirteen years! We had Shiekh Bahlool to thank for our good fortune. Every day since he had arrived had been full of joy. That was until our wounds were torn open yet again.

NINETEEN

It was noontime. I was finishing my homework when a *deh-bashi* came to our cell. "One of your family members has just arrived in the Dehmazang hospital," he said. "They've come from the *Arg*."

We were shocked. My brothers, cousin and I followed the *deh-bashi* to the hospital, anxious about what we would find there. When we arrived, we approached one of the hospital assistants.

"We were told that one of our family members was just admitted to this hospital. Where can we find him?" I asked.

"Follow me. He's in one of the rooms upstairs," said the assistant.

My curiosity and anxiety heightened as we followed the man upstairs.

"Right this way," he said as he approached one of the doors.

He turned the knob slowly, and when the door opened, a shock of excitement rushed through me as I looked at the face of my dear cousin, Yahya. I hadn't seen him since I was six years old, but I remembered the times Yahya's family would visit our home—moments of laughter, full of shared games and fun.

We all stepped forth, giving big hugs to our cousin, feeling blessed by this reunion.

"Finally you visit us!" Dastgir joked. "We thought you had forgotten about your cousins!"

Yahya laughed, saying there must have been a misunderstanding. "You were supposed to come visit ME, remember? Oh, you've always been the forgetful brother!"

We all laughed and joked together, probably the most we'd done in a while. But after the initial surprise wore off, I noted the pale complexion of my cousin and the obvious weakness of his posture.

With casual trepidation, I asked, "What brings you to the hospital?"

"I've been suffering from stomach pains for a long time," he said, "terrible pains. Dr. Mir came and prescribed me painkillers, but they didn't help. The pain just kept getting worse. He continued to increase the dosage, but that did little to help. He then knew my condition was much more serious. He sent repeated requests to get me admitted to the hospital. Finally, yesterday, it went through."

Suddenly, we heard a knock on the door. It was the doctor.

"*Salaam*, tomorrow a surgeon from the Ministry of Health will be coming to operate on you."

"What do you believe the issue is?" Yahya asked.

"Your symptoms seem to match some form of tuberculosis. The surgeon will need to operate on you immediately to ensure the disease doesn't spread," said the doctor.

My stomach dropped. I remembered how my older brother and cousins had died of tuberculosis. Samad had even come to the very same hospital and hadn't survived. I tried to suppress the memories and block out the image of Hamid's lifeless body in Sarai Badam. I couldn't. All I could think about was the death surrounding our lives and the danger for my poor cousin.

"I will check in on you later tonight," the doctor added. "For now, enjoy your time with your family." He too was making an effort at being light-hearted.

After he left, silence swept through the room.

"Don't worry, I'll be fine," Yahya assured us with a hopeful smirk. "I want to hear about you and what you have been doing all these years! You're all grown men now!"

His optimism lifted our spirits. We spoke of all the knowledge we had gained, especially from Sheikh Bahlool. Yahya smiled wide with fascination.

"I hope to meet and learn from Sheikh Bahlool after I recover from this wretched disease."

"We can teach you as well," said Dastgir.

"I prefer to drink the water from the top of the mountain," Yahya said with a chuckle.

We stayed with our cousin until late, laughing and sharing stories about life in Dehmazang. He told us about the *Arg* and mentioned that Janbaz Khan had also been suffering from illness. A silent worry arose within my brothers and I after hearing our uncle may be suffering the same fate. I tried to ignore my fearful thoughts of losing them to illness.

"We will come back and visit you tomorrow after the operation. Make sure to rest for now," said Ghaffar.

I watched my cousin get back into bed, turned off the light and closed the door. My shoulders hunched as I walked down the stairs. I felt my energy sink. I looked over at my brothers and noticed hardened faces covering sadness.

We made sure to see the doctor on our way out. "Your cousin will be done with his operation tomorrow at noon," he said. "You can come visit him anytime after that."

We thanked him and said goodbye, then headed back to our cell. As we all laid our heads down to sleep, one question overwhelmed the silence: *Will Yahya survive?*

The next morning, we impatiently counted the minutes until noon. I went to my class with Sheikh Bahlool, but I found it too difficult to focus on anything other than the anxiety I felt about Yahya. Shiekh Bahlool noted my distraction. "You're not focusing," he said. "What's the matter?"

"My cousin just checked into the hospital yesterday and has been diagnosed with tuberculosis. I haven't seen him for over a decade, and I feel anxious about his operation today."

Shiekh Bahlool paused for a moment. "Take as much time off as you need. It's more important to be with your cousin right now. It's also important to come to class focused." He sent prayers for my cousin, wishing him a full recovery.

My brothers and I continued to wait impatiently in our cell. Finally, it was noon. We scurried over to the hospital and found the doctor there with another man dressed in a white lab coat.

"Boys, I want to introduce you all to Dr. Humayon, the surgeon who treated your cousin. He came in from the Ministry of Health to perform the operation."

We greeted the surgeon with respect and hoped for good news.

"*Salaam,*" he said. "I have some bad news for you. Your cousin has been suffering from chronic intestinal tuberculosis. I had to make incisions and remove several parts of his intestines where I found decay; otherwise, the disease would spread even more rampantly."

Feeling my throat choke with fear, I asked, "Will he make a full recovery, sir?"

Dr. Humayon took a deep breath. I knew I didn't want to hear what he had to say next.

"Unfortunately, his disease has become chronic, and I don't think there's a good chance for him to make a full recovery," he told us. Our hopes were instantly crushed. I could see that Dr. Humayon didn't like being the bearer of bad news. "He's resting now, but you can visit him if you'd like," he said.

This time Yahya had been moved to one of the rooms on the ground floor. As we walked in, we saw him bandaged up, his face weak, and his eyes squinting. He could hardly talk, so we insisted he save his energy. We sat around him all day, praying for his recovery. When the time came for the daily prisoner count, we were once again forced to leave. We hated to leave him alone, but we at least took solace in knowing we gave Yahya a little more hope. Maybe that could alleviate his suffering.

We continued to visit Yahya every day. Each day he looked like he had gained more energy, but our conversations still lacked the energy and exuberance they had before his surgery. We held his hand and prayed together every night and did our best to reminisce on the joyous times we had shared together.

One late morning, we went to visit Yahya again. He looked very weak now, like he was barely hanging on. I tried to hold back my tears as I acknowledged what was coming. His voice was so weak that we had to lean close to hear him speak. I held his hand as he muttered, "We've gone through Hell since we were small children and although we've been put through miserable circumstances, I'm so grateful I got to spend my last days with you all…my cousins…my best friends."

The tears started to flow as I squeezed his hand, and they rushed faster as he squeezed back with the last bit of life he had left. Yahya took two final breaths and one big gasp for air that brought the room to silence. Then all the strength left his hand, and he was gone. I felt my heart shatter into a thousand pieces, and we all collapsed on the concrete floor sobbing for what seemed like an eternity.

A minute later, the doctor came in. He had nothing to say other than his condolences. He allowed us to stay in the room with our cousin for as long as we wanted. Struggling to hold back our tears, we thanked the doctor and stayed and grieved beside our cousin while the doctor waited outside for the Commander. We struggled to accept these were the last moments we'd ever see our dear cousin's face.

After an hour, the Commander of the Kabul police headquarters arrived at the hospital to officially certify Yahya's death. After he did the necessary paperwork, he turned to us and asked, "What do you think we should do with his body?" We were shocked. For the first time in our life, an official had asked us how to proceed with funeral arrangements for one of our relatives. I thought about all our other family members who were buried by soldiers in unknown graves. I knew exactly what to tell the Commander.

"We'd like to carry Yahya's body to Sarai Ali Khan for a proper funeral where our mothers and sisters can attend to him," I said.

"Okay," he responded. "I will talk to the warden about this." He left the room with his head down, a sign of empathy towards us, and a gesture that for once instilled in us a sense of hope.

About half an hour later while we were reciting the Holy Qur'an and saying prayers, the warden, Mr. Abdul-Khaliq, came and told us the bad news, "The Commander did not see it fit to carry the corpse to the female prison. I recommend you bury your cousin in the cemetery nearby."

Later, a few men came to take Yahya's body to prepare it for a proper Islamic burial. We waited in the lobby for about thirty minutes, shocked and heartbroken. I stared at the grey concrete floor, watching my tears collect into a small puddle. Ghaffar, Dastgir, and Azim were silently grieving as well. Then, a large black boot stepped in my puddle of tears. I looked up to see the Commander looking down at us.

"His body is ready for burial. Come with me."

The men had placed our cousin in a wooden casket. We loaded the casket on a lorry, which took us to a nearby cemetery. I had never seen so many graves in my life. Here, a *mullah* led funeral prayers as we buried Yahya *jan*. As we shoveled the dry dirt over his wooden casket, my heart grew heavy with grief. As I shoveled the last bit of dirt that would cover his casket, I said, "*Bamon-e-Khuda[67]*."

Upon our return, Mr. Abdul-Khaliq met with us to share his condolences. He also told us that the Commander had shared the request with some higher authorities, but it was they who rejected his proposal. I grew furious as I thought of the ruling regime and their stone hearts.

What injustice did we ever do? How can someone imprison a child? How can they kill the innocent and not even allow them a proper burial by family?

Once again we'd been hit with the cruel stone of inhumanity. The empathy shown by the Commander had actually given me hope that things were changing with our dictatorial government and their cruel political stance, but now I doubted things would ever change. It didn't matter if the UN had mandated that the end of the war meant the liberation of all political prisoners. I doubted we would ever be free.

---

[67] God be with you.

TWENTY

Nayeb-Salar Janbaz Khan.
Photo was taken before imprisonment in 1920.

The next time we received our laundry from our mothers, I wrote in the note that our dear Yahya *jan* had passed away and that we wanted to give him a proper burial, but the authorities wouldn't let us. The next week, we received a reply from Siddiqa, written on behalf of everyone there. She wrote that everyone was grief-stricken about the news. She also asked about our condition. I could sense they were worried about us.

The following weeks were filled with grief and memories of Yahya. I couldn't shake the haunting realization that I hadn't spent enough time with him.

One morning, my brothers and I were reading in our cell, waiting for our classes with Sheikh Bahlool, when a *deh-bashi* interrupted us. "You have another family member here from the *Arg*. He's in the hospital. You may want to come visit him immediately."

My heart sank. *Please, not again.* We rushed to the hospital, as fast as we could with shackles around our ankles. I just knew in my gut that this would be bad news. As we entered the hospital, the assistant was surprised to see us back so soon.

"We were told that another family member of ours was just admitted," said Ghaffar.

Another assistant appeared as my brother was speaking and told the first assistant he could take us to our relative's room. When we arrived near the room, he told us our relative was in a state of paralysis. Then, he knocked and opened the door.

There, lying on a bed, propped up by pillows from three sides, was Janbaz Khan, Yahya's father, our uncle. Janbaz Khan was one of the few elders in my family that had been spared execution. He was also the national hero who fought alongside Colonel Shir-Mohammed Khan to reclaim King Amanullah Khan's throne from *Bache-e-Saqaa*.

I was completely shocked to see my uncle in that condition. As a token of respect, each of us kissed his feeble hand and held it to our forehead. Tears formed in his eyes, but he remained silent, unable to move his body. As we introduced ourselves, he wept heavily, and finally with a raspy voice spoke Ghulam Jailani Khan's name. The two were cousins and had grown up together, experiencing all seasons of life. They fought together in the final Anglo-Afghan war and worked together to bring forth King Amanullah's vision for a new Afghanistan.

We leaned in close as he recollected the brutal executions of the members of our family. He told us in a voice rife with heartache about how Ghulam Jailani Khan, Shir-Mohammed Khan and Mohammed Mehdi Khan were dragged along to the gallows. He shared how terribly heartbreaking it was to watch the young teenagers—Mustafa, Rabbani, and Abdul-Latif—thrown off their feet as they hung to their deaths. Although I had heard these stories before from other political prisoners, hearing them from a respected elder made the dark reality of our family's tragedy sink even deeper.

We waited alongside Janbaz, praying for his recovery. It was getting late, and my older brothers insisted we let him rest. "We can come visit tomorrow morning," said Ghaffar. As we were leaving his room, the doctor called us over.

"Boys, unfortunately for your uncle, it's too late. We've examined him. He's suffered a stroke as well as some other ailments. Our tests show his internal organs are barely functioning. I'm sorry to tell you this bad news, especially after the loss you all experienced so recently."

I couldn't stand hearing such dreadful news. We begged the doctor to do something to save our uncle.

"I'll do whatever I can," he said.

Over the course of the week, we continued to visit our uncle daily. We prayed as a group to bring positive energy to his bedside. Meanwhile, the doctor and his assistants checked on our uncle regularly, but unfortunately, his health was deteriorating day-by-day.

One gloomy morning when we visited the hospital, we were greeted with concerned looks from the assistants. They said nothing to us, though, and instead left to check on other patients. My gut tightened; I knew something terrible had happened. Then, I saw the doctor walking down the stairs. He walked over to us, keeping his head down, avoiding eye contact.

"I'm sorry...your uncle passed away last night in his sleep. You can see him if you'd like. The Commander will be here soon to certify his death."

We all choked back our grief. Ghaffar led the way and opened the door for us. There on the small hospital bed was our uncle. Janbaz Khan was a true national hero, one who risked his life and gave his all for his country, and now he was dead because of the same man who had once called him Brother. I felt the rage boiling in my stomach, yet I was helpless to do anything about it. Minutes later, the Commander arrived and certified our uncle's death, offering his condolences. Then once again with a kind voice, he asked, "What would you like to do with his body?"

I immediately thought of the rejection of our previous request regarding Yahya.

"Sir, can we please have a minute to discuss this amongst ourselves?" I asked.

The Commander agreed, and my brothers and I muttered back and forth about our options. Despite our previous rejection, we decided to tell the Commander our true wishes: we wanted to carry Janbaz's body ourselves to Sarai Ali Khan so our mothers and sisters could see him. Then we wanted to bury his body in our ancestral cemetery in Charkh.

We pleaded with the Commander, telling him that Janbaz's family had been denied the right of visiting him while he was alive and that they should at least see him one more time before he was buried.

"It is said that a human being's extreme pent-up emotions of sorrow and grief can be released once they can see the face of their deceased loved ones once more. For this I beg you, please let us do this for his family," said Ghaffar.

The Commander listened compassionately and replied with a tone of sincerity, "Well, I don't think it's a good idea to take his body to the women's prison, especially since your mothers and sisters haven't seen him for so long. It would be a terrible shock for them to see him this way. I think it is better to have him buried wherever you choose, and then the four of you can go pay a visit to your mothers and sisters to give them the news and console them."

The Commander turned to Mr. Abdul-Khaliq and said, "Let these men visit their mothers and sisters for one day as per prison regulations."

When I heard this, I couldn't believe my ears. It felt like I was in a dream. All these years we had never received kindness like this from any of the higher authorities. Our requests were never granted. Now, the Commander of the Police Headquarters was in the hospital giving us his condolences and granting us an opportunity to reunite with our family. It was surreal.

Mr. Abdul-Khaliq arranged for the ceremonial washing of the body to be done the next day, and a *mullah* led the funeral prayers in the hospital. Afterwards, we were guided outside to bring the casket with us onto a coach that would go wherever we wished. We asked to first go to the house of Janbaz's brothers.

Twenty minutes later, our coach stopped outside the home followed by a cloud of dust. A group of our distant relatives came out with surprised looks, and when they recognized us, they welcomed us with loving embraces. "Thank God you're all alive and well, and now grown men!" they said.

"We're only permitted here for a short time, and unfortunately we have some sad news. Our beloved Janbaz Khan died yesterday, and we came to bring his body so everyone could wish him farewell and pay their respects," said Ghaffar.

Like a snap of a finger, the entire mood changed. Tragedy, heartbreak, and wails of grief overwhelmed the gathering. Each family member approached the casket, kissing Janbaz's forehead. After everyone had given their blessings and bade their farewell, a guard subtly pulled me aside, mentioning that we had to leave now to bury the body and return on time. We said our goodbyes, hoping to reunite soon. As we boarded the coach, a second coach took the casket and Janbaz's brothers for a proper burial in our ancestral cemetery in Charkh. As our coach began to move, I could still see the crying faces of the women and the grief-stricken faces of the men. I clasped my hands together and exhaled a helpless sigh.

We took a different route along several empty streets for half an hour until we finally arrived at Sarai Ali Khan. The prison guard stepped down from the coach and told the *qabchis* of Sarai Ali Khan that, under the direct orders of the Commander, we were permitted to visit our family.

"Come now, you may enter the *hawili*," said a *qabchi*.

Our family had no idea we were going to visit that day. When the *qabchi* went to let them know that we had arrived, we heard the excitement echo within the jail as our family members raced towards the main gate in jubilation. As soon as I locked eyes with my mother and sister, it was as if I was in a dream.

My mother and sister ran over to me, embracing me, kissing my cheeks and shouting with joy and gratitude. I looked over and saw Azim swimming in his own sea of affection and smiling. It was no dream. The moment was real.

This tremendously unexpected visit was truly a divine blessing for us all. For Azim and I, we had been away for a few years, but my older brothers had been separated for more than a decade from our family at Sarai Ali Khan. The joy at such a reunion was significantly more overwhelming for them.

"How were you able to come here for such a special surprise?" the women finally asked.

My brothers and I were silent for a moment, looking at each other to see who was going to deliver the bad news.

"The Commander allowed us to come visit you all, so we could inform you that our beloved Janbaz Khan died yesterday. His brothers just took his body to be properly buried in the ancestral cemetery," said Ghaffar.

Together, we all grieved for him, wishing we could see our uncle again. I looked around at everyone, trying to memorize the faces of my dear family. With all the loss I had seen, I wanted to absorb every ounce of this moment and keep their souls safe in the depths of my heart. That's when I noticed something else that broke my heart. Looking at our mothers and sisters, I could see, from their pale skin and bony jaws, they were all suffering from rheumatism. Years and years of imprisonment in such harsh living conditions had taken its toll.

Regardless of their physical state and their grief, they were in good spirits. Our mothers consistently expressed their gratitude to God for us being in good health. And in their usual motherly fashion, they reminded us that after hardship comes ease.

"We must have faith and trust that everything is bound to change," said my mother.

The joyous gathering ended sooner than I could comprehend. Before we knew it, the *qabchi* announced the Dehmazang guards were insisting on our return. Respecting the favor from the Commander, we quickly said our farewells before we were rushed back to the coach.

When we returned, Dehmazang felt emptier somehow. I could hardly sleep that night as I was haunted by images of my sweet family and their thin, bony faces. Their obvious suffering broke my heart.

TWENTY-ONE

We had a simple choice: suffer in boredom or study. So to make the most of our situation, we continued our studies with fierce commitment, directing all the emotion and intensity we could muster toward learning as much as we could from Sheikh Bahlool.

For the most part, we succeeded, but there was one thing interrupting our focus. Every week we saw fellow prisoners gaining their freedom. It was officially the end of WWII, and the UN had mandated the freeing of political prisoners after all. These releases happened one by one at first. Soon after, prisoners were freed by a few at a time. I couldn't help but think to myself, *when will it be our turn?*

One morning, as I was preparing to meet Sheikh Bahlool for my class, a *deh-bashi* came to our room. "The warden wants to see all of you in his office now," he said.

A flicker of hope sparked inside us. "Maybe we're going to get our release orders," I said to my brothers. "Maybe this is freedom!" Excitement and joy built up within us as we walked towards the warden's office. When we arrived, the *deh-bashi* ordered us to wait outside. A few minutes later, the door opened, and they welcomed us inside. We paid our salutes to the warden and sat down.

"I have some good news for you today," Mr. Abdul-Khaliq told us.

I tried to contain my excitement, but I couldn't help but grin.

"The Commander of the Kabul Police Headquarters has issued an order under which you are allowed to visit your family in Sarai Ali Khan once every fortnight. You can go any day you like except for Fridays because that is set for *mulaqat*."

Our excitement abated. Although this was still a great gift, we had hoped we'd be set free. After all, by now, many other prisoners had already been released.

The warden finished the meeting by talking to us about mortality and the perishable nature of life and how life is such a blessing. As great as the advice was, I didn't want to hear it. I felt like he could never relate to our situation. But then, his eyes began to water, and it seemed like Mr. Abdul-Khaliq was sympathizing with us. He became aware of his own emotion and immediately changed the subject, busying himself by organizing the papers on his desk.

"Just let me know when you'd like to visit your family, and I'll be happy to have your escort prepared," he concluded.

"Can we go tomorrow?" I asked with a bit of hesitation.

"Of course. I'll have a *deh-bashi* come and escort you all tomorrow morning."

We thanked the warden and exited the office together. As we walked back, we discussed this new order from the Commander. We took it as a good sign—a hopeful step in a process that would lead to our ultimate freedom. Azim interrupted those thoughts with some haunting questions.

"What if this is the most freedom we'll ever get? What if we are bound to suffer and languish here for decades to come?"

In truth, we all had the same thought.

"We have no other choice than to be patient and have faith," Ghaffar instructed. "For now, we have the privilege of being able to visit our family. Let us enjoy this gift and be grateful for it. After all, they've never let us have this opportunity before. This is a great first step. Our time for freedom will come soon enough."

I knew my brother was right. With the Commander's order, the doorway to freedom had cracked slightly open. I turned my focus to the joy of being with my mother, sisters, aunts, and cousins again.

The next morning we woke up early, so we were ready when the *deh-bashi* arrived at our door. "The coach is waiting for you outside."

We followed him, excited to surprise our family with yet another visit so soon after our last one. On the ride there, I started to wonder what the outside world was like—the one beyond isolation and the narrow roads between jails. I remained lost in thought until we arrived at the gates to Sarai Ali Khan. It was still early in the morning, and we figured everyone was eating breakfast indoors. As we entered the *hawili,* my mother just happened to be opening her door. She looked over to see us young men and screamed with excitement.

This caught everyone's attention, and soon we were again doused with love and affection. Our family was over the moon with joy to see us.

"What a great surprise! God is great!" My mother exclaimed, bursting into tears of gratitude and kissing my cheeks as if I were still her baby. "Thank God you are alive. I'm so happy to see you so well."

"We can visit you every two weeks now," I told her.

"Finally, some good news," my sister said as she hugged me tightly.

We spent the day sharing more stories, discussing current events, and telling them of the recent releases happening at the prison. They agreed it was a hopeful sign and said they would pray for our freedom.

I spent a lot of my time that day with my cousin, Habiba.

"I have a brilliant teacher in Dehmazang," I told her. "He's taught me advanced Arabic literature, philosophy, logic, and reasoning."

"Impressive, but I hope you haven't forgotten the French I've taught you," she teased me.

"Of course not, *Mademoiselle,*" I teased back.

We laughed together as we shared stories and the strangely funny moments of prison life. It felt so invigorating to be together as a family. By the end of the day, there was light in everybody's eyes. Despite the terrible atrocities we'd experienced, the one thing that made everything more bearable was that we had each other.

But as always, our time together came to an end. "It's time to go," said the guard.

We said our goodbyes, though there were fewer tears this time. "We'll see you in two weeks," we told them. As we left, I lit up with positive expectations, imagining the day we would finally be free.

But when we returned to *Dehmazang*, it looked even more abandoned. We learned political prisoners were being released in groups now. I asked a neighboring inmate why so many were being released all of a sudden. He looked down both hallways to make sure no guards were walking by before he spoke:

"We have a new Prime Minister, Shah-Mahmood. Apparently, Hashim became very ill and could no longer carry out his duties. Thank God. That bastard was a ruthless, stonehearted murderer. It seems the new Prime Minister has a bit more decency. He just released a large group of political prisoners today."

We felt more hopeful with this change in power. Afterall, Hashim had a terrible reputation for being a stonehearted tyrant. *Maybe this man will realize we've done nothing wrong and grant us our freedom so we can actually become productive citizens for our country.*

By the time the next few weeks passed, almost all of the political prisoners had been released, all except for my family and Sheikh Bahlool. Even the political prisoners in the *Arg*, the *Wilayet* detention center, and *Sarai Muti* prison had been freed—everyone but our relatives. Out of our entire family, only the four of us were given the extra leniency to visit our family once every fortnight. Everybody else had been left in the shadows.

Finally, there were no other prisoners to release. The following weeks went by slowly. Each day we anticipated our freedom, but it didn't come. This did not discourage Shiekh Bahlool. The emptiness of the prison only inspired him to teach us more. "There's less distraction now, so we have more time to focus on our lessons," he'd tell us. It also helped that the guards were more lenient with his teaching programs and didn't require us to be constantly supervised. Shiekh Bahlool was even allowed to sometimes come to our cell to teach my brother and me in a group.

One day, during one of our philosophy lessons, as he was searching his memory for examples in his quiet, contemplative way, I asked him, "Instead of thinking, could you join us in praying for us to be free like the other prisoners?"

Shiekh Bahlool paid no attention to my words and continued to ponder in silence, resuming his lecture after he had secured a few examples to illustrate the philosophical point of view. I wasn't sure if he had heard me or not, so I kept silent and tried to pay attention to the lecture. At the end of the lecture, he asked me, "Khaled *jan,* what did you ask me?"

"Nothing, I only asked that we pray to get our freedom like the other prisoners."

He was silent and looked up, stroking his beard in contemplation. "Let's pray that Almighty God may free us together so that we can finish these lessons outside of the prison, and if not, we ought to beseech His Almighty to keep both of us in this prison until we can successfully finish your lessons. That will be the real liberation."

I was stunned by such an answer, and somewhat irritated. *Why rot in this stinky cage when we can be free? Surely anybody with common sense would want to get out of this wretched place.* But my teacher was a wise man, and at that moment I felt the frustration and anxiety melt from my body as I thought more about the wisdom behind his answer. He was telling me to live for the present. And he was right. The emptiness of the prison had taken away distractions, allowing us to focus on what was most important, expanding our intellect. I needed to appreciate that.

I took this new focus with me, making the most of my studies. And then one day in October of 1945, a number of our relatives were set free. From Dehmazang, Anwar Khan, Ubaidullah, and Enayatullah Khan were all released, and from the *Wilayet* detention center, a few of my father's cousins were set free. At this point, I realized there were only five political prisoners left in Dehmazang: my brothers, my cousin, Sheikh Bahlool and myself.

TWENTY-TWO

During those long, empty, winter months, I noticed there were more frequent visits from specialists from the Ministry of Health. I heard more stories of criminal prisoners who checked into the hospital with less severe symptoms, only to see their disease spiral out of control. I began to suspect the Ministry's real intentions.

Instead of transferring sick prisoners to Dehmazang when their disease was manageable, the stonehearted wardens would keep ill prisoners in their cells at these other prisons until they were on the brink of death. Then, the warden would approve their request to be sent to Dehmazang where the facilities were not quite enough to support a full recovery. Thus, it was only a matter of time until the prisoner died.

The wardens just saw the hospital as a transition point to death for ill prisoners. They did not care about healing anyone. They only cared about being paid by the ruling regime and keeping their jobs. As for the doctors, it was an opportunity to research various diseases. The hospital was a laboratory, and we were the lab rats. This thought sickened me. Now I knew there had never been an intention to help Samad, Yahya, or Janbaz. They had just been part of a larger research project.

And then one day, I almost became one of these victims. Following weeks of chronic flu and difficulty breathing and sleeping, I checked into the hospital hoping for some help. After telling the hospital assistant what my symptoms were, he told me that a specialist for respiratory diseases would be visiting Dehmazang the following week. He said the specialist could see me to diagnose and treat my condition. I left the hospital, hopeful yet slightly pessimistic.

What if I end up being another research project?

The next week when I went to the hospital, I noticed an abnormally long queue. After 45 minutes, it was finally my turn. The visiting doctor examined me and said, "Your nose is fully blocked. There are some thick layers of tissue cluttered in the upper portion, but we cannot operate on it here due to insufficient facilities. I want you to come to Ali Abad hospital where I operate on my patients. I'll write a recommendation letter for you so you can be admitted."

This man was not like the other doctors at Dehmazang, and I was truly impressed by his magnanimity. With respect, I asked, "Sir, don't you know that as a prisoner, I am not allowed to visit another hospital?"

He put a compassionate hand on my shoulder and whispered into my ear, "I will write you a certificate. They will certainly let you undergo the operation at Ali Abad."

I thanked him profusely for his kindness, but all I could think about was the wall of rejections my family had faced in the past. "But the jail directorate has very strict rules," I responded. "Do you really think it will work?"

He looked at me with a kind smile. "Don't worry," he said, "Although your condition is not a serious one, I'm going to describe your problem as critical. They will definitely consider it if they have the slightest bit of a conscience."

He then wrote his name, specializiation, and a signed note on a piece of paper. The note read:

> *Should the jail director pose any objections, have him contact the head physician of Ali Abad hospital. I shall be here today, examining the patients until late in the evening.*

I expressed my sincerest gratitude to the doctor and left the hospital for once with a sense of joy. As I walked back to my cell, I read the doctor's recommendation letter and saw his name, Dr. Abdul Wahid Rasheedi.

When I read the name, I had this feeling I had heard it before. *Yes, Mohammed Sharif Rasheedi!* He was a fellow political prisoner who had recently been freed as part of the ongoing release program. I remembered all that I learned about the Rasheedis and the bond they shared with my family.

When Sharif jan was released, perhaps he told his family stories of prison and talked about my brothers and I. My name must have looked familiar to the doctor.

With a heart filled with tremendous gratitude, I headed for the warden's office to hand him my recommendation letter. I waited about 40 minutes outside the room, hoping it would all work out. When it was my turn, I was relieved to see the warden on duty was Mr. Abdul-Khaliq instead of the sadistic Duran. I gave him my letter and patiently waited as he read through it. Then he paused for a few seconds, and I perked up to hear what he had to say.

"Unfortunately, this is not up to me. I'll have to pass it to the Commander and follow his instructions. Wait outside the door, please."

I sat outside for another long hour, hunched over, staring at the floor. I struggled to stay positive as I flashed back to all the times my family and I had been rejected and ignored. Everything from being denied food and clean water during our first days at Sarai Badam to the denial of proper funeral services for our loved ones to the countless times our mothers pleaded with the qabchis to improve our living conditions.

Anxious thoughts tumbled through my mind until, finally, the door opened. "You can come inside now," said Mr. Abdul-Khaliq. I was given my letter and noticed it now contained a footnote:

The prisoner mentioned above shall be admitted to Ali Abad hospital through an official letter of inquiry from Dehmazang jail. The prisoner shall undergo an operation and be returned to the jail as soon as his treatment by the doctor mentioned above is over.

I was told to hand this letter to the prison administration so my admission to the hospital could be arranged per regulations. I left the office, relieved at my good fortune, but wondering why such a simple decision took an hour to make.

I delivered the letter to the admissions officer at the prison administration, and when he read it, he told me, "Well, you have to come here early in the morning to collect your letter of inquiry, and then you can go to Ali Abad hospital with an escort. As soon as your treatment is over, you must immediately return to Dehmazang."

"I understand. Thank you, sir," I replied.

I walked back to the jail hospital to find Dr. Rasheedi. He was still busy with patients, so as soon as I had the opportunity, I approached him to extend my gratitude. "Thank you, Doctor, I truly appreciate what you've done for me. How can I be sure to have you as my doctor at Ali Abad hospital?"

He quickly wrote out a statement and signed it on his official prescription pad, adding my name, my diagnosis, and a note stressing my urgent need for an operation.

"Give this to the prison administration, but you should know your condition is not critical, so don't worry." He shook my hand and said he would see me next week.

The next day, I went to the prison administration to obtain my permission letter. "You must bring your bedding and basic belongings for your stay," the officer said.

I obeyed and set off to my room to pick up a set of sheets, my toothbrush, toothpaste, and a few books. Ghaffar was there, so I told him I was being sent to the Ali Abad hospital.

"Tell the others I said goodbye," I told him.

"*Bamon-e-Khuda*," he said, embracing me goodbye.

I returned to the officer, who then appointed a soldier to escort me in a coach to the hospital. As I looked out the back of the coach, freedom looked like it was becoming more of a possibility. This was the first time I'd ever been taken to an environment outside of any prison. I smiled with new hope until I looked over and noticed the soldier staring daggers at me. Slightly intimidated, I focused on the dust trailing behind us, thinking once again of freedom and of how the doctor had told me everything was going to be okay.

In a short time, we arrived at Ali Abad hospital. I was stunned. Beautiful, pristine white walls made up the large complex, surrounded by five acres of lush garden. It was paradise. I walked in with my soldier, carrying all of my belongings. A nurse greeted me and, after checking me in, guided me to the cleanest room I'd seen in thirteen years. "This will be your room during your stay here," she said. My eyes widened, and I couldn't hold back my grin. I was so happy to be there. "You can leave now," the nurse said, nodding towards the soldier.

"No, he is my *bandi*[68]. I cannot leave him."

"You must. There's only accommodation for him here. Besides, he's under our supervision now. You can go back."

The soldier refused apologetically. He said he was under direct orders to never leave his prisoner. The staff tried their best to explain to him the hospital rules, but the soldier would not accept them.

This stirred up some commotion, attracting the head administrator of the hospital. After he learned about the dilemma, he told my guard directly, "Don't worry, I've signed this reply letter myself, and I am responsible for strictly monitoring the prisoner. As the nurse has stated, we don't have any accommodations for guards. After a certain hour, nobody is allowed to stay on the premises other than the patients, and the nurses and doctors on the night shift."

The poor, illiterate soldier could not fathom all of this professional reasoning. Since he had gone through military training, he had not been trained in anything except absolute obedience to his officers. He kept repeating the same sentence over and over. "Yes, you are right, but I cannot leave my *bandi* unless I am personally ordered by my officer." Every time I heard that word, *bandi,* it stung with a deep level of indignity. It made me feel like scum.

"I'll call Dehmazang's warden to settle this," the hospital administrator said.

The hospital administrator tried to reach the warden many times, but he could not get through all day. The soldier decided to spend the night outside my room, falling asleep with his back against the door. I woke up in the middle of the night hearing him snore, wondering if there would ever be a time when I wasn't under complete supervision.

---

[68] Prisoner.

The next morning when the doctors arrived, they heard about the incident with my guard. They came over to meet me and were surprised by how young I was and how long I had been in prison. It never occurred to me how my situation might look to the outside world. For me, growing up as a prisoner was just normal life.

I relayed to them the incident with my escort and how he wouldn't leave me alone. They assured me they would immediately resolve the issue. After a few hours, the doctor returned and told me they had spoken to the warden and resolved everything. The doctor gave the soldier 20 Afghanis and sent him on his way, then he turned to me and said, "I need to go check in on my patients. I'll return to visit you in the evening after my official duties are over."

When the guard finally left, I found myself suddenly alone in my comfortable room. I felt a huge weight drop off my shoulders, and for an instant, I actually felt free. Before I knew it, I drifted off into a long, restful nap.

When I awoke, it was evening. Through the window in my room, I saw doctors and other hospital staff leaving. Then I heard a knock on my door and rose quickly to open it. It was the same doctor from the morning, along with another young doctor. The new doctor introduced himself first, "My name is Mir Fakhruddin, and this is my colleague, Dr. Zamanuddin."

After exchanging friendly greetings, Dr. Fakhruddin asked a nurse to bring a few chairs into the room so that those who wanted to see me could sit. When I heard these words from Dr. Fakhruddin, I told him, "I am glad to meet you and His Excellency, Dr. Zamanuddin, and I am extremely grateful for your kindness and compassion; however, you should not bother yourselves bringing in chairs. I won't be having any visitors."

"The chairs are for us," Dr. Fakhruddin explained as the nurse came in with the chairs. "Dr. Zamanuddin, myself and the whole hospital are your friends, and we would like to ask you some questions if it is okay. Please lie on your bed, and we will take a seat beside you and talk for a while."

I was stunned they would treat me, a prisoner, which such regard. "Of course, what would you like to know?"

"Dr. Zamanuddin and I used to study in Najaat high school. All of the students there know what terrible things befell your family. We have been feeling terribly sorry for the miseries you've endured."

With sympathy and compassion, Dr. Fakhruddin named the young members of my family, such as Mustafa, Abdul-Latif and Rabbani, who had been brutally killed. He also mentioned Samad and Hamid, saying they had been his classmates. When I told them that Samad was my brother and Hamid was my cousin and that both had died of tuberculosis at young ages, the young doctors were shocked. The familiar silence of disbelief and grief that had become so familiar swept through the room for a long, sad minute.

Then Dr. Zamanuddin broke the depressing silence. "I am…so sorry. Please tell me, who of your family is still alive and where do they live?"

I informed him that of the small children who had since grown up, my elder brothers Ghaffar and Dastgir, and my cousin Azim were with me in Dehmazang. I then went on to tell him that all of the female members of my family were still being kept in Sarai Ali Khan.

"Damn this government," Dr. Zamanuddin responded. "What kind of animals would torture children like this?!"

Their compassionate outrage touched me, but I tried to change the conversation lest the wrong person be eavesdropping. After seeing and hearing of the brutal punishments of inmates in Dehmazang, I knew the danger we were in. Had someone passed their words to the higher authorities, it would not be surprising that this entire innocent group would be sentenced to five hundred lashes with an unspecified term of imprisonment. With the replacement of one brother by the other as Prime Minister, there had been no remarkable change in the overall policy of the ruling regime and the oppressive behavior of its officers.

I successfully redirected the conversation by asking these amiable doctors questions about the hospital and the staff. We chatted for a while, and then a nurse came in and placed my dinner on the table. I looked out my window and noticed the night sky had already swept throughout the city. With that, the doctors rose up to leave. "Enjoy your dinner," they said. "We're going home and shall see you tomorrow."

I said my goodbyes, feeling grateful for their compassion. For the first time since I had been imprisoned as a child, I felt cared for as a human being.

The next morning, they escorted me to the operating room. I felt relieved to see the room was much more hygienic with more advanced equipment than the operating rooms at Dehmazang's hospital. That relief was followed by sorrow. *If only my brother and cousins could have been taken here. Maybe they would still be alive.*

I was in bed staring at the ceiling when I heard someone come in. It was Dr. Rasheedi. He came in wearing a long, clean *chapan*[69] and greeted me with a broad smile. He grabbed a syringe and said, "I'll need to put you under anesthesia for the operation. I'll just be removing some of the excess cartilage in your sinus, which has been making it difficult for you to breathe. The procedure should last about one hour. It won't be anything serious. You'll feel fine in no time!"

He injected me with the anesthetic and I quickly grew drowsy before falling into a hallucinogenic trance. Time slowed, and then I was out.

I woke up later that night disoriented in my room and noticed I couldn't breathe through my nose. Something was blocking it. I stared at the ceiling for some time until it melted away...

...I heard a child crying. His back was to me, and he was standing on the edge of a cliff. I called out to the child, but he didn't respond. I could see the little boy was sobbing heavily. I walked towards him slowly with my right hand extended. "Hey, what's the matter?" He couldn't hear me. "Hey, child! Answer me!" I kept walking towards him, yelling for his attention. Finally, I patted his shoulder, and he slowly turned around with his hands over his face and tears running down his cheeks. "They're gone," he muttered. "They're all gone." He lowered his hands, and I saw the child was me. "They're all dead!" he screamed. I looked past my childhood self and down the cliff at a pile of bodies below. I recognized many of the faces. I saw the bloodied corpse of my dear uncle, Ghulam Nabi Khan, and

---

[69] A loose, long-sleeve coat.

next to him, Ghulam Jailani Khan. I saw the faces of my other uncles, Janbaz Khan and Shir-Mohammad Khan, my oldest brother, Samad, and my cousins, Habib, Hamid, Mustafa, Rabbani, Abdul-Latif, and Yahya. I also saw Abdul-Khaliq and his father, Khuddadad Khan. The clouds darkened and a heavy rain fell on their faces. This storm formed a flash flood, and it began to fill the pit. In no time, a big wave was heading toward us. I grabbed the child, and we braced ourselves for impact. The wave hit us, and we were swept underneath a giant deluge of violently rushing water. I grabbed the child and kicked my way to the surface. But something heavy was dragging him down. I looked and saw shackles around his legs and bubbles coming out of his mouth as he screamed, sinking into the abyss. I swam down after him, but it was too late; he had already disappeared into the darkness. The current was growing now and I started kicking frantically, desperate for air. Then, I too was caught. I felt the chains go around my ankles and drag me down. I looked up at the surface to see distorted faces looking down at me. It was the faces of all the prison officials and commanders that had locked me away. They were laughing. I could see their lips mouthing the word *bandi*. I swam harder, but the chains were too strong. Helplessly, I screamed for air…

"Air! I need air!" I gasped, jolting awake. I looked around frantically, trying to understand my surroundings and saw Dr. Rasheedi staring back at me.

"Don't worry, it was just a nightmare," he told me. "Your breathing is uncomfortable because of the cotton in your nose, but I did that to prevent any bleeding. If you come with me to the *pansement*[70], I can remove it."

I went with Dr. Rasheedi to the *pansement* where he carefully removed the cotton swabs. I started to feel some pain as the anesthesia was wearing off, but he was right: With the swabs removed, I could breathe again.

"All done," he said. "Let me accompany you back to your room." After we

---

[70] The room where wounds are dressed.

made it back, Dr. Rasheedi gave me a choice. "It's up to you whether you want to be discharged now or remain in bed for a few more days." I didn't even need to answer. At seeing my face light up at the prospect, he patted me on the shoulder and smiled, "We would be more than happy to have you here another few days."

I was overjoyed at the privilege, but when I thought back to the smelly, humid prison cells in Dehmazang, and the cruel, sadistic warden, a feeling of guilt washed over me. I knew I was a just and honest person, but I did not know myself as a free person anymore. I felt in some way like I did not belong outside those dirty prison walls anymore, and that I should not take advantage of the kindness of these doctors, especially if their actions could be misconstrued and put them in harm's way. I decided to speak up.

"I love being with free and civilized people," I said to the doctor, "but don't you know sir? I'm a political prisoner, and I'm not allowed to stay any longer than is necessary. There would be no justifiable excuse for such a delay."

At that moment, Dr. Fakhruddin came into the room, and when Dr. Rasheedi told him of the situation, he assured me not to worry. "The other doctors and I would like to listen to your stories, so we're going to take care of this issue with the warden so you can stay here a bit longer. Don't worry," he reassured me.

I thanked both the doctors and smiled in relief. When they left, I rested and dozed off again, thinking how lucky I was to be here. I awoke later to a sharp knocking at my door. It was the soldier who escorted me. A sudden uprush of anxiety sank my optimism like an anchor.

"I must remand you to Dehmazang now," he said waving a letter at me. He handed me the letter to read, and I noticed it was addressed to the head doctor of the hospital.

"This is for the head doctor to make sure he wants to discharge me now," I replied. "You should take it to him."

The soldier looked at me with a squint of suspicion, but he turned abruptly on his heel to do as I said.

My heart sank. For a few hours, I had gotten to experience paradise, and now it was being taken away, replaced by an interminable sentence in a dank, pest-ridden cell. After a few minutes of deep anxiety, Dr. Fakhruddin returned with my guard. "We cannot discharge you now," he said. "We need you to stay here for at least one more week. The wounds inside your nose are fresh, and that can lead to further bleeding or possible infection, making you susceptible to illness or even death. This has all been stated in the head physician's letter." Dr. Fakhruddin explained all this in plain language so the guard could understand. Then, he gave the guard some money and sent him off. After the guard was far enough away, Dr. Fakhruddin looked over to me and winked. "I told you, we've got you covered."

I smiled as gratitude swelled in my heart.

TWENTY-THREE

With the soldier gone, I finally felt like I could freely enjoy this paradise surrounded by friendly, civilized, and educated people. Each day, when the doctors finished their rounds, they'd invite me to come and sit with them and have me tell stories about what the people had endured in Dehmazang. They cringed with empathy as I told them about the brutal beatings the prison officers imposed on the prisoners. I was about to share some of the cruel torture tactics as well, but thought better of it. My gut instinct warned me not to tell anyone, for if word got out, I too could be subjected to torture.

When they asked me what my daily life in Dehmazang looked like, I told them about my studies. "Well, I have one German class, then one Arabic literature class, and one philosophy class every day."

They were stunned. "How? From whom?" they stammered.

"My brother teaches me German, and a wise man named Sheikh Bahlool teaches me Arabic literature and Philosophy. We meet every day. My brother has a German textbook, but Sheikh Bahlool teaches me simply from his extraordinary memory." I told them how Sheikh Bahlool could recite hundreds of poems for hours. When I noticed how engaged they were, I felt valued. These free people were actually listening to me. I had never felt this important in the entire fourteen years I had spent in prison.

"How long have you been studying in prison?" they asked.

"Since I was first imprisoned in Sarai Badam at age six. My aunt decided to set up a school and run it in secrecy to make sure we children would not remain illiterate and uneducated." I went on to tell the story of how Ku Ku *jan* started our school, how we started by writing with pebbles on dirt, and how she convinced the *saqaa* to bring us school supplies. I could see in their eyes how moved they were by my aunt's dedication.

"Enough about me," I said. "I would like to learn about your lives. This is truly the first time I've felt free since I was six and I want to know more about your world."

They told me their experience with the school system, how they graduated, got their jobs and now worked here. "Your stories are much more fascinating though," they concluded. "How were you able to make it through all this?"

I paused and looked down as I remembered the wounds and the heartache that I knew would never leave me. "Every day I focus on how I can learn and improve myself more than the day before," I said looking up again. "That is my secret." I felt my voice echo with that sobering truth, and I saw the light in their eyes. They were humbled by my answer.

"Thank you, Khaled *jan*, for sharing your stories with us," they said. "They are very inspiring."

My chest lifted as my heart swelled with something I hadn't felt in a long time: pride. "It's my pleasure, gentlemen," I responded with a smile.

Aside from these moments talking with the doctors, I loved spending time just observing the free people walk to and fro in the hospital corridors. I enjoyed the open air, the enormous garden, and the delicious food. One day, while I was walking in the spacious yard, a desire came to me: I wanted to walk as if I was a free man. It was so difficult for me to fathom, but for the first time since I was six years old, I did feel somewhat free. I looked to make sure nobody was watching me. When I saw I was alone, I began to walk, pretending to be a free person like anyone else. The thought of this caused jubilation to rush through my veins. I pumped my fists in the air. In my mind, I shouted, *I'm free! I'm free! I'm free…at last.*

The feeling was short lived. In a heartbeat, the week was over. My escort appeared again with a letter demanding my return to the prison. I let out a sigh of disappointment as I felt the dreadful reality of prison coming toward me; I didn't want the fantasy to end. Fortunately, Dr. Fakhruddin intervened, once again delaying my discharge from the hospital by stating that I needed to be there for two more weeks for observation. The guard grunted and saw his way out. When the guard left, Dr. Fakhruddin came to my room and told me that he'd taken care of the matter.

"You know, Khaled *jan*, you are an unusual person," he said before leaving the room. "Most people see this hospital as a prison, yet you treat it as if it is an orchard, a blessing. You are an extraordinary person, and you deserve to enjoy more of that freedom."

I felt blessed. I thought of how for fourteen years I had been deprived of even the most basic human rights, subjected to extreme physical and psychological pain. Being at Ali Abad made me feel like a nightingale who had escaped its cage and was now perched on the branches, chirping songs of joy with the other birds. I knew this was a favor I'd never forget.

But alas, the next two weeks flew by faster than the first. At the dawn of the fourth week, a *mubasir*[71] and the same guard came into the hospital. They approached us as the doctors and I were speaking freely with one another around a table. As we all turned our attention to them, our smiles faded.

"It's time for you to go," the guard barked at me with anger.

Dr. Fakhruddin came to intervene again, but the *mubasir* barked at him with a rude, aggressive tone. "We must return this *bandi* to Dehmazang immediately, so you better not argue," he yelled, slamming his fist on the table. "Have him discharged immediately or I will take him without your permission!" Then the *mubasir* turned to me and ordered me to go with the guard to my room, collect my belongings and prepare for my return.

Witnessing the awful behavior of the *mubasir*, I wanted to prevent any future headaches for the hospital. "Ok," I said. "Let me thank these doctors and say my goodbyes first."

I told the doctors it was ok to discharge me now. I left with the soldier to collect my modest belongings. I then returned to the doctors and bade them farewell, thanking Dr. Fakhruddin and Dr. Zamanuddin profusely. "You will never know how much it means to me for you both to have treated me the way you have," I told them.

---

[71] Prison guard.

"Of course, you are our friend," they told me.

Friend. I liked the sound of that, to be a friend of the free.

"C'mon *bandi,* it's time to go back to where you belong!" the guard yelled again. His words stung my soul, but I knew the *mubasir* and soldier were getting antsy, so I followed them. We boarded the coach and left towards Dehmazang.

As we drove back, I thought about my brothers. I wished they could experience the freedom and dignity I had experienced at Ali Abad. I thought about my mother and sisters and how they deserved to live in such comfort. Oh, how I missed them. I thought about my father. I wondered how he must feel, being out in the free world, yet exiled from his family. I pondered what it meant to be a prisoner. I had felt like a free man at Ali Abad. Every time I studied and learned something new, I also felt free, the same freedom I felt when I played and laughed. I understood then, while prison is a solid place, being a prisoner is a state of mind. So I decided in my mind that, even though I was returning to Dehmazang, I was no longer a prisoner. I now wanted to live like a free man.

TWENTY-FOUR

When I arrived in my cell, I asked my brothers and cousin if there had been any news about our release. They gave me looks of shock, almost as if I was a different person. "Are you daydreaming or what? You'd better tell us about Ali Abad hospital. What happened with your operation, and why are you so late?" Dastgir asked in an eager tone.

I told them about the paradise I got to enjoy, all the people who walked like free men to and fro in the corridors. I told them about the cleanliness of the rooms, the advanced medical equipment, and the way patients were treated. I told them of the delicious food we enjoyed and the spacious, lush garden. But most importantly, I told them of the kindness of the doctors, especially Dr. Fakhruddin and how he intervened to let me stay in that paradise to share my experiences with them. I told my brothers these stories until the late hours of the night. "It was truly paradise," I concluded. "I felt like I finally got a taste of what freedom feels like. I don't have any particular reason to say this, but when I was there, I felt like soon enough, we will be free men."

"*Inshallah,*" we all said as we fell asleep.

Waking up that next morning in Dehmazang made me realize how spoiled I'd been in the hospital. I felt somewhat guilty, knowing I had been in such a paradise while my brothers, Azim, and Shiekh Bahlool had languished in these putrid cells. Worst of all, Dehmazang's emptiness was even more haunting than before. Silence echoed through the halls. It felt like the entire prison had been made just for us. Although I had just left my friends at the hospital, I felt forgotten by society. I went to study with Sheikh Bahlool to take my mind off the harsh reality we lived in. Listening to my dear teacher's philosophical lectures again brought me some ease.

When I returned to the room, Ghaffar told me, "We must go to bed early tonight. Tomorrow we'll visit the family." *What a relief*, I thought. After the sudden emptiness of Dehmazang, a home visit was the perfect remedy. I was excited to tell my mother and sisters about my experiences at Ali Abad hospital.

The next morning, we made our way to Sarai Ali Khan. When the gates opened, we were lavished with love and affection. A crowd gathered around me as I recounted my surgery, the beauty of the hospital, the warm-hearted way I was treated, and the sweet scent of freedom. The day went by quickly. By the time I had a chance to breathe after all the storytelling, I could see the night sky already peering over the horizon. The guards entered and urged us to say our goodbyes.

"I'm glad to hear you are well, my son," Mother said as she gave me a hopeful hug.

As our lorry took off, I looked back out at the dust trailing behind us. I thought of all the messages Mother had written me over the years, how she would remind me not to lose hope. *Hope...I don't want to hope for us to be free. I want us to be free.* Frustration boiled in my blood. I let out a quiet sigh as I looked up to the autumn night sky. My shoulders slumped as I thought of the boredom of jail. Aside from a family visit once every fortnight and new lessons from Sheikh Bahlool, we were in a state of limbo. *Perhaps, Mother is right. All I can do is hope.*

Another harsh winter came. Depression and gloom spread throughout the empty corridors of the jail. The once lush bushes were now barren, and the songbirds that once sat on the tree branches now trembled on the snow-covered ground as they searched for grain to eat. I imagined this was how thousands of poor Afghan families were spending their winter days, hoping for a greater future, but always suffering in the end.

TWENTY-FIVE

Myself. Photo was taken after release in 1953.

It had now been eight months since Shah-Mahmood had been appointed as Prime Minister. The days slowly passed as I battled conflicting thoughts of hope and fear. I hoped for freedom yet I feared that I'd languish in prison until the day I died. To reassure myself, I'd often recite the verse from the Holy Qur'an: *Verily, there is ease with difficulty.*

The cold was so severe during these winter months that I contracted pneumonia, which led me to be bed-ridden in Dehmazang's prison hospital. I longed to be transferred again to Ali Abad, but unfortunately, Dr. Rasheedi was not around. I spent days lying in my bed, imagining and dreaming of a better life. Then, a miracle happened.

It was a late December day in 1945 when Dastgir came to visit me. He sat on a chair next to my bed and read his book, occasionally checking to see if I was ok. All of a sudden, Azim entered the room hyperventilating with excitement. "I was alone…in the room…and a man came in… and then he congratulated me…for freedom! The release *firman*[72]…he saw it…*Wilayet*. I got so excited! I didn't know what to say or do…so I brought him here."

We perked our heads up. With wide eyes, my brother stepped out of the room to talk with the messenger.

"I'm a *hazir bash*[73]," I overheard the man say, "in *Wilayet*. Today, I saw Mohammed Sarwar Khan, Head of *Wilayet*, take a *firman* out of his drawer and give it to his secretary. He told the secretary to deliver it along with a special letter from the Prime Minister to the Warden of Dehmazang.

"'Which prisoner does this *firman* belong to?' the secretary asked Mohammed Sarwar.

"His Highness said, 'It doesn't belong to one person, but rather a whole family—the family members of Ghulam Nabi Khan Charkhi and his relatives.'

"When I heard this," the soldier continued, "I came out of the office, pretending to fulfill some other mission…but I rushed over to congratulate you on the good news, and to get my *shirni*[74]. If you need more assurance, one of you may come with me to the warden for confirmation."

Without a word, Dastgir immediately left with the soldier. Azim looked over at me and yelled with more excitement than I'd ever heard from him before, "Freedom!"

I laughed with joy. "We better keep it down. Don't jinx us," I said to my cousin. Just hearing this news made my symptoms start to disappear. I sat up

---

[72] Decree.

[73] Guard.

[74] Literally, sweets; in this case it is customary for the bearer of good news to receive some sort of a present, such as candy, an invitation for dinner, etc.

with more strength and energy, waiting patiently and eagerly for Dastgir to return.

Finally, he came back. "Our release *firman* has not reached the warden yet," he said, "but when I went to Mr. Abdul-Khaliq Khan with this soldier, he picked up the phone and called the Head of *Wilayet* and asked him about its authenticity. After he hung up the telephone, he congratulated me on the validity of the news.

"'According to His Highness,' he said, 'your release *firman* is to reach the Dehmazang prison administration in two hours' time, after which your family shall be free to join the rest of your family.'"

We all felt intense jubilation. *Finally! Finally! Freedom here we come!* I excitedly thought of all the possibilities that would become available to us. At last, I'd be deemed a citizen, a human being. My brother then turned to the soldier and said, "Dear brother, we don't have any money to give you for sharing the good news with us, but you can come to our room and take whatever you'd like." The soldier understood. After all, we had been prisoners for over a decade. He agreed and waited by the door, eager to follow us and receive his *shirni*.

I readied myself for discharge from the hospital, and in my excitement, I pleaded with Dastgir to accompany me to Mr. Abdul-Khaliq's office.

"I want to ask Mr. Abdul-Khaliq if we can have permission to visit our family with a guard and inform them of this news. When our release *firman* arrives, we could send the guard back," I said excitedly. My brother did his best to calm me down, stating that we should wait for the release *firman* and then see our family as free men.

I stared at him with pleading eyes, and he realized I couldn't maintain my excitement. "Ok, let's go," he finally agreed.

On the way, we went back and forth, debating on what to say and how to say it. My cousin and the messenger waited by the door as my brother and I went in.

"Mr. Abdul-Khaliq, I've come to ask for your permission to visit my family with a guard to inform them of this divine blessing we've been granted," I said.

He stared at me in bewilderment, noticing how excited I was. "I have no objection," he said with a smile. "You shall be free as of today when your release *firman* arrives. Then you can leave as free people. If you go now, though, you will have to be brought back to prison as per regulations in order to be officially discharged. It's your choice."

With overwhelming joy, I responded, "I prefer the latter, sir."

He arranged everything with the clerk, and I was free to go. First, my brothers and I had to give the messenger his *shirni*. On the way to our cell, I still couldn't believe this was reality. I questioned whether we had truly just received our freedom, if we were even in prison right now, or if this was just a dream. Walking down the hallway, I looked into the other cells. The grim, dark, and hopeless faces of the criminal prisoners stared back at me. I remembered the first day I walked into Dehmazang with Azim, trying to keep my composure when I felt nervous by the stare from these men. Looking at them now, I felt compassion.

"Can we walk faster, please?" the soldier from *Wilayet* urged. He was in a hurry to get his *shirni*. We were only too happy to oblige.

"Here we are, take whatever you like from our room," Dastgir said to the soldier. The man hastily eyed everything in the room until his attention locked onto a red, checkered rug.

"I'd like to have that rug," he said shyly.

We hastily agreed, and he folded the rug and stowed it under his arm as he left with a greasy expression of gratitude. Ghaffar stared at the interaction, clearly confused by the sudden intrusion and our smiling faces. "What's going on?" he asked.

"Freedom," Dastgir said.

"Freedom!" I yelled.

"Freedom?" he asked in disbelief.

"Freedom!" we all triumphantly yelled as we embraced our brother with joy.

I quickly changed out of my hospital clothes into my normal clothes and raced to the escorting guard. The lorry drove off, and I stared at the trailing dust. This time, I saw my shackles vanish with it. I envisioned what my life would look like now that I was a free man.

When I arrived, I was surprised to see my father's cousin there. My mother rushed to embrace me, "We've heard the news," she said. "What a spectacular day!"

We cheered in excitement.

"It looks like I beat you to tell the news," said an uncle of mine whom I hadn't seen in years. We embraced as free people. The atmosphere was vibrant with happiness. We cried, laughed, and thanked God for this precious blessing.

With such intense joy, time passed by in an instant. Soon after, my brothers and cousins joined us in the afternoon without a guard to escort them. They had processed their paperwork and were now officially free men.

Then, at five o'clock as dusk fell, the *qabchi* arrived with a message for me. "You must go back to Dehmazang and fulfill your discharge formalities," he ordered.

Anxiety overwhelmed me. *What if this means I have to stay in Dehmazang longer?*

"Look, all my brothers and cousins have been set free," I pleaded.

"No, you must come immediately. These are the rules, and you must abide by them until you're officially free," he ordered.

I knew he was right. I just didn't want to go back. I wanted to forget the life I had just left. I didn't want to see Dehmazang ever again. Still, I obeyed and followed him into the courtyard and toward the gate.

Suddenly, the Sarai Ali Khan gate opened. A squad of seven guards appeared in an orderly row. They lowered their guns in a military salute, and the Commander of Kabul's security headquarters entered in full military dress and long, black Wellington boots. He spoke briefly with the *qabchis* before strolling towards me with his security guard. I paid him a salute.

"I would like to go inside and have a chat with the mothers and sisters," he told me.

I'm saved. Please let this mean I don't have to go back. "Sure, follow me please," I responded.

I led the Commander into a room where he searched for a seat. We didn't have any chairs, so he sat on a *rakhtkhab*[75]. We all gathered to listen.

"Congratulations, you are now all officially free citizens," he told us. "You have been allotted the old estate of the King of Bukhara—a huge property with a garden, located in the vicinity of Qala-e-Futuh; however, since it's very cold now, it will be better for you to stay here until the weather improves. Once that happens, we'll provide vehicles to transport you there with your luggage. You'll live there temporarily until the case of your other properties is solved. In addition to all this, your daily ration has been raised from two Afghanis to six Afghanis according to the *firman* issued by the Prime Minister."

He then stood up to leave, saying farewell to everyone. We were glad to hear that someone working closely with the ruling regime had officially announced our freedom in person. This made it real for me. On the way out, the Commander told the same guards who had lived with us since I was child that their duty as prison guards was now officially over.

"You must go join your unit now," he said. "These people are free, and they can now go wherever they want. Those who wish to visit them should not be barred from entry." He then looked over at the *qabchis* and then to us. "Do you need them still?" he asked.

"Yes sir," Ku Ku *jan* replied. "We need them to take care of the gate and lead our visiting relatives into the *hawili* until we find someone to do the job."

"Fine," the Commander agreed. He then turned to the *qabchis*, "When you are no longer needed, you must return to the *Arg*."

I saw the generosity of the Commander and thought I better grasp this opportunity. "Sir, I came over with a soldier from Dehmazang under the condition that I return to be officially discharged once the *firman* arrived. However, I really don't want to return. I have all my belongings, and my whole family is here already living as free citizens."

He paused and turned to my guard. "Tell the warden I sent you and that this young man is free," said the Commander. I could tell the soldier disagreed with the order, but he could not object. Dismayed, he left for *Dehmazang*

---

[75] A roll of bedding clothes including a mattress, pillow and a quilt or blanket.

without me after paying the Commander a farewell salute. In gratitude, everyone gave the Commander a respectful handshake before he left.

Just as we were about to re-enter the *hawili,* another coach arrived. To our surprise, we saw Rahman, son of Janbaz. I smiled wide from ear to ear, grateful to see him after nearly 15 years. We rejoiced with a big, warm embrace. "How's the rest of your family?" I asked anxiously.

"They're all fine," he answered. "They're staying at an uncle's house in Deh-Afghanan and will come here tomorrow or the next day." We all went in and Rahman was lavished with affectionate embraces. My heart smiled with delight to see this joyous reunion. We sat around one of the houses and chatted for hours, hearing Rahman's stories from life in the *Arg.*

The next morning, the *qabchi* informed us of meetings the Commander had arranged for us with various important government officials. "The Commander has set up an appointment for the men of this family to visit with Prime Minister Shah-Mahmood tomorrow afternoon. A coach will come pick you up and escort you there," he said.

My brothers and I wondered what this could be about "Maybe it's about getting our land back," Dastgir said. I hoped so. But a fearful thought entered my mind. *What if we're not actually free? What if we're just going to be detained elsewhere?* I swatted those thoughts away like a pesky mosquito.

That night as I went to sleep, I realized something. I didn't have a chance to say goodbye to my teacher, Sheikh Bahlool. In my extreme excitement and eagerness to be free, I forgot about everything else. I thought about the last conversation we had before I entered the hospital with pneumonia. We were studying Philosophy, using an Arabic textbook, and he talked with me about how all of life is impermanent, that the only thing that continues to exist is this vast Universe. I hoped he'd be free soon as well, and that we'd be able to have a conversation as free men, out in the world. But Sheikh Bahlool was already free. He lived life like a free man, no matter where he was. That, perhaps, was the most important lesson I learned from him.

The next day, all the formerly imprisoned men of our family, about a dozen of us in total, left to visit the Prime Minister. I was apprehensive. This man and his family had been the ones involved with causing tremendous suffering for my entire family for all these years. They killed my uncles Ghulam Nabi Khan, Ghulam Jailani Khan, and Shir-Mohammed Khan. They killed my cousins Rabbani, Mustafa, and Abdul-Latif. They killed Abdul-Khaliq and Khuddadad Khan. Samad, Hamid, Habib, Yahya, and Janbaz Khan died prematurely because they unjustly imprisoned us. I secretly hoped we would receive some compassion and empathy after all the suffering we've endured by their hands. We all hoped the Prime Minister would at least be honorable and reinstate our properties.

We arrived at three in the afternoon and hesitantly walked down the polished corridors of *Sadarat*[76]. When we reached the Prime Minister's office and knocked on the door, there was a long, dull silence, then the door opened, and an assistant appeared. "Come in," he said. We stepped in and saw Shah-Mahmood organizing papers at his desk as if he was about to leave. When he saw Janbaz's brothers, he stood up to warmly welcome them with an embrace. Shah-Mahmood knew Janbaz Khan very well, that is, before he and his family decided to imprison him.

A brother of Janbaz then introduced each of us. We then approached the Prime Minister who held his hand out in a way that demanded us to kiss it. I tried to hide my repulsion as I kissed his hand and he kissed my forehead. After we all greeted him, he had us stay standing as he walked behind his desk and began to speak for a few short minutes, ending with these words: "You belong to Afghanistan and Afghanistan belongs to you, but from now onwards, be mindful of your life." He then picked up his hat from his desk and bade us farewell.

Be mindful of my life? What about you? Since when has it been mindful to imprison children and publically execute teenagers? His words made me furious. He had said nothing of our properties, instead choosing to deliver veiled threats. But I locked these emotions away just like he and his family had locked me away for over 14 years. After we made our way out of the building, Dastgir put his hand on my shoulder. "I think that's just his way of saying we're free."

---

[76] The Consulate of the Prime Minister.

PART II

A depressed mind is familiar with the night of strangers.
In the battle between us and me, thoughts become blood.
Close your eyes of neglect, and open your intuitive eyes.
The caravan of life has no time for delay.

From: **"Open Your Intuitive Eyes"** – Khaled Siddiq

TWENTY-SIX

One of our housemaids, nicknamed Khanum, with the children of Ghaffar, Zohra (left) and Latifa (right). Photo was taken after release in Kabul, 1955.

Over that next week, we had several more meetings, one of which was a lunch invitation at the home of the Minister of the Royal Court, Ahmadshah Khan.

On that day, after we had our traditional greetings, Amadshah told us, "I have collected some wild animals. Would you all like to see them while we wait for lunch to be prepared?" We nodded our heads and followed.

As we walked through his zoo, I was most fascinated by the African lions and Bengal tigers, and the cubs that were playing with each other within the confines of their cages. I looked one lion in the eye and felt a surge of sympathy. *I know how you feel.*

"Come, there are more animals," our host said. "Here are exotic birds, wolves, and monkeys." We sauntered, moving from cage to cage, observing each of the animals. Then, I saw some figures running to us from a distance: Afghan shepherds. They were the most fascinating dogs I had ever seen in my life. They ran towards us cheerfully and powerfully as their long, silky golden-brown hair flowed gracefully with the breeze. Ahmadshah ordered them to sit, and they immediately obeyed. "You may pet them if you'd like," he told us. My brothers and I played with the hounds, petting their luxurious fur and playing fetch with a stick. After a few minutes, a servant came down. "Lunch is prepared your Highness," he said.

We followed Ahmadshah into his large dining room, seating ourselves in exquisite chairs around a long table. All sorts of amazing foods and delicacies were brought out to us in abundance. "Let us begin," he said with a smile.

As we ate, Ahmadshah talked about his friendship with my father and Ghulam Nabi, reminding us of the time when they had all worked together in the court of King Amanullah. We could tell he was sincere. He showed great empathy for our suffering, and he seemed like a good-hearted and cheerful man. After our meeting, I pondered if he and other members in the government actually felt sympathy for my family, but perhaps were unable do anything about our situation because the King and Prime Minister viciously ruled as tyrants.

The next day, the Commander showed up again. This time he came to give us a serious message. "My brothers, I do not consider it in your best interest to receive too many visits from your friends and relatives. It worries the government. I think you'd better move into Qala-e-Futuh as soon as possible. Being sufficiently far enough, it will lessen the number of visitors you receive during the cold weather. Meanwhile, the government will not feel threatened. You should, from now onwards, be more cautious in your life and try to avoid any move which might cause a headache for the government."

So, as it turned out, we were not as free as we thought. This was all just another form of control, and for a moment, we wondered if our new home was just another prison. Still, we did not want to risk going back to the darkness of Dehmazang. My brothers and I addressed the Commander with the utmost humility. "Sir, you know what's in our best interest better than we do. Whatever you think is right, we are ready to do. If you could get us moved there along with our modest appliances, we shall be grateful."

"Very well," said the Commander. "I will send you as many vehicles and laborers as you need. You should try to pack up your luggage and be fully prepared to move by the weekend."

So on December 28th, 1945, the eighteenth day of our life as free citizens, we left Sarai Ali Khan for our new home in Qala-e-Futuh. On that day, our former attendant, Khaja Mohammed, came from Charkh village along with another one of our caretakers. They brought two of their sons and replaced the rude government-appointed *qabchis*.

They were followed by a number of *pishky*[77] soldiers arriving in military trucks. "We've come to help with your move," said their leader.

We packed our belongings, boarded four lorries, and headed towards Qala-e-Futuh. Snow fell heavily around us as we made our journey out of Kabul. As I looked at the giant piles of snow accumulating, I thought back to the cold, winter days in Sarai Badam when my brothers and I had created snowmen.

Throughout the long drive, my mind wandered between the past and the present. I thought about every time I had boarded a lorry in the past. I remembered the drive from our home on Andarabi Street to Sarai Badam, the move from Sarai Badam to Sarai Ali Khan, the transition from Sarai Ali Khan to Dehmazang, and then the short visits to Sarai Ali Khan and Ali Abad. I hoped this would be the last time I'd ever need to be transported by soldiers. I held my hand outside the lorry, catching some snowflakes. They melted as they met my warm skin. I hoped our suffering would melt away like the snowflakes.

---

[77] A man who is conscripted into military service by a draft.

We arrived at a large estate. The panoramic spread and the huge building looming over us took me aback. I could see a number of rooms, a large yard, and a green sylvan garden spread across twelve acres of land. In some way, it reminded me of our home on Andarabi Street, although this was much larger. It was obviously a royal estate. Seeing the large plot of land brought a smile to my face. *That will be one beautiful garden come spring time*, I thought.

As the trucks came to a halt, we stepped off with our belongings. To our surprise, a lady and her two sons opened the front door of the mansion. Before entering our new home, the Commander called us together.

"The King of Bukhara, Said Alim Shah, had his retinue and servants live here. The royal family moved to this city after the King's demise and the sale of his entire estate to the government. After they settled in here, the servants and attendants who had accompanied them from Bukhara asked the new government to let them live in these houses until they could build homes in some other corners of the country. However, the property has now been allocated to you until further notice. When this decision was made, all of the royal servants and attendants evacuated the place except for a small family— a lady and her two orphaned sons. The lady pleaded with the government to let her live here with her sons and assured them that she would be glad to work as your attendant. You have the option of letting them remain or making them leave as the rest of the servants did."

We looked at the helpless lady and felt so much compassion for her as if all our misery was expressed through her eyes. "Of course, she may stay with us as long as she'd like," I said.

We took the woman and her children like family, telling them they had nothing to worry. A wave of happiness came over her face, and she offered her prayers of goodwill and gratitude. The Commander smiled warmly at our decision. He shook hands with us, saying goodbye before disappearing into the snowy fog. Watching the soldiers leave was an incredible sight. Finally! We felt free—free from the constant supervision, free from the intense restrictions, free to live happily as a family.

We entered the mansion and divided the rooms equally amongst all the families. "With such a vast space, how will we be able to cover the ground with our limited number of carpets?" Dastgir asked as a joke. We laughed with gratitude. What a much better problem to have!

Night fell across Qala-e-Futuh quickly, and unfortunately for us, the power was out. We made due with candles and a few hurricane lamps, but we desperately looked forward to the next morning's sunrise so we could explore all the corners of our new home. That night, we fell asleep in our half-carpeted rooms, huddled around *sandalis* to warm ourselves in the frigid weather.

During our first week in our new home, I learned more about this village. Qala-e-Futuh resided in the Char Dehi district, and its inhabitants made their living through farming and raising livestock. Most families lived in mud-brick houses and usually had an acre or two of land and a few cows and sheep. The majority lived in poverty.

The transportation system of the village consisted of four cow-drawn carriages. Each carriage would leave at dawn towards Kabul, returning each evening. Other than that, there was no transportation system for people to commute between the city and the village. People who lived here hardly left, and others rarely visited.

Qala-e-Futuh was one of the villages outside the distribution area of the state-owned power companies. Consequently, we would have to make due with our candles and hurricane lamps for as long as we'd live there. For water, there was a nearby stream that crossed a number of orchards and passed through our *hawili*. To be safe, we boiled the water first before we drank it, usually storing some of it for nighttime. None of these issues really posed any concern for us, especially compared to the way we had suffered in the past. I felt humbled as I learned how millions of people in Afghanistan lived in poverty outside of prison.

Even though it was terribly cold and difficult to commute to our new town, we regularly had friends visit us. Upon hearing about our release, they could not hold back from seeing us and paying their respects. They'd frequently invite us to their homes and arrange dinner parties. Thus our days and nights in Qala-e-Futuh were filled with joy and happiness.

With each passing day, we grew more and more optimistic about reclaiming our former estates and lives. Eventually, the winter season loosened its grip and gradually gave way to spring. It seemed like every living being was vibrating with happiness as the Earth put on its fresh green dress. For us no longer languishing in our prison cells, it was a rebirth.

As the weather continued to warm, more relatives came and visited, often staying a few nights to a week with us each. We made trips occasionally to the city to visit our relatives as well. They'd do their best to entertain us and create evenings filled with joy so we could recover from our long years of suffering. These gatherings went on consistently until one day in May.

On that day, Abdul Azim Khan Ulumi, the Governor of the Char Dehi district, came to visit us. My brothers and I invited him inside the house where we sat together for *chai* before he began to speak.

"My father was on very good terms with your late uncle, Ghulam Nabi Khan, who I also considered as my uncle," he said. "My family has always felt sympathy towards you and your long years of pain and suffering. Today, I've been sent by the Commander to inform you that the government, due to deteriorating security conditions in the country, wants to take care of you as required by government policy. Therefore, a squad of seven *pishky* soldiers has been assigned to guard you around the clock. This is so you can remain safe from irresponsible people trying to cause chaos in the country."

"Sir, I'm sure we're more than fine," I said. "We're out on rural farmland. There is no crime here. I don't see the need for soldiers."

He went on to speak about a few incidents that had happened recently in the area, one that led to the death of a shopkeeper. It felt like he had made the story up to cover what was really happening—we were being placed under increased surveillance.

"I personally feel the government's decision is in your best interest and I don't see any reason why it should last very long. As soon as your properties are reinstated by the government as stipulated in His Excellency, the Prime Minister's decree, you will be able to return to Kabul and no longer be bothered by such restrictive measures."

He then went on to talk about our regular visits with relatives and friends, asking why they had been so frequent. He told us this had aroused the government's suspicion and resentment. Suddenly, his tone changed from one of respect and reverence to one of warning. "Whoever wants to visit you will have to obtain written permission from the Commander of the Security Headquarters," he explained; "otherwise, the guards will not allow them in. Similarly, when you want to visit the city, you will have to obtain prior permission for that, as His Excellency put it, all your comings and goings are strictly being monitored by the government."

This last directive came as a shock to all of us. It wasn't what we had been promised. As the months passed, our meetings with friends gradually slowed down until we were not allowed to go into the city at all. That's when I realized we had never been freed, just relocated. This wasn't freedom. This was house arrest.

TWENTY-SEVEN

Dastgir (left) and I (right) in the garden of Qala-e-Futuh, 1947.

This period of limbo gave me time to think about my future regarding marriage and family. In prison, I couldn't give such things much thought, but now that I was outside those walls, I noticed a lot of attention from women who wanted to marry me. "Khaled *jan,* you are so handsome and intelligent. When will you choose a wife?" they'd ask me with hope. Their compliments were flattering, but I knew exactly who was in my mind: Habiba *jan*. She was the most beautiful, kind, and loving person I knew. She was a real angel.

So, on a beautiful spring day, I asked Habiba to go on a walk with me. We walked through the lush green garden talking about our days at Sarai Ali Khan and all the memories we shared. Suddenly, I paused and faced her. "Habiba *jan*, I have something important to tell you," I said. My heart was racing with anticipation and love. "I want to marry you," I said with a bright smile.

She playfully laughed. "You're joking!"

My eyes widened. "No! I am serious! I want to marry you," I responded in earnest.

"But I am nine years older than you. Don't you want a wife your age…if not, younger?"

I held her hands in mine. "No. I want to be with you."

She smiled joyfully. "I accept."

I was thrilled. My heart raced with jubilation. We returned to the house shortly afterwards to tell everybody the news.

The next day, our family prepared a humble marriage ceremony for us, and Habiba and I joined as husband and wife. Although we didn't have much, our wedding day was filled with joyous celebration. That wasn't the only wedding. Dastgir also married Kobra, the daughter of Ghulam Jailani Khan. Our mothers cried with happiness at these unions. As the days continued, love filled the air as more marriages happened amongst our relatives. It was not long after that many of the wives became pregnant.

When I learned Habiba was pregnant, I was both joyful and disheartened—joyful because I would be a father, disheartened because my child would be born under house arrest. That's why I decided to name her Bereshkai, meaning "light." Her birth meant a new life for all of us.

When Bereshkai was born, she brought light to our eyes. Soon after her birth, my brother Dastgir had his own daughter—Kobra. It was such a joy to watch these two grow up. My sisters and cousins all wanted to babysit them. "Khaled *jan*, let us take care of them. You go continue your studies," they'd tease me.

During that time, we received another surprise, a letter from my father. I was in Kabul at the time, visiting some family friends, when a man notified me with an urgent message. "Khaled *jan*, the Governor of Kabul requests you come visit him. He has something very important for you," he said. I wondered what it could be. *Perhaps some news about our properties being restored to us?* I went with the man to the Governor's office.

"Khaled *jan*," the Governor greeted me. "I was in Berlin this past month, and I met with your father."

Father! None of us had heard any news about our father for the past twenty years. Hearing that somebody else had recently seen him was a tremendous surprise to me. "How is he, sir?" I asked.

"He's in good health, *Nam-e-Khuda*[78]. I have something for you, a letter from him to your family."

I was overjoyed to hear about my father, and when the Governor handed me an envelope, I held onto it like it was the most precious object in the world. "Thank you, sir. Thank you very much!" I said with sincere gratitude. *A letter from my father! I can't believe it!*

I wanted to open it immediately, but I knew I had to wait until I got home where we could read it as a family. When I arrived back in Qala-e-Futuh, I ran inside, shouting, "Father wrote us a letter! Father wrote us a letter!" Like excited children receiving gifts on *Eid*, all the adults rushed over to me.

"Open it already!" Dastgir exclaimed.

I opened the letter and began reading my father's precious words. He asked about us, how we were, where we were, and he told us how he was thinking about us all the time. He wrote that he was well and that he wanted to introduce two people to us—our half-brothers, Ahmad and Zaid. He included pictures of them with their names written on the back of the Polaroid. He had remarried during the years of exile to Huriya *Khanum*[79], the sister of Queen Soraya and sister-in-law to King Amanullah. He wrote that the Governor mentioned we were all free now and that he had been praying for us every day. At the end of the letter, he asked a more serious question: *Who is still alive?*

---

[78] In the name of God.
[79] Mrs.

Dastgir ran to grab a new sheet of paper and a pen. "Khaled *jan*, let's respond immediately. How can we get this letter to him?"

"I can ask the Governor. He's the one who went there and gave Father's letter to me." I replied.

I began drafting a response from all of us to my father. I told him I was now married to Habiba and had a child, and I mentioned the news of the other marriages and Dastgir's child. I told him we were all fine and lived in Qala-e-Futuh, and that we all missed him. I shared with him the unfortunate news about Samad's untimely death, along with my other cousins and Janbaz Khan.

The next week when I was in Kabul, I paid a visit to the Governor's office. I thanked him profusely again for providing such a blessing to us. I asked him if there was any possibility to send our letter to my father. "Of course, Khaled *jan*. I will bring it to him on my next trip to Germany. That will be in a few months," he said with a smile.

A few months later, I heard the news that the Governor had returned from his trip. I made my way to Kabul, eager to see what news he had. It was another letter from Father. In this letter, my father said he was happy to hear about all the marriages and his new grandchildren. He wrote some formalities, asking again how our life was, telling us that he was doing well and that he missed and prayed for us every day. The tone of his letter was formal, but we understood why. He feared what would happen if the Intelligence Office found out we were sharing too many details or opinions.

Still, for my next letter, I decided to write something more personal from myself to my father. I wrote this letter under candlelight while everyone else was asleep, and as I thought deeply about what I wanted to tell him, I was overcome with emotion.

Dear Father,

I miss you so much. I've been thinking about you every day. I'm so sad to say that I can't remember your face or the last time I was with you. I don't want you to be a faded memory in my life. I want to spend time with you. I want to know you. How can I visit you? How can I spend time with you?

I continued writing, tears dropping from my eyes, some onto the letter. These were feelings that had been closeted for the past eighteen years, and they came pouring out of me. When I was done, I folded the letter and hid it in my book. The next week, I brought it to the Governor, asking if he could again do me the favor of delivering my words to my father on his next trip to Germany.

The response from my father took some time. It wasn't until six months later that I heard the Governor had returned from his latest trip to Germany. When I saw him, he had another letter from my father. This time, it was written just for me. I opened it immediately upon leaving the Governor's office.

My father's words were less emotional than mine. The entire letter was much more formal. In regards to us seeing each other, he simply wrote, *I will see what I can do.* I understood his caution. I knew from his previous letters that his utmost concern was our safety and livelihood. That night, I told my wife about his response. I didn't want to tell my brothers, not yet. "Have faith, Khaled *jan,*" she said with a comforting voice. "You two will reunite."

There were no letters from my father for a while after that. Instead, we had other surprises come along. Dastgir had another daughter, Parwin, and Ghaffar and his wife Aziza had their daughter, Zohra. Soon enough, Qala-e-Futuh became a playground full of joy with kids running and playing in the garden and through the halls of our home. It reminded me of my childhood days, before our imprisonment, when I'd play with my brothers and cousins in our home on Andarabi Street. I was glad at least that the children had the freedom to play and have fun, that they were in a healthy environment and didn't have to starve or see the corpses of their loved ones. If I had to live through watching them experience that, I don't know how I'd be able to bear it.

TWENTY-EIGHT

My wife, Habiba *jan*, working with UNICEF, 1951.

Over the next year at Qala-e-Futuh, our most profound source of joy came from raising our kids and watching them grow. Despite these gifts life brought to our family, we couldn't deny our reality. In the evenings, the same conversations echoed through the halls, and the same fearful thoughts played in my mind. *Will we ever be free? How long will we be stuck here?* The large, luxurious estate began to look more like a comfortable cage. I thought of the beautiful lions and tigers caged in Ahmadshah's home.

We brainstormed ways to make the best of our situation. Some of us decided to find jobs at national agencies. I hoped to enroll in school and finish top in my class so I could pursue foreign scholarships. Remembering the kind doctors I had met at Ali Abad hospital, I daydreamed of becoming a doctor like them and serving people.

Just like anyone else, we all longed to join the caravan of life and climb ladders to success, so we petitioned the authorities to at least grant us the freedom to work and study. Unsurprisingly, our petitions were ignored. Instead of letting this discourage us, we waited a few weeks before petitioning again. Still nothing. We continued petitioning, but there was still no change in the government's position.

Seasons changed, yet the days remained the same. No promising news or words came from Mr. Ulumi about the restoration of our property or any of our freedoms. Soldiers continued keeping us under strict supervision at all times. It turned out that Mr. Ulumi's prediction of a short period of supervision had been wrong.

We continued to petition, pleading for some sort of work in the national organizations, or at the very least to have a small increase in our daily rations to cover our most basic expenses. Sadly, all these efforts were in vain. Whenever we asked whether they'd received our petition, they always barked at us with negative responses.

During this time, Shah-Mahmood went on a trip to Europe and Daoud stepped in as acting Prime Minister. As such, he would go to the Ministry of the Interior once a week to personally hear people's complaints. The petitioners would sit in long queues on wooden benches in a large room built just for this purpose. Then the *Mudir-e-Arizin*[80], who had a list of names in his hands, would rise and say, "Whenever I call up a person, he or she must stand up before His Highness, the Minister of the Interior, Daoud Khan and describe their problem to him. When His Highness hears your complaints, His Highness will give me instructions from which I'll take the appropriate measures."

---

[80] Head of Petition.

Despite the many comments I'd heard from others about Daoud being a harsh man, not prone to giving permission, I left for the city one afternoon seeking an audience with the new leader. The next dawn, when the air was still crisp, I rushed over to the Ministry of the Interior and wrote yet another petition, getting myself a slot just near Daoud's desk in the second row of the complainants. After waiting for a few hours, a great commotion arose in the complainant's room, signaling the arrival of Daoud Khan. A group of aids, both in military uniform and in plainclothes, dispersed around the room to monitor the crowd of petitioners. Daoud Khan entered after them under a military salute from the waiting officers and soldiers. All petitioners stood up as a sign of respect until he reached his desk.

The Head of Petitions officer read out the names of the people from a list. One by one, each complainant stood up and explained the content of his petition before His Highness and the attending audience. The Head of Petitions officer took the petition from the person in question and jotted down a short note at the bottom of the document at Daoud's discretion. He then said to the complainant, "Come to my office tomorrow and get the response for your petition."

I waited patiently for my turn, and when it arrived, I stood up, introduced myself and began speaking. "Sir, I come here today asking for permission to work and for my family to have our properties restored as we've been promised."

Daoud Khan turned to the Head of Petitions officer and said, "Ask the Governor of Kabul to provide his records."

Like the rest of the petitioners, I was told to return the next day. The Head of Petitions officer made the note at the bottom of my petition and told me to collect it the following morning.

The next morning, I went to the Petitions office to receive my petition. It had no approval, only the note at the bottom asking the Governor for my records. I picked it up and rushed to the office of His Excellency, Governor Shah Alimi and managed to meet the Governor after a two-hour wait.

Being a good acquaintance of the elderly members of our family, the Governor of Kabul welcomed me warmly and promised to do whatever was in his power to solve my problem. "Come visit me in about a week's time," he said. "That'll give me enough time to sort everything out."

A week passed. Then another week passed. And then another two weeks passed. Each time I came to Kabul, it seemed that Governor Alimi had done nothing. I grew increasingly frustrated by the frequency of requests I had to make to the Commander to let me travel to the city. The Commander would sometimes approve my application when he was in a good mood, but when he felt short-tempered, he would bluntly reject my request without reason.

During that time, some friends came to visit us. They reminded us not to lose hope. One friend told us that he knew a Minister who had connections to an important government organization. He insisted on taking our petitions by hand to him. He tried once a month, but it always ended with him returning empty-handed, feeling frustrated and angry in his own right at the cruelty of the ruling regime.

One day, another one of my friends told me about a man named Syed-Akbar Khan. This man worked for the Ministry of the Interior as the Head of the Police Department. When I heard the name, I immediately remembered a man who had served his jail term with us in Dehmazang: Brigadier Syed-Ahmad Khan. I remembered a conversation I had with him about how he studied in the Turkish military while my uncle Jailani was serving as Afghanistan's ambassador in Ankara. During our conversation, he had spoken of Syed-Akbar Khan, who he described as a very bright and talented student. The mention of this man's name ignited hope that maybe this new Head of the Police Department might remember my uncle and his excellent support for all the students. I knew I needed to go to him immediately.

I sent a request to the Governor to leave for Kabul. A slow week later, I received my permission to leave. A carriage took me to the city, and once I arrived at Syed-Akbar's office, I was directed to line up behind all the other petitioners until an official called me inside. I nervously prepared what to say and prayed this would be my pass for being able to study or work, and for my family to finally have our properties back. I watched anxiously as the line moved a few feet every few minutes. My palms were sweating by the time it was my turn. "Next," said the official. I wiped my palms on my jacket and entered.

"Come in, please," Syed-Akbar told me as I stepped forward and put my petition papers on his desk. He picked them up and glanced through them. "Oh, you're from the Charkhi family," he said. "I knew your uncles." He then looked over at the official. "Please close the door and make sure nobody comes in for a while."

When the door closed, he offered me a seat. "My sympathy and condolences to you and your family. I know you have all suffered terribly, and I hope I can do my best to support you. Fortunately, I have a personal relationship with the acting Prime Minister," he said with compassion. "Next week I will talk with His Excellency Daoud Khan about your problem and I feel very optimistic I can do something for you. You should come back and visit me the following week."

"Thank you, sir. I visited Daoud Khan before. He asked for the Governor of Kabul to give him my documents, but I never heard anything back."

Syed-Akbar nodded and indirectly told me that my dossiers had been overlooked due to Shah Alimi's fear of Daoud Khan.

I understood and stood up, thanking Syed-Akbar profusely. "I say this from the bottom of my heart. I greatly appreciate your help," I said before I left.

On my way home I was filled with conflicting thoughts. Sometimes I felt optimistic about the promises I heard, and sometimes I felt that I'd never be granted my freedom. Syed-Akbar's support made me feel optimistic. I could feel the sincerity of his help. But in the end, I knew the ruling regime had all the power. To know that other officials were afraid of bringing up my family's name to those in power told me the ruling regime still held views of hatred towards us.

The next week when I visited Syed-Akbar's office, I tried to remain hopeful about receiving good news. When the office opened the door for me, Syed-Akbar stood up from behind his desk and walked up to me, giving me a warm hug. "Please leave us alone and hold the other petitioners back for a while," he told the official. When the door closed, I could see a look of frustration on Syed-Akbar's face. "Daoud is an unreliable, two-faced person. You just can't count on him," he ranted in anger. "The son of a bitch did not listen to me about your case. You better wait until the old man, Shah-Mahmood, comes back from his trip. At least he is somewhat more reasonable."

From there, Syed-Akbar tried to conceal his emotions. "Please extend my sincere regards to your respectful family, and try to visit me as soon as you hear about the Prime Minister's return. I will do whatever I can to help," he said with empathy. I expressed my gratitude to him and got up to leave. Although this was unfortunate, it was no surprise. I took the rejection in stride. For my family and I, it was just another obstacle.

When I returned home that evening, my brothers were eagerly awaiting news. They were surprised by how kind and sympathetic Syed-Akbar was, especially since he was a government official none of us knew. "We have to wait until Shah-Mahmood returns and reclaims the reins of power from Daoud," I told them. I hoped that Shah-Mahmood had visited the United States and Europe where he'd be exposed to a world where human rights were encouraged and protected. I hoped that if he had those experiences, he'd at least have some more empathy.

I counted the days and nights, waiting as patiently as I could for Shah-Mahmood's return. Finally one afternoon, word came to us about his arrival and return to power. Just to be on the safe side, I waited a few more weeks, knowing he would have many visitors and VIPs wanting to meet with him in the early days of his arrival.

Three weeks after the Prime Minister's return, I obtained another permit from the Commander to visit the city and meet with Syed-Akbar. When I entered his office, Syed-Akbar was warmer than ever. He embraced me and spoke to me very casually like we were two best friends. He spoke about his good memories with the elder members of my family, and he was particularly effusive when he mentioned my uncle Nabi's gallantry.

"Don't lose hope," he encouraged me. "God is great. I'm glad you're here. However, your petition is still in my file. During the next week, when I meet His Excellency Prime Minister Shah-Mahmood Khan, I will certainly talk to him about your matter and will do my best to solve your problem. Come to me at week's end."

I was highly impressed and encouraged by Syed-Akbar's steadfast support. I shook his hands with sincere gratitude before leaving his office.

TWENTY-NINE

After another week, I found myself in back in line waiting for a meeting with Syed-Akbar. As soon as he saw me, Syed-Akbar greeted me with his typical warm words. "My dear brother, I did my best to make His Highness consider restoration of your property and freedom, but I only managed to get you a work permit, allowing you to work in the national and private organizations. I am extremely sorry that I could not fulfill all that I promised and what I know you deserve as your absolute right."

I was blown away…speechless. I felt so much delight to hear the words "but I only managed to get you a work permit." I shouted with excitement, "Did you really get me a work permit in writing?"

He was taken aback by my exuberance. "Yes, you will be able to go ahead with your work, but I will be doing all my best as well to restore your confiscated property. I'll spare no effort in this regard." Then, remembering my question, he qualified his statement. "To be clear, His Highness has not written anything himself at the bottom of your petition, but he has given me oral instruction. Don't worry, though. I will try to have your petition signed by *Sardar* Shah-Mahmood Khan so you will not face any difficulty when applying for a job in the future."

"And how does that process work?"

With a big smile on his face, Syed-Akbar spoke calmly, "My dear brother, be patient. I have considered all aspects of the issue. You should write a petition for each male member of your family and get them to me as soon as you can. If possible, do it today."

I thanked Syed-Akbar and rushed outside to the *areeza navees*[81] outside the gates of the Ministry of the Interior and got four pieces of official paper to write new petitions for my brothers, cousin and I. When I was done, I ran back to Syed-Akbar and submitted the petitions to him. He glanced through the letters and then looked up at me. "Ok, come back to me tomorrow afternoon."

I couldn't help but ask, "What about the women of my family? What if they want to look for a job as well?"

Syed-Akbar took this in stride. "They won't have any problem. As soon as the male members of your family can work freely, the ladies' problems will be automatically sorted out," he said.

The next day when I saw Syed-Akbar, he greeted me with a bright, happy face. "You are free. From now onwards, you are allowed to apply for a job anywhere. Here are your petitions and *Sardar* Shah-Mahmood Khan's signature."

I turned my eyes to the petitions to see the Prime Minister's approval myself:

It has been considered. In order to make his livelihood, the petitioner can work in governmental and non-governmental organizations.

Signed by: Shah-Mahmood Khan

I smiled in disbelief at my family's sudden good fortune.

But Syed-Akbar offered one more unexpected blessing. "I know you've had a squad of soldiers who've been guarding you all this time. Would you like them to remain with you in Qala-e-Futuh? If not, I will tell the Commander to send them back."

I could not believe my ears! "Dear sir, I've been with those soldiers since I was six, more than twenty years! Honestly, we cannot bear looking at them for even one more day. Besides, our former attendants and their children

---

[81] Petition writers who helped the illiterate write their petitions.

would be more than happy to come and look after us."

"Very well. I will write a letter to the Commander today to send the soldiers back to their regiment."

And just like that, my family was finally rid of the pesky, overbearing watchdogs who had ruled our lives for decades.

With enormous gratitude, I thanked Syed-Akbar for all his extreme generosity and left with my petition papers. I couldn't help but think of how his kindness reminded me of the doctors at Ali Abad hospital. I felt a joy dancing in my heart as it sang the tunes of freedom. When I arrived home that evening, my brothers were overjoyed at my news.

"We are free to work now!" I exclaimed, smiling from ear to ear as I pulled out the work permits. We celebrated with hugs, all thanks to the benevolence of Syed-Akbar. Finally, we were free to start our lives.

We each wasted no time figuring out which paths we would take. Dastgir's name had appeared as a *pishk,* so when the letter came in, he immediately agreed to register for military service without a second's hesitation. However, when he went to enlist, they did a full background check on him, and according to the laws, political prisoners could not be armed soldiers. So Dastgir found employment with the Ministry of Public Works. There he worked as a civil servant in road construction in exchange for thirty Afghanis and six *seers*[82] of flour a month.

Dastgir soon learned that the Ministry of Public Works desperately needed translators, especially since all the survey texts for the roads were written in German and English. When the Minister of Public Works found out that Dastgir was fluent in both languages, he appointed him to the translation department. As for Ghaffar and Azim, they went to the Ministry of Finance and found jobs there.

I chose not to work with governmental agencies. Instead, I went to Mr. Hanifi, a close friend from Charkh village who managed the transportation unit of a large textile company, to ask for his recommendation. When he saw me, he smiled with relief, "Thank God you are finally free from troubles.

---

[82] A unit of weight measuring seven kilograms.

Thank God you can finally be the owner of your destiny." Upon telling him my skills, he gladly supported my idea of working with a national agency.

"I prefer the Afghan National Bank and Textile Company over any other national organizations," he said. "You should go to Mohammed Omar Khan. He's the Acting Chief of the National Bank, and his department also manages the Textile Company. Also, as far as I know, Mohammed Omar Khan was on very good terms with your father, so I'm sure he'll do his best to help you. Let's go see him," he said.

Together we left by car to the National Bank to meet with Omar Khan. I was getting more and more excited with each passing minute. In all the years of languishing in prison, one of the main things that helped me through all the suffering was the thought that what I was learning in jail was going to help me get a great job someday. Having a job would make me feel like a true citizen, something that, at the time, was foreign to me. Now, it was all becoming a reality.

We arrived at the bank and were immediately led to Omar's office. As soon as Mr. Hanifi introduced me, Mohammed Omar stood up to embrace me warmly. "Please sit my friends," he insisted before he went into elaborate detail of how close he and his brother were with my father. "So what brings you here today?" he asked.

"I apologize for my unexpected visit at this time," Mr. Hanifi said. "But Khaled *jan* has recently obtained the Prime Minister's approval for work and wishes to find a job in one of the national organizations. I came here today to ask for your consultation."

I gave my work permit to Omar. He read it thoroughly and then turned to me. "Ok," he said with a pause. "I will need a week to consider this. Would you mind telling me what skills you have and what you have studied?"

"I am twenty-five years old," I said. "I could neither do my traditional schooling nor join any other official educational institute due to various obstacles that I'm sure you're well aware of. However, I worked hard in prison and tried to learn as much as possible. I believe I can work as a petition writer in Farsi. I also know German and Arabic very well. Also, I have an average fluency in English and French."

"Well, just stop by my office after another week. That will give me time to consider all aspects of this," he restated. We thanked Omar and left the office somewhat hopeful.

On the way to the car, Mr. Hanifi shed some light on Omar Khan. He explained that, though Omar was a very kind person, he was far-sighted at the same time. "We have to be patient to achieve our goal," he advised.

The following week, I went to meet with Omar Khan. I saw him get a checkbook out of his drawer. He casually began writing, then handed me a check for 1,000 Afghanis and apologized for not being able to do anything at the time. He suggested I meet him the following week. I was extremely touched by his gesture, but I put the check back on his desk. "Thank you very much," I said. "Excuse me if I am too bold, but I am fine. I am here to seek a job and work to earn my money. It's okay. I can come by next week," I said, kindly refusing his charity.

Upon my refusal, he broke into tears, got up and hugged me tightly. His throat was tight and unable to vocalize his grief. "You never knew the level of my friendship with your esteemed father," he pushed out his words. "He is still famous as *Aghai Gul*[83] among our family members. You are my nephew, Khaled *jan*. Please accept my humble gift."

Because of my high respect for Omar Khan, I accepted his check and returned home feeling grateful and somewhat guilty. I was disturbed by my actions. I didn't know if it was the pride of youth or just my inner nature. I felt like I had humiliated myself by accepting his gift. These thoughts haunted me all the way home.

The week quickly moved. Soon, it was time to revisit Omar Khan. This time I went with Mr. Hanifi, with whom I shared the details of what had happened the week before. When he heard my story in detail, he repeated, "Remember, he is a far-sighted man. *Inshallah*, everything will go alright."

When we arrived at Omar's office, he presented me with great news. "I'd like to introduce you to the Afghan Textile Company. It will provide you with a better future with more fringe benefits." He then turned to Mr. Hanifi and asked, "How do you like this idea?"

---

[83] A nickname my father had.

"Well, the company is opening a big factory in Gulbahar, and that factory alone will require five thousand workers. With much of the machinery coming from Germany, they'll also be bringing some German engineers to manage the factory. With Khaled *jan*'s fluency in German, I believe he'd be a great candidate for a translation role," said Mr. Hanifi.

Omar agreed and picked up the phone to call the President of the Textile Company. "Mr. Serajuddin! Mr. Hanifi is going to bring you someone who says he can read and write in both Farsi and German. Can you see what job openings are available in your company—scribe, head scribe, and translator—and find him a slot somewhere." He then hung up and returned my petition and Shah-Mahmood's approval letter. "Both of you should go to Mr. Serajuddin with these documents and see what comes."

"Thank you very much, sir!" I said, expressing my deep gratitude.

Mr. Hanifi and I left for the Textile Company, feeling optimistic about the opportunity. We arrived and met with the Vice President of the company.

"Is Mr. Serajuddin available?" Mr. Hanifi asked.

"There was a pressing issue, so he left," the Vice President said. "He will be back in an hour or so, I think. Could I help you in any way?" he asked.

"We have come from the office of Mohammed Omar Khan at the National Bank. He spoke with Mr. Serajuddin about a position for Khaled *jan* here."

Mr. Hanifi then gave a formal introduction about my father, my family background and me. The Vice President turned to me and stood up with widened eyes.

"You are most welcome, sir! I'm more than happy to get to know you, for you do belong to a very respectable family. I personally cherish some good memories of your uncle Ghulam Jailani Khan when he used to manage the military corps in Herat. Now, please tell me how I could be of service."

"Thank you, sir. I'm looking for a job," I said as I showed him my work permit.

The Vice President rang the bell on his desk, calling the attention of a clerk, and asked him to bring the hiring supervisor.

A minute later, the supervisor stepped into the room. "Mr. Izzat, this is

Khaled *jan*. He's been sent here today by the acting chief of the National Bank. He's interested in working with us, and as far as I know, you need a German-Farsi translator. If this is true, please go and discuss this matter together. If agreed, consult with the Head of the Translation Department to determine Khaled *jan's* salary and position."

"Very well," said Mr. Izzat. "Let's go to my office to sort things out," he told me. We went to his office, sat down and he began to interview me. "So which university did you attend?" he asked.

I started to feel doubt creep in about getting the position. "I never went to university, sir. All my childhood I was imprisoned. I have a work permit, though, which has been approved by the Prime Minister," I said with hope. "I believe I will be able to handle any type of office work such as accounting or writing, and I will be happy to do translation work if you have an open position. I am fluent in German and Farsi."

With a smile on his face, Mr. Izzat said, "This is a wonderful coincidence. We recently announced an opening for a German-Farsi translator in Anees Daily[84]. Yes, we urgently need someone who can translate between these two languages as the company does all its correspondence in German with the branch of the National Bank in Munich. If you're ready to come on as a contractor, we can sign an agreement on an as-needed basis, but it will entitle you to no career development or promotion. However, if you prefer to work for the company as a graded-employee who can be promoted, the company also offers that option."

"If I want to be employed as a graded-officer, which grade would I be employed at?" I asked, wondering if my lack of educational certificates would get in the way.

"What I can do is start you at the grade we give our college graduates. This paygrade will compensate you with 800 Afghanis per month. If you wish to do this, you need to talk to Mr. Nizam about your job duties," he said.

I was overjoyed. "Thank you very much, sir!" After my meeting, Mr. Nizam came into his office. He welcomed me into the company and paid tribute to my family elders. "You can start tomorrow," he said with a smile.

---

[84] A newspaper in Kabul.

THIRTY

Habiba *jan* among her colleagues at UNICEF
(first-row, second from the left), 1951.

I felt new optimism enter my life. Having spent so much time in prison, I was used to obsessing about what people would think of me should I ever be free. I feared the false propaganda of the media would portray my family in a negative light, and would, therefore, affect all of our futures and the lives of our descendants for generations.

To my surprise, my experience was quite the opposite. Most people were fair-minded and understood that many educated and intelligent people who had fought for social justice had been imprisoned unjustly. They had sympathy for the suffering my family went through. I was even more humbled by the younger generation.

One day, I learned that the Ministry of Education turned our home on Andarabi Street into a high school. When the young students found out the university site belonged to our family and that in one corner lay the body of three martyrs—Ghulam Nabi Khan, Ghulam Jailani Khan, and Shir-Mohammed Khan—they all joined hands and held a memorial service, praying and reciting verses of the Holy Qur'an. As part of their memorial service, they prepared bread and *hawla*[85], giving them to people passing by. I was deeply touched when I heard about this.

After over 20 years of dark winter, spring had finally come. My brothers and I were promoted to greater jobs with better salaries. My wife took a job with UNICEF and then with the Ministry of Public Health. My female cousins likewise became nurses and my sister became a high school teacher.

Eventually, we left Qala-e-Futuh, moving into our respective homes and apartments. Finally, we had left house arrest behind. A year after the move, my son Farid was born, and my daughter Bereshkai began attending school.

When I saw my daughter begin her studies in freedom, the sight brought grateful tears to my eyes. I used to fear my children would never be allowed the right to an education. Thank God they now had that chance. Life suddenly seemed brighter than before. I knew the freedom we had craved for two decades had finally come.

---

[85] A local food made of fried sugar, flower, and oil, often prepared for charity purposes.

PART III

If I am proud of existence,
You are the proof of all time.
You are meaning and expression.
You are the essence and the proof,
You, who is the substance and the absolute,
and the reason for the innate and the living.

From: **"You are meaning and expression"** – Khaled Siddiq

THIRTY-ONE

One alarming day, my niece, Dastgir's seven-year-old daughter, Parwin, was rushed to the hospital, suffering from sudden and severe knee pain. At the hospital, the doctors diagnosed her with gonalgia and suggested two treatments: Either they could plaster cast her leg, and she'd be bedridden for the rest of her life, or they could amputate. Neither option was acceptable to her parents.

Dastgir learned he could take Parwin to Germany where the medical treatments were significantly better. He found out the Ministry of Public Health allowed patients to leave the country so long as doctors could certify the disease was not treatable in Afghanistan. He managed to get a letter excusing him and his daughter to leave the country.

One of the requirements for getting a passport was to introduce a *zamin*[86]. The *zamin* was supposed to fully guarantee the receivers of the passport and undertake the responsibility of the traveler's journey abroad and back home. If the owner of the passport did not appear in due time, the *zamin* would be asked to summon them as soon as possible; otherwise, he would have to remain in jail until the person he had guaranteed appeared before police. Mohammed Yunus, a friend from Charkh, offered himself as Dastgir's *zamin*. Meanwhile, my father, who was still living in Berlin, arranged appointments with specialists to take care of Parwin upon her and Dastgir's arrival.

After over twenty years of separation and exile, my father would finally be

---

[86] A guarantor.

able to see his son. I hated to admit it, given the circumstances, but I slightly envied my brother. I had never had the privilege to create memories with my father, yet my brother was able to see him again. I suppressed the thought, instead focusing on being happy for my brother and praying for my niece's recovery.

When the German doctors examined Parwin and heard the diagnosis and proposed treatment from the Afghan doctors, they were in shock. They vehemently denounced the diagnosis, stating that what the Afghan doctors suggested was a crime, like cutting off a hand because of a splinter in a finger. Fortunately, they were optimistic they could treat her.

Two weeks after my brother left for Germany, I woke up early to the ring of my doorbell. I put on my robe and walked downstairs to see what was the matter. I found Yunus standing outside my door with a police officer. Soon after greeting us, Yunus asked anxiously, "Has Dastgir *jan* returned from his trip?"

"Not yet, why?"

"I was just summoned by Kabul's security headquarters, and they asked me to look for Dastgir *jan* and ensure them of his return. If he has not come back, this gentleman is obligated to take me back to the headquarters where I have no idea what lies in store for me."

"Why?" I asked the police officer with surprise. "What is the matter? My brother has committed no crime. He has taken his child abroad for treatment, using a legal passport. I assure you he will return soon and resume his job in the Ministry of Public Works."

Yunus was so worried that he paid no heed to my words and just kept repeating the same sentence again and again. "Please come along and rescue me from the police…Please…I cannot go there alone. They have asked me to bring either Dastgir *jan* or one of his family members to the security headquarters."

"Okay," I said. "I will go with you. Let me put on my clothes. Please come in and have some breakfast while I get dressed."

Yunus pointed to the police officer and asked, "What about him?"

"He is welcome too. He is also our brother."

Yunus entered the house with the escorting police officer, regaining his composure a little. I got dressed quickly, and after some breakfast and *chai*, all three of us went to Kabul's security headquarters. When we reached the Passport office, Yunus introduced me to the officials saying, "The person I had guaranteed is still not back, but here is his brother."

"Where is your brother?" asked one of the officials with a hard expression. "The authorities are furious with us. Our branch manager has been dismissed from his job, and we have been punished with a salary deduction, all because of your brother."

"What's the matter?" I asked. "My brother has simply taken his ailing child to Germany, and may I remind you he has done so with all the required legal documents and security clearances. I assure you he will return soon."

When I finished speaking, the official in charge spoke up. "I know very well that your brother has done nothing wrong. When we submitted his file to a commission for further investigation, they could find nothing wrong with his passport. However, a letter arrived from the *Sadarat's* Intelligence Office, dismissing our manager and punishing all other employees with a salary deduction for ten days. According to this letter, you all are banned from leaving the country. The fact that your brother was able to do so revealed that the director and the other Passport Office staff were not diligent enough in reviewing his application. So, they were punished, and now we must ensure that your brother returns. Now, let's go to the Commander of the Security Headquarters. He is anxiously awaiting news of your brother's whereabouts."

Yunus, the police escort, the official from the Passport Office and I went straight to the office of the Commander, Mr. Ataullah Khan. He came from a well-known Afghan family and was very polite. As soon as the officer in charge began talking to him, Mr. Ataullah interrupted him. "I know him," he gently said. "I am in the loop. Would you mind waiting outside with these two (referring to Yunus and his escort) for a while?"

Once the two of us were alone, Mr. Ataullah began speaking to me in a very informal manner. "I know your brother, Dastgir *jan*, has done nothing illegal; however, you know well where the government stands in relation to your family. Please tell your brother to come back as soon as possible.

Otherwise, I am afraid to say, you and your family may again be in trouble. It is the *Sadarat's* Intelligence Office that has raised this issue, and we are in no way involved."

"Very well," I told him. "Please give me some time, and I will write to him to return soon and put an end to this whole mess. I hope you will inform the relevant office to no longer summon the person who guaranteed my brother. From now on, I promise to be available in his place whenever required."

Impressed by my cooperation, Mr. Ataullah Khan accepted my request. When he called the others back in, he said to the officer in charge of the Passport Office, "Do not summon the *zamin* of Dastgir from now on, for his brother has promised to show up whenever required. Grant Dastgir a respite of one month so he has time to make travel arrangements and return."

Although the problem seemed to be temporarily solved, this incident reminded me of the ruling family's continuing strict stance against my family. I suddenly recalled Shah-Mahmood's words: *Afghanistan belongs to you, and you belong to Afghanistan.* I was now acutely aware that only half that statement was true—we belonged to Afghanistan.

On my way home, I reflected on the phases of punishment they had bestowed upon us. The first phase was to kill, exile, and imprison the patriarchs and any men capable of sparking a revolution. The second phase was to have all the kids grow up in prison isolated from educational institutions. The third phase was more isolation, this time living for five years in impoverished conditions under close supervision with no opportunity for work. And now the fourth phase: banned at all costs from leaving the country. There seemed to be no way out of the never-ending injustice. The only thing we could do was to make the most of our lives, be patient, and trust that someday things would change.

As soon as I got home, I wrote a letter to my brother, informing him of the trouble that had erupted since his departure. I feared that if he took more time than the government allowed, something terrible would happen to all of us. But before finalizing the letter, I had second thoughts. The government said he had a month, and I really wanted to let my brother enjoy his reunion with our father so he could return home with peace of mind. So I put the letter aside, and ultimately, I chose not to send it. I decided my brother should be with our father for as long as he wished. He deserved that.

At the end of the month, a police officer came to our house with a subpoena, ordering me to appear at the headquarters. With an escort, I returned to the Security Headquarters where the Commander interrogated me. "Where is your brother?" he demanded.

"He's still in Germany. His daughter needs more time to rest after her treatment," I said, making up an excuse.

"There is no reason for him to be so late," he said, rejecting my answer.

Then he softened…I could see it in his eyes. He turned to me again and said, "Tell your brother to come back as soon as possible; otherwise, the Passport Office will be under mounting pressure and will have no choice but to bother you again. We don't want the case to turn in an undesirable direction," he said with some compassion.

He then looked over to the accompanying officials. "Grant him a respite of two more weeks and do not disturb me up until the end of the deadline."

The Commander's words triggered a flood of terrible memories in my mind. I thought of the day we had all been imprisoned. I thought of the executions of my uncles and cousins. I thought of the brutal whippings and beatings the prison guards imposed on the inmates. This time, I took his message as a grave warning. Without hesitation, I wrote a letter to my brother, telling him to return to Kabul immediately so we could avoid further persecution.

One week after sending the letter, I received a reply from my brother. He promised he'd return at his earliest convenience, and he kept his word. A week later, he arrived with his daughter. He told me of the great joy he had with our father and uncle Aziz. "I met our two younger brothers," he told me with delight. "Ahmad and Zaid. They are both pursuing their studies in Germany. I hope we can go together sometime soon and visit."

My excitement dimmed at his last words. "We are banned from leaving the country, Dastgir. That is why I had to hurry you about coming back. I don't know when we'll ever be able to leave again."

He looked at me in disbelief. "I thought we were free," he said, clearly confused.

"Apparently not as much as we thought," I sighed with disappointment.

THIRTY-TWO

Six years passed by working with the Afghan Textile Company. I was promoted several times, and before I knew it, my salary grew from 800 Afghani to 5400 Afghani per month. The former President was no longer there; instead, an engineer named Mr. Shansab was now in charge.

One day an office assistant knocked on my door, requesting I go to Mr. Shansab's office to discuss a pressing issue. I thought it was going to be something related to the company, but when I entered his room, he had a gloomy expression on his face. He asked the assistant to close the door and started rubbing his forehand with his hand. "Please sit, Khaled *jan*," he said. A wave of silence filled the room as he paused, looking at the floor deep in thought.

Anxious thoughts flooded my mind. *Did I make a mistake? Will I be fired? What if someone, out of jealousy, told the President something terrible about me?* Finally, the President broke his silence.

"Khaled *jan*, have you ever requested the Textile Company or the National Bank to provide you with a scholarship to study in Germany to get more experience?"

"No. Never." I was shocked by such an inquiry. I started to think maybe he had some good news for me, but I tried to contain my excitement.

"Today, I received a call from a man who did not introduce himself. He had an exceptionally hoarse voice. He was less than welcoming and talked indecently. When I picked up the phone, he asked if I was the President of the Textile Company. I said, 'Yes.'

"With no etiquette, he replied, 'I am speaking from the Ministry of the Interior. We heard that you had provided one of your employees, Khaled, son of Ghulam Siddiq, with a scholarship to study in Germany. This man is banned from leaving the country and is under scrutiny. You must keep him under close watch and avoid giving him the chance to go abroad.'

"He repeated those words again and again and never let me ask him about the matter. When he finally stopped talking, I asked him to please introduce himself.

"Then he yelled at me, 'Why the hell do you want me to introduce myself. I am just telling you that the man is banned from leaving the country and is under scrutiny. You have to inspect him as well.'

"I wanted to interrupt him, Khaled. I wanted to say, 'Talk to me like a human being! What nonsense are you barking about?'

"But he never let me have a word and kept on repeating his orders. Finally, when there was a pause, I grasped the opportunity and told him, 'You work for the government; therefore, it is your duty to inspect and scrutinize. The Textile Company is a commercial enterprise. We cannot inspect our employees nor poke our noses into their private matters.'

"I wanted to ask him his name and phone number, but he interrupted me with his hoarse voice, 'I've informed you, and now the choice is yours.' And then he hung up. You can't imagine how crazy he made me, this stupid man. What crime could you have committed that would merit a call like this?"

I sighed, "My crime was that I languished in prison for almost fifteen years. Then, I spent five years in isolation with my family in Qala-e-Futuh under the direct control of the government, unable to even work. Finally, with great difficulty, I managed to get my work permit and find employment with your company. If any of those things are crimes, then I must admit that I am a criminal. Other than that, I can't remember having committed any crime that would warrant such persecution."

Mr. Shansab became silent for a long time. Then, he said, "You are a free man now. The Textile Company reserves no right to intrude into your personal life. You deserve to work with peace of mind."

Despite Mr. Shansab's sympathy, this experience stung me. I felt like a nuisance that the ruling regime would go so far as to inconvenience others just because I was connected to them in some way. When I returned home that night, I told my wife and Dastgir, both of whom just shook their heads in disbelief. But we all knew the truth: there was nothing we could do about it.

So I remained at the Textile Company, and in 1951, when my company planned to lay the foundation for their new factory in Gulbahar, they held a big event and invited many of us employees to participate in the festivities. We gathered in a lush green area near the Shotal River on a beautiful spring day. Having made all the arrangements for the ceremony, we waited for Prime Minister Shah-Mahmood to arrive to lay the cornerstone of the factory with his own hands.

Armed soldiers lined both sides of the main road in preparation for His Excellency's arrival while a large number of police officers watched the attendees from every vantage point. At last, a long line of cars entered the facility honking in celebration, and in the distance, a motorcade appeared that we all knew carried the Prime Minister.

I was busy working with my colleagues to arrange the dining tables when I saw Mr. Hanifi approaching me. He put his hand on my shoulder, guiding me away from the crowd. "Khaled *jan*, I'm extremely sorry to have to relay this message from Mohammed Omar, but he asked that you not be present when the Prime Minister arrives."

"Okay," I said blandly, pretending not to care. "I'm not really interested in being seen in public anyway. Also, I'm tired. I will go rest." Mr. Hanifi could see I was hiding my disappointment and gave me a look of sympathy.

I left for the Shotal River where I found a giant boulder to sit on. I stared at the gushing water with my feet dangling over it. A nostalgic feeling came over me. I remembered the French writer, Lamartine, and his famous works, *The Lake* and *Poetical Meditations*. I began talking, almost murmuring to the rushing waters, complaining about the unjust way of the world, especially the way I was treated by the government and the way men bowed down to them in fear.

As dusk fell, the ceremony came to a close. Once I saw that all the national leaders had left, I returned to my friends and colleagues, trying to forget the Prime Minister's pettiness. Still, I was bewildered that someone could maintain such a grudge.

As the days went on, I heard more disheartening stories of government corruption. Members of the ruling family would forcibly buy people's agricultural lands for incredibly low prices, and nobody dared disobey their orders.

I knew the truth. The government did not care about the people. They only cared about themselves. Key governmental posts were allocated exclusively to the ruling family members, and if the ruling family had no people to appoint, they appointed their distant cousins and friends from the Mohammed Zai tribe, their ancestral clan. All of those related to the ruling family were exempt from paying taxes, customs duties, and electricity bills. They were also given a car with a personal driver, and a monthly salary called the "continuous salary" from the Ministry of the Royal Court. All this money came from customs duties, municipality and utility bills, and taxes imposed on farmers and poor segments of the population. The nepotism in the government was blatant and rampant.

Although the incident at the groundbreaking celebration left me with a bitter aftertaste, I had much to be joyful for. I decided to focus on enjoying the freedoms I did have and continued building a great life for my family.

Time went on. My brothers and I progressed in our careers. Dastgir had an exciting opportunity when the German government offered to sponsor a delegation from the Ministry of Public Works to visit some of the construction companies across West Germany. Of the three people chosen to go on the trip, Dastgir was one of them. The Deputy Minister presented the list to Daoud Khan, who was now the official Prime Minister. He removed my brother's name from the list, only approving the other two. We were all disappointed, although we were used to this. Instead, we focused on happily living. Unfortunately, we were soon faced with another tragedy.

It was a silent night in 1953 when my dear aunt Ku Ku *jan* died. We were in Paghman at my uncle's home. She was lying in bed when she suddenly stopped breathing. Her high blood pressure and heart issues had finally caught up to her, and she suffered a heart attack. Dr. Mir, the same doctor who had treated us all those years in Sarai Badam and Sarai Ali Khan, happened to live by us, and we had remained in regular touch since our release. I drove to his house immediately, asking for him.

"Dr. Mir, Ku Ku *jan* has had a heart attack," I said.

Before I could continue my sentence, he insisted I take him to our home. We drove to my uncle's home in Paghman, and Dr. Mir checked my aunt. When he looked up, all of our hearts sank. "I'm sorry everybody," he said. "It's too late for her."

Everybody broke down beside Ku Ku *jan*. Habiba held her hand in tears, and her cries broke my heart. My children sobbed alongside her. I drove the whole family to Kabul in my cousin's jeep and brought Ku Ku *jan's* body to my house. Dastgir, Azim, Siddiqa, Mastoora, Ghaffar, my mother, my wife, my kids and I all mourned together for the rest of the night.

The next day we prepared for her funeral ceremony. Ku Ku *jan* was our hero. Had it not been for her valiant efforts and leadership, we would have remained illiterate. We would've suffered much more and eventually lost hope. We wouldn't be the strong souls that we had become. But Ku Ku *jan* had saved us. A mother to us all, she played a fundamental role in us overcoming our imprisonment. May you rest in peace my dear Ku Ku *jan*.

THIRTY-THREE

Every year since my brother returned from Germany, I had applied for a passport in the hopes the ruling regime would lighten up their stance towards my family. The process always began with me going to *Wilayet* prison to fill out a petition. These trips to the prison haunted me, knowing my family members had languished there for fifteen years. I always wrote the petition rapidly so I could leave the grip of those dark memories as fast as possible. I'd then go with my *zamin* to several police stations to pass the security clearances. After I was officially cleared, I'd go to the Passport Office and give them all my documents. The Head of the Passport Office would then send my documents to the *Sadarat's* Intelligence Office for approval. Unfortunately, I was always met with the same cold rejection letter:

"We do not give Khaled Siddiq permission to have a passport."

There was never any reason or explanation, just old resentment influencing their decision-making. I always tried to forget about it as I waited for the following year's attempt. Besides, my life was brighter now. I had a great family with four adorable children who all had the privilege of attending school. I had a great job with a high salary and a vibrant social life. This all inspired a newfound optimism in my life, leading me to believe that these denials wouldn't last forever—that eventually the ruling family would drop their grudge against my family and let me see my father.

One day, I received a surprising phone call at work. It was Sahibdaad Khan, a close friend of my father who had served as the official photographer for King Amanullah Khan. "Khaled *jan*, can you visit me after you're done with work today?" he asked.

"Yes of course, is there anything wrong?" I replied, thinking he needed help because of his deteriorating health condition.

"No, I'm fine. Just come over as soon as you can. I'll talk to you then."

I rushed to his house immediately after work trying to guess what news he had for me. His friendly wife welcomed me when I arrived, and after she led me to his room, he requested that she leave the house for some time. He then lowered his voice, as if he didn't want our conversation overheard by anybody.

"I want to talk to you about a serious matter," he said, "so serious that I could not communicate this with you over the telephone. I strongly urge you not to share this with anyone, be it family members or friends. No one."

I nodded my head, and he continued in a low voice.

"My friend, Ali Mohammed Khan, came here for a visit yesterday. He spoke about his trip to Germany and mentioned how happy he was to spend a couple of days with *Vizier Sahib*[87] in Berlin." (Sahibdaad would always refer to my father as *Vizier Sahib* because he was the Minister of Foreign Affairs during King Amanullah's era.)

Sahibdaad continued, "He said your father was in a very good health, which is a blessing for us all. When he asked your father if there was anything he needed, your father told him, 'I have a son, Khaled, who wishes to visit me. Unfortunately, all of his attempts to get a passport have resulted in years of rejection. If you can help him get a passport to visit me, I will be very grateful.' Ali asked me to find you and give the message to you. So, *Inshallah*, we will do our best. You need to write a petition to the higher authorities and bring it to me as soon as you can. And once again, don't tell anyone. If word gets out, it can jeopardize our initiative."

I couldn't believe my ears. I was speechless and grateful. I felt my heart jump a beat as I stood up and profusely thanked Sahibdaad. Then, I immediately left for *Wilayet* prison and filled out a petition.

When I came the next day with my petition, he told me, "Great. Now you

---

[87] A term of respect for a Minister.

must wait one week for me to come back with an answer."

One week was nothing for me. After 25 years of dealing with the regime, I had developed a lot of patience. I went through my workweek thinking about my father, imagining what it would feel like for us to meet each other for the first time. Emotions welled up in my body at the thought of it.

At the end of the week, I had heard no answer from Sahibdaad. I thought about contacting him, but then I decided to wait. Instead, I continued visualizing the reunion with my father, trusting that soon enough it would happen. Another week passed, and by now I was starting to get pessimistic. Still, I did my best to maintain hope. Finally, on the third week, Sahibdaad brought me a message from the Minister of the Royal Court, "I'm sorry Khaled *jan*. I couldn't get you your passport," he said with failure in his face.

I should've figured. The past 25 years had shown me that I'd be more likely to see donkeys fly than the ruling regime softening their hearts.

Instead of dwelling on the disappointment, I again focused on making the best of my life at home, realizing I could always try the next year. However, before the next year came, another blessing intervened in my life. One day, Abdullah Khan Malikyar, a kind-hearted man who had served as the Deputy Prime Minister during the reign of Daoud, came to the Jangalak Factory[88] to order some furniture for his home. The Textile Company had hired a German engineer to manage the furniture section of the Jangalak Factory, and this man personally took down Mr. Malikyar's order while I translated for the both of them.

After he placed the order, Mr. Malikyar put his hand on my shoulder, guiding me away from the others. "I have recently returned from a trip to Europe where I visited your respectable father," he said. "*Alhamdulillah*[89], he is doing fine. I have some important news for you. I want you to come to me tomorrow morning before I head to my office. We can have breakfast and discuss this matter a bit more."

I was surprised that such a high-ranking official would be so kind to me,

---

[88] Jangalak factory was a part of the Textile Company.
[89] Thank God.

and I was honored at the invitation. "Thank you, sir!" I replied with excitement.

The next morning, I drove over to Mr. Malikyar's home in the luxurious neighborhood of Shahr-e-Naw. Over a breakfast buffet, he gave me a great deal of invigorating news. He began by talking about his friendly ties with my father and the great time they had together in Berlin. "I promised your father I would do my best in getting you a passport. I need you to write a petition to the Prime Minister today and bring it to my office in the Ministry of Finance."

Besides being the second highest authority in the cabinet, Mr. Malikyar also had a close familial relation to Daoud Khan: his daughter was married to Daoud's son. Knowing this, I felt very confident this time I would get my passport.

The next day I brought my petition to Mr. Malikyar at his office. Enthusiasm thrummed in my heart as he took the paper. "Very well. I will let you know soon about your passport," he said in a calm, confident voice.

A few days later I got a message through the VP of the Textile Company that Mr. Malikyar wanted to see me at the Ministry of Finance. *So soon?* I went there immediately.

As I made my way to his office, I noticed something strange I had never seen before. Everything looked different. The people, the city, the world. It was all lighter and brighter somehow. I saw smiles on people passing by. I saw birds flying in synchronization across clear skies. There was delight everywhere. Then, I realized that it wasn't the external world that had changed, it was me. After 26 years of being deprived of my human rights, after more than six years of persistently applying and being rejected to see my father, I felt like I would finally receive all the freedoms of a normal citizen.

By the time I entered Mr. Malikyar's office, I could hardly hide my smile. He noticed and welcomed me warmly. "I'm glad to see you in such high spirits. Fortunately, I have great news for you. Yesterday I shared your passport problems with the Prime Minister in the presence of the Minister of the Interior. His Highness said that he has no objection to you visiting your father."

Joy rushed in, and in my excitement, I could hardly speak properly. "Has His...has His Highness...signed my application?"

"Unfortunately, I did not have it with me ...never mind... I will do it myself." He began searching for my application among a pile of papers on his desk, but he could not find it. He then picked up the phone to call the Minister of the Interior.

I could hear him speaking to the Minister, reminding him of the earlier day's meeting with the Prime Minister. "...Yes, Khaled, son of Ghulam Siddiq. You heard His Highness say he should be given a passport so he can visit his father in Germany, right?" He paused to listen, and then said, "Ok, thanks, I am going to send him to you."

Mr. Malikyar hung up the phone and turned to me with a serious look.

"If you can go to the Minister of the Interior right now, your application should be complete."

On the drive over, I could not stop myself from shouting with joy. *Finally! Finally! Thank God!* When I entered the Minister of the Interior's office, he greeted me warmly. "His Excellency, the Deputy Prime Minister, has told me everything about your case," the Interior Minister said. "Now, tell me if you have brought any written instructions from His Excellency, Mr. Malikyar."

My shoulders slumped. "No, I haven't. His Excellency wanted to give a written order, but he did not remember where he had placed my application. After the telephone conversation, he told me to visit Your Excellency."

He paused and began thinking for a while. Then, he picked up the telephone and called the Governor of Kabul, informing him of Mr. Malikyar's instructions. Still holding the phone, he turned to me and said, "Please go to His Excellency, the Governor of Kabul. He will issue you your passport."

The Governor was well aware of my background and the number of times I had applied for a passport. When I arrived at his office, he spared me the time of saying the details. "The Minister of the Interior has given me instructions over the phone. It would have been much better if you had brought a written order from His Excellency. Anyhow, I'm glad you can finally achieve your goal. Now, you must go to the Head of the Passport Office. I shall instruct him to give you a passport."

I was still in the doorway of his office when he phoned the Head of the Passport Office and overheard him as I slowly walked out. "He will be coming to you right away…yes…you should issue him a passport as per the Minister of the Interior's telephone instructions. He will tell you the rest when he is there…"

Night had fallen over Kabul as I drove to the Passport Office. Excited and anxious, I pulled into the parking lot and took a deep breath. I looked at the entrance feeling that this would be the time I finally beat rejection. I walked in, realizing I hadn't eaten since breakfast. I had been too focused on getting my passport. I knocked on Mr. Shoaib's door. He welcomed me into his office.

"I think you have hit the target this time! Come and tell me what you have done."

Without taking a breath, I told him all the details. "Excellent! Well, the workday is over now. Come here tomorrow early in the morning with two photos. I will try my best to prepare your passport."

"Very well," I said. "I will see you tomorrow. Thank you, sir." I shook his hand.

That night I couldn't sleep. I had too much excitement rushing through my veins. I thought about how I would finally see my father for the first time in my life. I imagined the conversations we would have. I imagined how proud he would be to hear about how much I had learned growing up. The last time I had seen him, I was two years old, and it was like a faint dream. Even though I could hardly remember him, I respected him deeply. He was the reason I did my best to be as great a human being as I could be, someone he could look to with pride and proclaim, "Yes, that's my son!"

I woke up early the next morning, still buzzing with excitement. As I entered the Passport Office, I watched Mr. Shoaib take a blank passport out of his drawer and start writing my name and information on it. He then handed an *ingit*[90] to his office assistant and told him to get my security clearance from all the police departments as soon as possible. As the office

---

[90] Passport application.

assistant was leaving, Mr. Shoaib addressed his assistant again, "Listen," he said, "if you see that any of the other departments are delaying the process, tell them to call me. You have to get these signatures by the early afternoon today and bring the form back to me." He then turned back to me, "If you have something to do, you may go now, but come back in two hours. Your passport should be prepared by then. The form I gave to our office assistant to get your security clearance is only a formality. I know you don't have any criminal case against you. Nonetheless, it is better to have this form in your file, just in case an authority asks."

"Ok," I said. "I have some other things I can tend to, but this task is far above all of them."

Mr. Shoaib nodded laughing. "I know how terribly you have suffered in the past, and I know how hard you've tried to get this passport, but this time you will not have any trouble. You will get your passport as soon as you return." As I looked behind, I saw a long line of people impatiently tapping their feet and checking their watches. I left Mr. Shoaib's office to occupy myself with errands.

When I returned two hours later, Mr. Shoaib had already prepared my passport. Handing it over to me, he said, "The only signature left is that of the Commander of Kabul's security headquarters. It is your responsibility to retrieve this. When you get it signed, bring it back here so I can register it and give it a serial number."

As I reached Kabul's security headquarters, a commotion erupted in the yard of the compound. I saw the Commander rush out of the building into a car and speed off into the dust. I entered the building and was greeted by an office clerk.

"Do you know where the Commander went?" I asked.

"I'm not entirely sure," the clerk answered, "but I think some important foreign guest is due to arrive in Kabul today. He may have gone to welcome him."

"And when does he return?"

"I have no idea."

I went back to the passport office to explain that the Commander was out of the office. Mr. Shoaib was busy collecting the papers scattered on his desk. "Did you get his signature or not?" he asked.

"No," I replied. "When I reached his office, he had already left the headquarters. Some office assistant told me the Commander went to join the welcoming team for a visiting VIP."

"Oh yes," said Mr. Shoaib. "I forgot to tell you that Soviet Premier Khrushchev is due to land in Bagram Air Base today. All the high-ranking officials, including general directors, are supposed to be at Bagram before his arrival. Never mind. Come back tomorrow. Things are going to be alright."

After another night of restless anticipation, I went to the headquarters the next day and received the Commander's signature with ease. I was now one step away from obtaining my passport. The thought of this kept me buzzing with excitement until Mr. Shoaib silently handed me a letter from the Intelligence Office.

To Kabul Passport Office! We received your letter of inquiry. We would like to draw to your attention that the Intelligence Office does not agree that Khaled, son of Ghulam Siddiq, should go abroad.
(Signature of Ghulam Rasul, Head of the Intelligence Office).

When I read the letter, I erupted in anger. "What!" I shouted. "Is the position of Rasul Khan higher than that of the Prime Minister?!"

"I am very sorry," Mr. Shoaib said. "The Passport Office shall not issue a passport for any Afghan citizen unless the Intelligence Office approves their application. I was under the assumption you were already cleared, so to fulfill my own duty, I sent an urgent letter of inquiry to the Intelligence Office asking for their immediate confirmation. I really don't know what is behind this. I think you should go to the Deputy Prime Minister today and inform him of what has happened."

Mr. Shoaib then took my passport and put it back in his drawer. Having to hand my passport over to him was demoralizing, but I could tell he did not want to cross any lines with the ruling regime. If he did me a favor and they found out, it would cost him his job.

I was in shock, and my heart was heavy as I somberly left the Passport

Office. I drove in a slow daze to the Ministry of Finance and asked to meet again with Mr. Malikyar.

As I entered his office, Mr. Malikyar looked at me with a kind smile on his face. "How is everything?" he asked. "When will you be leaving, *inshallah?*"

"Not anytime soon, Your Excellency. I've been denied again."

Mr. Malikyar was stunned. He immediately picked up the phone to call the Head of the Intelligence Office. Outraged on my behalf, he told Ghulam Rasul the whole story of how I had already gotten verbal approval from the Prime Minister with the Interior Minister as a witness, and still, my application had been denied. He paused and listened to Rasul. I could not hear what was said on the other end, but Mr. Malikyar seemed more taken aback with each passing moment. "Yes…yes…yes…" he repeated. "Okay," he concluded. "I will send him to you."

He turned to me, silent and wary. "Ghulam Rasul Khan says you have a case with the Intelligence Office. I don't know what that is about."

"I have no case other than time in prison as a child."

"You should go to the Intelligence Office. It is most likely a misunderstanding. Anyway, they will let you know." While he was saying this, I could feel he was surprised by what Rasul had told him. There was something fishy going on.

I arrived at Rasul's office the same day and once again related my story. In the end, I emphasized that the Prime Minister had already approved my application.

Rasul listened intently, and when I stopped, he said, "Sadly, when I asked His Highness about your application, he told me to postpone it for the time being."

I had no more questions. It was clear the ruling family still had not given up their grudge towards my family. I simply thanked him and left his office.

On the way home, I wondered if Rasul had even consulted Prime Minister Daoud about my case. I knew how fearful people were of him and how concerned they were about keeping their jobs. Mentioning my family's name could irritate the Prime Minister, causing him to react in abusive ways. His family had become notorious for that.

Each day, I thought about what I could do to influence a change in their decision. On the third day, I wrote a letter to Prime Minister Daoud.

Your Highness!

As His Excellency Deputy Prime Minister and the Minister of the Interior informed me, Your Highness had kindly approved my application for a passport. His Excellency, the Deputy Prime Minister and the Minister of the Interior communicated Your Highness's message of approval to the Governor of Kabul. As per regulations, the Passport Office has sent a letter of inquiry to the Intelligence Office to make sure they agree with the issuance of my passport. But the Head of the Intelligence Office has not agreed. As a result, I have not been given a passport.

May I ask, has Your Highness really approved my application for a passport to visit my father or not?

Yours Sincerely,
Khaled Siddiq

That same morning I went to Prime Minister Daoud's private home and gave my letter to Karim, his special attendant. Karim and I knew each other well because of his marriage with a member of my family. He took my letter and guided me into a booth inside the gate. "Wait here," he said. "I will let you know soon." He then made his way towards the *harem serah*[91] and returned within minutes.

"I've given your letter to His Highness. He read it thoroughly, from start to finish. Unlike other letters that His Highness usually tears up and throws into the dustbin, he put yours into his pocket and said he had approved your application then, but he won't now."

I thanked Karim for providing me with such a clear-cut answer and tried my best to appear indifferent to the situation. But then I heard myself say, "I was expecting such an answer."

---

[91] A home that was for all the women; often a man's wife and daughters.

When I left Daoud's house, I bumped into an old friend of mine, Habib. He worked as a civil engineer with the Ministry of Public Works. At the same time, he worked unofficially for Daoud, and of late, he had been doing some construction work for His Highness.

"What are you doing here?" he asked me with surprise. "When are you leaving for Germany?"

I was fairly surprised when he asked this question. No one apart from my family members and a few very close friends were aware of my travel plans. "Nothing in particular," I said evasively. "I wanted to see His Highness to say my farewell. I must go now. Great to see you."

I felt disappointed, not because of the constant barriers the Intelligence Office had created for me, but because the Prime Minister was the sole person who held the destiny of Afghanistan and all its people in the palm of his hands. He called himself the "strongest Prime Minister"[92] and kept all other Ministers and Provincial Governors under his scrutiny. No one would dare do anything without his permission. *Why would a leader, who held full political, economic and military might in his hand, feel so threatened by a person like me, bereft of any political and economic power?*

Once again, my long cherished wishes and aspirations had turned to ashes, and the efforts made by a respectable member of the government, Mr. Malikyar, had been all in vain.

To crush the poor is the way of the world.
Bidil! Feel not insulted by the starers[93].

Another year passed without any hope of visiting my father until one day when I received a letter from Germany. It was from my half-brother Zaid,

---

[92] It was the same statement Daoud had made in a radio address in Kabul when Pakistani-Afghan relations soured over the Pashtunistan issue.

[93] This is a verse from Bidil, a famous Persian poet. In this verse, he may want to say that the world is ungenerous and cruel; it crushes helpless people, and what one should do is to raise his head, stand up to the miseries of life, and not humiliate himself by begging and showing cowardice.

and he stated that our father was in the hospital after suffering a stroke. I erupted in rage, and then profound sadness settled in. *I've never had a conversation with my father, and now because of Daoud, I might never be able to.*

I could hardly function at the office that day. When later that day, I was in a colleague's office discussing a health care insurance program for the employees at my company, my colleague, Dr. Sharq, noticed my troubled expression. "You look sad today," he said. "What's going on?"

"Nothing. It's ok," I replied, trying to hide my feelings.

"C'mon, tell me, please. Let me see how I can help," he pushed.

Finally, I told him everything: the letter, the bad news about my father, how much I missed him, how much I wished to see him at least once while he was alive, and how I could not do so because the government had persistently denied me a passport for seven years. When I finished my rant, I apologized for not being able to control my feelings.

Dr. Sharq was silent for a while. He then mentioned that strokes had different phases: they could be light or severe. He hoped my father's stroke was a light one and prayed to God for his speedy recovery. He then asked, "When would you like to visit your father?"

"Tomorrow, if I could," I said, startled by his question.

"Very well. If you could write an application to the Prime Minister and give it to me either in the *Sadarat* or when I come here tomorrow evening, I will try to get it approved by *Sardar Sahib*[94]. But mention all your reasons."

"I don't think I'll be able to come to your office in *Sadarat*, but my application will surely be ready when we meet here tomorrow evening," I said.

The following day, I wrote a petition to the Prime Minister asking him to approve my passport application for family health reasons. I prayed for this to be the last time I would ever have to petition for my rights. I knew it would be terribly difficult for me to recover from the grief if my father passed away without me ever getting to see him.

---

[94] Daoud Khan and other members of the Mohammed Zai tribe were often referred to as *Sardar Sahib*. *Sardar* translates to "leader", and *Sahib* is a polite way to address a man.

I waited impatiently for the evening to come so I could meet with Dr. Sharq and give him my application. I thought of the past and became utterly hopeless, feeling almost sure that my dream would never come true. However, when I thought about Dr. Sharq's high position as the Prime Minister's special secretary, I dared to hope that somehow he would be able to do something.

The day passed slowly. As the evening approached, I felt some relief that I could now meet with Dr. Sharq. When I handed him my application, he read it and said, "Very well. You have explained everything very concisely. Rest assured, I'll bring you good news...*inshallah*."

Dr. Sharq called me a few days later, telling me he had gotten my petition approved by Daoud. I was once again in disbelief. I never expected to hear such news. Encouraged, I left the office immediately. "I'll be absent for a few hours," I told my colleagues as I rushed out and made my way to Dr. Sharq's office in the *Sadarat's* Special Secretariat.

When I arrived, Dr. Sharq offered me a seat next to him and instructed one of the clerks to bring my application number and hand it to me. He then turned to me and related the process of how the Prime Minister had approved my application. "Well," he continued, "I was reading some applications to His Highness. When I read your application, His Highness said, 'Give him a passport,' and I went on reading other applications. When we finished the rest of the applications, he turned to me asking, 'What did I say about Ghulam Siddiq's son?'

"'Your Highness approved it.'
"'Ok, but send his application through the Intelligence Office.'"

Hearing the words "Intelligence Office" shattered my hopes. I tried not to look frustrated and thanked Dr. Sharq before I left for the Intelligence Office. To my disappointment, the Head of the Intelligence Office was not available that day.

I waited for a few days, hoping my application would be sent from the Intelligence Office to the Passport Office. I went to Rasul's office, hoping he might have good news. He did not. "I received your application from the Special Secretariat," he said, "but when I took it to the Prime Minister for further processing, he said it should be postponed for the time being." I could not listen to any more of this. I could not take any more rejection, especially considering the critical condition of my father. I thanked him in a grey tone and left the office numb and defeated.

That evening, I met Dr. Sharq and told him the whole story. He thought for a minute, pressing both sides of his head with his forefingers and thumbs. "No, it's wrong," he said firmly and somewhat agitated. "I know His Highness. He never takes back his word once he approves something, but when he rejects something, he does it straight away. If Rasul Khan said such a thing, he must have made it up himself."

"But what could the reason be? There is no personal animosity or grudge between us."

"It is not a matter of a personal grudge," replied Dr. Sharq. "Some people are so circumspect that they don't have the guts to mention your name before high-ranking authorities, lest they lose their position." Speaking sympathetically, he added, "Never mind what he told you. Try to write another application to His Highness. I am going to verify the validity or invalidity of this statement."

Although I felt incredibly humiliated by the piling of rejections and did not believe Dr. Sharq would be able to change anything, I chose to put aside my doubt and wrote another application. I delivered it to Dr. Sharq the following day. "Don't worry," he said, "His Highness comes here once a week to answer people's petitions. When he is here this week, I'll get your application approved, *inshallah*," he said with confidence.

I went back to my work, still wondering about my dad and his health condition. Every day after work, I went to visit Dr. Sharq, eagerly expecting an answer but to my disappointment, he would always say His Highness was busy and had no time to read people's petitions. The week ended and I felt the last flickers of hope fizzle away like a candle snuffed out by the cold wind.

During the start of the next week, I received comforting news from Zaid: my father's stroke had not been too severe. In fact, he had already made a full recovery and been discharged from the hospital. *It's not too late.* My anxiety dimmed some and I decided to wait until Dr. Sharq contacted me. Fortunately, during the following week, I received his call. "Could you please stop by my office?" he said. "I'd like to have a word with you." I took his tone as a good omen and went to his office immediately.

When I saw Dr. Sharq, my heart beat with anticipation of his news. "I spoke with His Highness about you," he began. "I told him, 'Khaled's passport has not been issued, so he has written another application, asking for your kindness.' His Highness interrupted saying, 'I already approved his passport application.' As I heard him say this, I wrote at the bottom of your application, 'Khaled's passport is to be issued,' and then put your application before His Highness. He signed it. Now, an official letter from the Special Secretariat Office, attached with your application, shall be directly issued to the Governor of Kabul and given to you personally. You are to hand it over to the Governor. He shall instruct the Passport Office to issue you your passport."

"What about the Intelligence Office?" I asked.

"Khaled *jan*, it's all taken care of," Dr. Sharq reassured me.

He then turned to one of the office clerks and said, "Issue the letter I told you about—the one directly to the Governor of Kabul. Attach it to that application and give it to this gentleman and get his signature in the registration book."

The clerk nodded and had me sign the registration book, indicating I had received an official letter. I did so gladly, wondering if this could really be happening.

The office clerk left and returned with the letter in a sealed envelope, on the back of which was written, "Directly to the Governor of Kabul."

Addressing me, Dr. Sharq said, "I already told you that Rasul Khan's statement was not valid. He has, in no way, consulted His Highness a second time. That is why we are not going through the Intelligence Office this time. Now that you have His Highness's signature on your application, I'm sure there will be no more obstacles in your path."

I shook Dr. Sharq's hand with immeasurable gratitude and left for *Wilayet* to meet with the Governor, carrying the most valuable letter of my life. As I approached *Wilayet*, I thought of my time at Dehmazang. The idea that one day I would be holding an official letter with the Prime Minister's signature approving my passport application was almost impossible to imagine.

When I arrived at the Governor's office, he greeted me warmly. "Come into my office and have a seat, please," he said. When he read the back of my envelope—"Special Secretariat Office, directly to the Governor of Kabul"—he smirked at me, "I think you have brought a decree for us this time." He then opened the envelope, looked at my application signed by His Highness and thoroughly read the letter from the Special Secretariat Office. "My guess was true," he said in serious tone. Then with empathy, he said, "*Zindagi migozara*[95]."

He took his pen and wrote: "To be processed as per His Highness's instruction." He returned my letter, smiling as he said, "You may give that to the Passport Office now. Then your task will finally be done."

I raced to the Passport Office; my entire being was vibrating as I thought about the reality of seeing my father. When I arrived, I met Mr. Shoaib with tremendous excitement. "Now that you have such a powerful document," he said, "there will be no problem, I assure you. But it is too late today. Tomorrow, you should bring two passport photos, and I'll do my best to prepare your passport in one day."

Anxiety flooded me again that maybe the Intelligence Office would change their mind, but I put my faith in Mr. Shoaib's words and left for home. I could hardly sleep that night. The thought of how close I was to freedom, to reuniting with my father, kept me stirring all night. Upon waking the next morning, I rushed to get the two passport photos and delivered them to Mr. Shoaib's office. "Come back in one hour. I'll have everything finalized and prepared," he told me.

I didn't know where else to go. I had only come to Kabul for one reason. I paced back and forth in the lobby, until I got tired of that. I sat and read the newspaper, twice. Finally, Mr. Shoaib opened his door. "Khaled *jan*, I have something very special for you," he said.

At last, after eight years of hoops and hurdles, rejection and humiliation, I received my passport. I was overjoyed. Ironically, I received it just before

---

[95] Life goes on.

Eid. I remembered how in the past, *Eid* had just meant a time when I got shackled and confined in my cell. That day, I saw the holiday as a divine blessing.

But an anxious thought also came to my mind. *What if the higher authorities reconsider their decision?*

Without a second thought, I rushed to the ticket agency to buy the earliest possible flight to Germany. The Soviet airline, Aeroflot, had one Kabul-Moscow flight every week. For me to arrive in West Berlin, I had to spend one night in Moscow and catch a flight from there to East Berlin. Fortunately, I found a flight that left the following morning with a few remaining seats. I bought the ticket immediately.

Hearing the news, my boss told me to stay there as long as I wanted, and that I'd have a job with them whenever I came back. He wanted to make sure I had plenty of time to be with my father. "Thank you, sir, thank you so much!" I then left for home where I told the great news to my wife. She was so happy for me and helped me pack my suitcase. As we gathered the luggage, I glanced again at my passport and my ticket for Germany. I was unable to believe that, after three decades of separation, I was finally going to see my father.

THIRTY-FOUR

From left to right: Myself, Parwin *jan* (my niece), Ghulam Siddiq Khan (my father), and Kubra *jan*. The man standing is Ahmad Siddiq (my brother) at my father's home in Berlin, 1962.

Dawn peeked through the curtain in my bedroom as I cinched the knot of my tie before my departure. "Are you ready?" my wife asked.

I smiled, "Yes." My children lined up to wish me safe travels. One by one, I hugged them, kissing their foreheads as I said, "Be well."

I drove with Habiba to the airport. Although snow had fallen the night before, the road felt clearer than ever that day. I arrived at the airport feeling a bit rushed. Habiba told me to write to her often. We embraced for a long moment, savoring this blessing. "Goodbye my dear," I said, kissing her farewell, and then I turned and hurriedly made my way to the boarding area.

When I entered the plane, the reality of the moment rushed through me. I was free. I was about to fly in an airplane for the first time. I was heading to a new country. And I was about to see my father. I tried to calm myself down by looking out the window. As we took off, the once vague image of conversing with my father became clear in my mind. *It's real; it's finally going to happen.*

My first connection was in Tashkent, Uzbekistan. We were told that there'd be a delay due to harsh weather conditions. A swarm of people rushed to the telephones, phoning their loved ones of the news. When I went to call my father, the telephone operator told me it wasn't possible. "Sorry, sir. There is no way to call West Germany from here." *Why?* I wondered. The operator didn't give me any further explanation.

I waited some time for my next flight, losing myself in a book. When it came time to board, giddy excitement welled up again. The hours on the plane flew by like minutes, and before I knew it, the plane had landed in Moscow. I got my luggage and left to spend the night in a hotel. I couldn't sleep, though. I was too excited.

I spent the evening reading in the coffee shop of a nearby hotel. When I saw two military men speaking German, I approached them for a conversation. They told me about the political situation in Germany. I was curious to hear more, so after the coffee shop closed at midnight, I invited them to continue the conversation in my hotel room. They had some vodka and cigarettes, and the three of us drank shots and smoked as they told me more about German politics, occasionally cracking jokes.

I asked the men, "Why was I unable to speak to my father on the phone from Tashkent?"

"The Soviet Union does not have access to West Germany," one of them explained. "They're not communists."

At the end of the night, I brushed my teeth a few times, trying to conceal the smell vodka and cigarettes on my breath. I wanted to make the best impression when I met my father.

I woke up to an unexpected snowstorm, and when I arrived at the airport, I was informed the flight had been postponed until the afternoon. Impatient to leave, I tried to distract myself with another book.

Finally, an airport official announced our flight was now boarding. My heart began to pound with excitement. In my incredibly anxious state, I could no longer read or sleep. All I could do was sit still as my mind flooded with thoughts of all the things I could finally tell my father.

A few hours later, the pilot came over the speaker, "Due to inclement weather, we'll have to make a temporary stop in Dresden," he announced. *More delays.*

After we landed in Dresden, almost everybody rushed over to a nearby call office, telling their family and friends about the redirection. When my turn came, I gave my father's number to the telephone operator. "I am sorry sir. I cannot put you through to this number. Your number is from West Berlin, and we are in the DDR[96]."

I started to realize the harsh restrictions the Soviets had imposed on the East Germans. I felt sympathy for them; I knew far too well how it felt to be isolated. I spent a few hours in the Dresden airport, waiting for the weather to improve so we could fly to East Berlin. Finally, the clouds dissipated and we took off.

When I got off the plane in East Berlin, I was under the impression that I would meet one of my family members in the airport. I didn't realize the Communist regime had banned all West Germans from being able to enter the East Berlin airport terminal. I was appalled at the idea of a nation with people sharing the same culture and language being completely separated from one another.

As I passed customs, a female police officer read my name and looked up at me with surprise. "Mr. Siddiq! I have a note here saying I should send you in a taxi to where someone is waiting for you."

---

[96] Deutsche Demokratische Republik.

I only had one person in mind—*Father*. "Thank you very much," I said and followed her outside the terminal. It was snowing heavily again, and there was a long line of people waiting for taxis. An ordinary car stopped near us, and the police officer told me to get in. I thanked her for her help and entered the car. We sped off into the snowy traffic.

"Where should I take you?" asked the driver.

"To the wall near the Border Control. I will manage the rest myself."

As we approached the Border Control, the driver suggested we get out of the car. "I will carry your luggage to the gate," he insisted.

"Why?" I inquired.

"My car is not a taxi, and if the police find out I am using it as such, I will be severely punished."

I could see the desperate look of the driver. "Yes, of course," I said. I could relate to his situation and the situation of all East Germans. For many of them, their old lives had been shattered by the new Soviet regime, and their economy was in ruin. It made sense there was a black market. Before I took my suitcase from the driver, I thought to ask him about the taxi fare, but I suddenly changed my mind and took a US twenty-dollar bill out of my pocket.

"Is it enough?" I asked, showing him the note.

He quickly grabbed it, hid it in his pocket and stepped happily towards his car, thanking me profusely.

After going through customs at the gate, I officially crossed into West Berlin. I found several taxis lined up along the road, waiting for passengers coming from East Berlin. I showed my address to one of the drivers.

"Ok, let's go," he said.

By the time we reached my father's house, night had fallen over the city. When I rang the doorbell, a German couple came out. I was confused, but then thought maybe they were Father's guests.

"Good evening," I began. "Is His Excellency [97] here?"

The couple knew who I meant and said, "His Excellency has gone out

---

[97] I already knew that my father's German friends called him "Excellency."

looking for you." With this, they took my suitcase, paid the taxi fare and guided me into the house. As I entered the hall, the first person to see me was Huriya *Khanum*, nicknamed Bi Bi *Khord*, my stepmother and the mother of my half-brothers. Her sweetness and nurturing heart welcomed me with a warm embrace. I kissed her hands. She kissed my forehead. "Where were you, Khaled *jan?*" she asked. "Everybody is out looking for you. Didn't you see your father or any of your brothers on the way?"

I didn't, but I was somewhat out of my senses, immersed in a sea of joy. "No. I had your address, so I got a taxi and came directly."

The telephone rang. "Your father," she said, already hurrying towards the phone. She was right. It was my father. "Khaled *jan* is here. Come back home and don't worry, everything is alright."

I felt my heart beating faster. I listened for the doorbell, and my eyes remained on the hallway.

After what seemed like an eternity, the bell finally rang. I jumped up, hurrying towards the door. The German man opened the door. I rushed outside towards my father who was halfway across the yard. I met him in a long embrace.

I felt like I was floating outside my body, watching our emotional reunion from above. After three decades of misery, imprisonment, persecution, and injustice, my father and I had finally been reunited.

I tried my best not to break down in tears, but I already felt the tension in my throat and the water in my eyes. Then, the dam broke loose, the tears just poured out, and I sobbed uncontrollably. As the Persian poet, Rahi Moayeri, says:

Shaky tears shall not retreat.

"Come in my son, everything is okay now," my father said as he held my hand and guided me into the house. I could see the German couple and Bi Bi *Khord* wiping the tears off their faces. I tried to change the mood by speaking about my flight delay.

Suddenly, the doorbell rang again, and two tall, striking young men entered the house. They were my brothers, Zaid and Ahmad. "Hey!" they screamed in excitement as they rushed to hug me. "Which way did you come from? How did you not see us in the arrivals section?"

I learned there were several entry points into West Berlin and that my father had been waiting at the Aeroflot ticket agency in East Berlin, since my family thought I would have some challenges getting around the East Berlin airport. They had also prepared for the worst by having my cousin Dr. Usman wait for me at the subway station, while my brothers waited for me at the bus station. We laughed at how I had evaded all of them in my dazed arrival.

Shortly after meeting my brothers, another Afghan family rang the doorbell. It was a mother, a young girl, and two toddlers. They were relatives of my father's friend and had come to Germany for medical treatment. They couldn't speak German nor did they have a place to stay, so my brothers and father helped by taking care of their needs. My family's generosity touched my heart.

We all sat in a circle with my father next to me as he asked me endless questions about what had happened to us during our imprisonment. I tried to keep the answers short and made a conscious effort to avoid the horrific details. I knew my father was suffering from high blood pressure and chronic diabetes, and I didn't want him to suffer upon hearing about the cruelty we had experienced. Still, he kept asking questions, wanting to listen to every detail of our story.

As I went into some of the harsher details, I saw the visiting Afghan family burying their faces into handkerchiefs, crying ceaselessly. I asked my father for permission to change the conversation. He agreed, and so I told the story of the man who had driven me to the border. They all burst into laughter when I told them that I had paid him twenty dollars. "That was a bonanza for him!" said Zaid. I found out that one US dollar was equal to four West German DM, and one West German DM equaled five East German DM. So the amount I had given the driver equaled four hundred East German DM—a considerable amount for such a short taxi ride.

The next day, I went on a walk with my father through Thielpark. We sat down on a wooden bench, staring out at the pond as he told me the truth about the events that led to our cruel suffering. He told me how they had all worked with King Amanullah, and how as a team they were on the verge of creating a brighter, more modern Afghanistan. He explained how Nadir Shah had written letters to guarantee the restoration of King Amanullah's throne, thanking my father profusely for our family's contributions, all before betraying them and the entire country. I was outraged. "What happened to you during this time?" I asked.

"I was immediately removed from my post as Ambassador and exiled as an Afghan Political Refugee," he said with disappointment. "I was so worried after hearing about the death of my brother. I prayed for you and the family's safety. After a year of isolation, I felt utterly helpless. I knew if I returned to Afghanistan, they would kill me on the spot. I had no idea about any of your whereabouts and after sending many letters and never receiving a response, I feared they had captured you. I went on *Hajj*[98] in desperation, where I spent six months seeking God's mercy and guidance. Unfortunately, I received neither. Eventually, a friend found me in Mecca and urged me to move on with my life. He stated that my family wouldn't want me to suffer like this. I left, bereaved and heartbroken.

"I couldn't sleep at nights. My brothers, my wife, my kids, all of my dear cousins and nephews and nieces…you were all taken away from me. I remember the day your mother wrote to me about your birth. I wish I could have been there. I wish I could've been there in your early years to see you grow up. After all of this happened, I feared I'd never get to see you or anybody in our family ever again."

I began to tear up as I responded, "Father, perhaps it was best you were here. Who knows what Nadir Shah or Zahir Shah would've done to you had you been in Afghanistan at the time," I said.

Part of me dearly wished as well that my father had been home when I was younger. Growing up, I had only heard tales of him. He was like a legend in my eyes, and truthfully, he still was. But by him staying in Germany, he had survived, and I was just so grateful that I could finally be with him.

---

[98] A holy pilgrimage to Mecca.

THIRTY-FIVE

From left to right: Kubra *jan*, myself, my father, Helen
(Dr. Usman's wife), and Tahira *jan* (Ahmad Kabir Siraj's wife), 1962.

The following days carried on routinely. I'd have breakfast with my father, brothers, and stepmother. Afterwards, while Zaid and Ahmad left for college, my father and I would go on a walk around Thielpark. We'd walk for about an hour and spend another hour sitting on the bench by the pond. We'd talk about each other's lives and share stories, using our time to bond as father and son. I was most fascinated by his stories of working with King Amanullah before all the turmoil came with Nadir Shah and his family.

On one of our walks, my father told me about what had happened to him, my brothers, and stepmother there in Berlin after the war. In 1945, when World War II ended, and the occupying Allied Forces marched into Berlin, the Soviet soldiers began looting the houses of the Nazi party members. Not knowing which houses belonged to Nazi generals and officers, they began looting the homes of the foreign diplomats as well, arresting most of them and taking them to Moscow. Of these people were Allah Nawaz Khan, the Afghan Ambassador, my father (though he no longer held an official post), my brothers, Ahmad and Zaid, who were much younger at the time, and my stepmother, Huriya *Khanum*.

The Soviet soldiers put my father in one of the Moscow prisons and put Huriya *Khanum* and her two children in a hotel under their custody. Those diplomats, such as Allah Nawaz Khan, who were identified through their embassies, were released soon after, but my father, whose diplomatic passport had already been confiscated by the Afghan government, could not prove his Afghan identity and thus remained in prison. By the time the higher Soviet authorities found out about my father's arrest and imprisonment in Moscow, two-and-half-years had already passed. At the time, the Allied Forces were in negotiations with the Soviet Union about the division of Germany and its capital, Berlin. Hence, there was no time to investigate the cases of individuals languishing in prisons.

However, having finally learned that my father was a well-known Afghan political figure, the high-ranking Soviet authorities apologized for the irresponsible treatment by their soldiers and released his family. They provided him with a car and sent him back to Berlin to be with his family, accompanied by two officers who would help to retrieve his belongings, which had been plundered by the Soviet soldiers. In the end, the only thing he could get back was his house and some old, useless appliances the looting Russian soldiers had tossed into the backyard. Among the appliances, there were some letters tucked in a small leather suitcase left out and exposed to the elements for the two-and-a-half years of my father's imprisonment. Because of this, many important letters, including the correspondence between him and Nadir during the Civil War, were damaged by rain, making major portions of them unreadable.

I got to know my father with such depth on these daily walks around Thielpark. As we strolled and talked, I'd pinch myself to see if I was really awake. After our walk, we'd return home for lunch, joined by my brothers and my cousin, Hassan. My brothers would bring my uncle, Abdul Aziz Khan, from his home to join us, and I'd often be swept by a sense of unbelievable gratitude. *I'm with my father and my uncle! How lucky I am!*

We ate rice with potatoes, cooked spinach, beef, chicken, eggplant, and salad. Afterwards, one of my brothers would take my uncle back to his home, while the other left for college. My father went to take a nap. I passed the time reading German newspapers on the couch. My stepmother usually remained busy, cooking or cleaning in the kitchen, or making arrangements around the house.

I often took this alone time to write letters to my family in Kabul. I'd write to my wife about all the joys in Berlin, stories with my father and uncle, and I'd ask about her, the kids, and if she needed me to send her any money. My wife would write back, telling me the news in Kabul and about how the kids were doing, often reassuring me that she was good with money at the time. Before leaving for Germany, I had sold our 1955 Chevrolet Bel Air. It was in excellent condition and I had made a great profit with it. I split the money from it with my wife so she could take care of the family during my absence.

When my father would awake from his nap, we'd talk in the living room until just before dinnertime. By then, my brothers would return, and my cousin Hassan would join us as we all shared a light meal together.

After dinner, we'd watch television together, often world news or funny shows. There was one show we watched and one scene in particular that I knew I would never forget. A man took his father, who was recently having difficulties with his vision, to an optometrist. His father's vision issues made it challenging for him to shoot his rifle accurately, which really bothered him. The optometrist asked the man if he could read the letters on the wall. The man said, "No." The optometrist made the letters bigger. Still no. He made them even bigger. Still no. He made them so big that someone would have to be blind not to see, and still no. "Sorry, there's nothing I can do for your father. He's clearly blind," the optometrist said to the son.

The son grabbed the optometrist by the collar and said, "I brought my father here so he can see better, not read. He's not blind. He's illiterate!" My brothers and I laughed uncontrollably.

On Sundays, all my father's friends and relatives in Berlin would come to his house. My cousin, Usman, would come with his family and kids as well. For me, these gatherings were cheerful and high-spirited events. Because of these gatherings, I became acquainted with many highly cultured Afghan personalities residing in Germany. My father enjoyed a high popularity among all the Afghans living in Germany. He was also known by notable German personalities as a highly patriotic Afghan politician.

As the weeks followed, I wanted to make more use of my time in Berlin, so I began attending the Berlitz language school and took English and French classes. During my French classes, I thought of Habiba and our morning lessons at Sarai Ali Khan. I had truly come a long way since those desolate days of prison.

I also began taking dance lessons at a dance studio. I learned the cha cha, the waltz, the tango, the rumba, and more. I listened to music by The Beatles, and my brothers and cousins, Hassan and Usman, took me out on the weekends to dance clubs and bars (although we didn't drink alcohol).

One weekend, I was invited, along with my father and brothers, to Mr. Mayer's birthday party. Mr. Mayer was the patent holder of the cigarette lighter. He was a very wealthy and successful inventor and businessman. For his 60th birthday, he had a three-night birthday party. The first night was for his high-ranking political friends. The second night was for his diplomatic and personal friends. The third night was for the young men. We were there for the third night.

When we arrived in the backyard of Mr. Mayor's estate, we found a large "60" written in lights and nearly 70 people mingling together. My father went around, introducing me to everyone, saying, "This is my son. He speaks German very well."

Throughout the night, people took turns on stage delivering happy birthday speeches to Mr. Mayer. I noticed Arabic messages written on the blue-white plates. I read one to my father, and he, in his excitement, said to me, "Can you go on stage and read that to everyone, out of respect for Mr. Mayer's birthday?"

"Of course, father," I said with a stroke of pride.

After a few more people spoke, I got up on stage and said my happy birthday wishes to Mr. Mayer, stating I had something I wanted to read for everyone. I read the Arabic message for the crowd and then reread it, translating it into German. There was applause from the crowd and I was met with smiles as I walked off the stage.

My father sat proudly with a big smile on his face. His eyes were shining with pride. "*Afarin*[99], Khaled *jan!*" he told me.

A swell of emotion flooded my chest. For a moment, I remembered all those days in Dehmazang, learning Arabic from Sheikh Bahlool and German from Dastgir. I remembered the thoughts I'd had, how I had encouraged myself to make the most of my horrid situation and learn what I could to become a more knowledgeable person. I remembered how much I had been motivated by the dream of making my father proud by speaking with him in German and Arabic. And now, here I was, living it. What was once an improbable dream was now a heavenly reality.

Myself (center), Dr. Usman (far right) and his wife (second from the right), and Huriya Khanum (far left) at Mr. Mayer's birthday party.

---

[99] Bravo.

THIRTY-SIX

Experiencing life in Germany made me reflect on life back in Afghanistan. In Germany, I learned what it meant to live in a country with a democratic government. I witnessed freedoms foreign to what I had experienced in Afghanistan. Here, the citizens cared about their country, and the country truly cared for its citizens. There was a general feeling of mutual trust in Germany. All of this was a stark contrast to the despotic and autocratic government run by the ruling family of Afghanistan, who oppressed people, committed social injustices, and encouraged widespread racial and class discrimination.

I realized that the tragedy of a nation begins when it is ruled by a tyrant who controls or tries to control all aspects of people's lives, putting him in the position of determining the destiny of individuals as to who should live or die, who should be imprisoned or free, who should be subjected to torture and who should be given luxuries. When a government does not build ties with its people and respect the national interests of the country, it is certain the dream of progress and development will remain a dream.

Sadly, my precious time in Germany was coming to an end. Although it was a dream come true to be with my father, I had to return home to be with my family. During the final two weeks of my stay, I took a trip to Hamburg to visit a friend and do some gift shopping for my family. During my time in Berlin, I had received letters from my family, one from my youngest son, Siddiq. He wrote that he was thankful to God for my health and that I could see my father in Germany. Then, he asked me to bring some gifts for him, particularly a toy boat.

My friend in Hamburg, who I nicknamed *Malim*[100], was a teacher from Kandahar. He too was planning on returning to Afghanistan; however, he was going by car. The idea intrigued me, so I purchased a dark blue Volkswagen Bug, and we decided, after my visit to Hamburg, we would caravan together across the continents. When my brother Ahmad heard of the trip, he came to me and asked, "Khaled *jan*, would you be willing to take my friend Guenther with you to Afghanistan?" Guenther was a classmate and good friend of Ahmad's. "Yes, of course," I replied.

Before I left for Hamburg, my father told me he was going to a spa and wellness retreat for a few weeks. On our last day together, we went on a final walk around Thielpark. As we walked, I became acutely aware of the temporal nature of life. Acknowledging that my time in Germany with my father was coming to an end, at least for now, made me emotional inside. We walked back home where I had one final lunch with my father, brothers, stepmother, and cousin Hassan. Afterwards, I spent some time with my father, alone. We didn't say too much; it was more the bond of being with each other. Eventually, Guenther arrived, and it was time to leave.

"Goodbye my father," I said.

"Goodbye my son," he replied. "Take care of yourself. It's a long drive to Afghanistan. Are you sure you're ok to drive the whole way?"

"Yes, I'm fine, father," I said.

I gave him one big hug before walking towards the car. *Wow*, I thought. *Thank God for this wonderful time I've had with him.*

Guenther and I entered my Volkswagen, and we drove off towards Hamburg. Over the next two weeks, I spent most of my time shopping for my family. I bought a large blue and white model boat for my son, Siddiq, and clothing and chocolates for the whole family.

When it came time to leave Hamburg, *Malim* said he'd direct the way by driving in front of us, but that he needed to make a stop in Berlin. I was overjoyed by the notion. I asked *Malim* and Guenther if it was ok that I say one final goodbye to my father. The two were fine with it. *Malim* followed

[100] Teacher.

Guenther and me to the spa hotel where my father was staying. There, I saw him in the living room area. He was wearing the same suit he'd worn most days I'd been with him. He was surprised to see me. "Khaled *jan*! I thought you had left already!"

"We're on our way to Afghanistan right now. I just wanted to come and say goodbye one last time before I left," I said.

"I'm glad you came, son," he said.

We chatted together for a few minutes. I asked him how his time at the spa was. "It's great," he said. "Oh. If you'd like to, you should meet with Ubaidullah, the brother of Amanullah. He's living in Istanbul, so it will be on your way."

He told me he'd contact Ubaidullah on my behalf, and for me to call him tomorrow at 4 p.m., so he could give me his number. I agreed, and we said our goodbyes.

"Thank you, father. See you soon," I said.

That night, Guenther, *Malim* and I drove to Austria, just past the border, and stayed in a hotel. The next morning, we walked outside to find my Volkswagen missing.

"I think it's stolen, Khaled," said *Malim*. Guenther was distressed when he heard this.

"Maybe it was just towed," I said.

"No, you see, there are other cars parked here. You didn't park illegally," said *Malim*.

I called the police, and they made a report. "I'm sorry, but it's probably stolen, sir," the police officer confirmed. Fortunately, I had bought car insurance with the car. I called up the insurance company and reported the issue. Then I called the tow companies, but none of them reported having my car. Guenther and I lost some belongings, but fortunately, we had the majority of our things with us in the room. We talked it over and decided it was best to carry on with the trip. So we crammed all of our stuff into *Malim's* silver Ford Taurus and drove together en route to Afghanistan.

Later that afternoon, I called my father and obtained the contact information for Ubaidullah, King Amanullah's brother. Guenther heard about my plans and admitted he was eager to explore Istanbul. So Guenther and I talked that night about staying in Istanbul for some time instead of driving straight to Afghanistan with *Malim*. The following morning, I called Ubaidullah to confirm our plans.

"Salaam *Kaka*[101] *jan*, I'm Khaled, the son of Ghulam Siddiq," I said.

"Oh, Khaled *jan*! Yes, I know you! Your father has spoken many great things about you! Please come and stay with us. There are many great things to see here in Istanbul," he said. He shared his address with me, and I told him I was bringing a friend and that we'd be there in two days.

Malim split ways with us after dropping us off at Ubaidullah's home in Istanbul. "Good luck with the journey," I told him.

"*Tashakur*[102], Khaled *jan*," he said.

We bade him farewell and then took our luggage with us to the door of Ubaidullah. I rang the doorbell and was met with a smile and a wide embrace. "Khaled *jan*, I'm so glad you came," said Ubaidullah.

Ubaidullah introduced Guenther and me to the rest of his family. We sat around the living room having *chai* with snacks. "Tomorrow I'll take you to a museum," said Ubaidullah. We were excited.

Over the course of the next two weeks, Ubaidullah took us to countless museums and mosques throughout Istanbul. I saw ancient Greek and Egyptian artifacts, and Ubaidullah, well versed in the history and fluent in German, informed Guenther and I about it all.

At the conclusion of our second week in Istanbul, Guenther and I decided it was best to get moving towards Afghanistan. We bought train tickets from Istanbul to Erzurum, and in Erzurum, we bought bus tickets to Tabriz, and then took another bus from there to Tehran. In Tehran, we bought flights to Kabul.

We arrived in Kabul in the late afternoon. Through every place I visited, I carried Siddiq's toy boat through customs. When Siddiq finally saw me at the Kabul airport walking out with a boat, he lost himself in excitement. He ran to me, hugged me, took the boat, and then ran away. One by one, my children, Berekshai, Homa, and Farid, and my wife Habiba embraced me. We had been apart for six months.

My brothers Dastgir and Ghaffar were also there, along with my sisters

---

[101] Uncle.

[102] Thank you.

Siddiqa and Mastoora, and my mother. Azim and my other cousins had come as well. I introduced Guenther to everyone before we all left to my home, where we enjoyed a large family dinner.

The following day, I drove to the Textile Company. The President asked me about my trip. I told him that it was amazing, like a dream come true. "I'm so happy for you, Khaled *jan*," he told me with a warm smile.

"Is my position still available?" I asked.

"Yes, of course. You can go start tomorrow," he said.

"Thank you, sir," I said.

My family and friends very warmly welcomed Guenther. When I was working, Guenther would show magic tricks to my children. Siddiq was most fascinated by one particular trick of his, where he'd light a piece of paper on fire, crumple it in his hands, and then pull out a brand new piece of paper from the same hands. After work and on the weekends, I'd take Guenther out to gatherings, events, and historic places in Kabul. He stayed with us for a month before he returned to Berlin.

A few months later, after I had settled back into my normal life, I received a letter from Zaid. He told me the sad news: my uncle Abdul Aziz had died from a stroke. His death was hard for us all, especially since most of us weren't fortunate like Dastgir and me to spend time with him in Germany. Most of the family hadn't seen Abdul Aziz since before we were imprisoned, but it was still hard to accept that we'd never see him again. We heard he was buried in a Muslim-Turkish cemetery in Berlin.

The first few weeks were challenging, but we adjusted, just like we always did after a family tragedy. Then, one afternoon, a few months later, I received the worst news of my life: my father died.

I almost fell to my knees when I read the words in Zaid's letter, "Unfortunately, our dear father died today," Ahmad and Zaid wrote in the telegram.

Father…no…it's too soon, I thought, leaning against a wall to hold myself up. We had only just spent time together, and he was gone. His passing was too painful for me to comprehend.

Immediately after, I received a second telegram. My brothers were coming to

Kabul to bury Father in a cemetery according to his wishes. I was the one who had to tell my brothers, sisters, mother, and wife the news. It was an emotional night. We spent it recounting our memories with our beloved father.

It took ten days to receive approval from the officials for Ahmad and Zaid to bring my father's body to Kabul. Even with my father's death, the ruling family still held strict regulations towards us Charkhis. Fortunately, something must've softened their hearts, and they allowed my brothers to come. We held a funeral ceremony the day they arrived. Hundreds of people showed up—family, friends, political officials, and more—all expressing their condolences to my family and paying respect to my father, recounting all he'd done for them and Afghanistan.

My father's passing was extremely difficult for me. Every night I'd dream about him and wake up in tears, gasping for air, grasping for his fading image. My heart remained heavy with grief. Most often, I dreamt about our walks around Thielpark. I remembered the conversations we had, about his life and his prior work with King Amanullah. I remembered looking at him, and looking at the surroundings of Thielpark, thinking it was all a dream, something like heaven. My night terrors would continue, night after night.

My cousin, Hassan Khan, the son of Ghulam Nabi Khan, 1939.

My cousin, Dr. Usman, the son of Ghulam Jailani Khan, 1950.

My brother, Ahmad Siddiq, 1958.

My brother, Zaid Siddiq, 1963.

Myself in Hamburg, 1962.

From left to right: Ahmad (my brother), Abdul Aziz Khan (my uncle), myself, and Parwin (my niece) at my father's home in Berlin, 1962.

From left to right: Zaid (my brother), myself, and
Ahmad (my brother) in Berlin, 1962.

My cousin, Dr. Usman, and me in Berlin, 1962.

My dad and me at his house in Berlin, 1962.

PART IV

The city's abandoned, and the sky is dark.
There is no captain to guide the ship home.
What happened to the chivalry of warriors?
Desire became blood and a sigh in the throat.
A new spring was expected, but autumn came instead.
This lawn has become a tulip meadow—the blood,
A floral shroud.
O wise ones, help us console.
O lovers and mystics, bring us manly movement.

From: **"Abandoned City"** – Khaled Siddiq

THIRTY-SEVEN

The summer of 1962 burned hot. Political changes came as conflict grew between members of the ruling family. Prime Minister Daoud Khan and his brother, *Sardar* Mohammed Naim Khan, the then Foreign Minister, were forced to resign from their posts as Zahir Shah tightened his grip on power and exercised his influence in the formation of the government. As such, he changed Afghanistan's Prime Minister three times in the next ten years, selecting ministers for the first time outside the family. He also played a considerable role in the selection of the Parliament and Senate, as well as the appointment of other key government officials.

The conflict between the two brothers and Zahir Shah reached its peak in 1964, after the codification and enactment of the Afghan Constitution that year. Article 24 of the new constitution stated that Zahir Shah's uncles and cousins could not be heir to the throne. A tense atmosphere filled the household of the royal family as Daoud held secret meetings with his supporters, preparing himself for a coup against his cousin, Zahir Shah.

However, with instructions from Zahir Shah, the government went to great lengths to reduce the influence of Daoud Khan in any sphere of government affairs. The current Prime Minister dismissed or demoted most of the pro-Daoud government officials in an attempt to isolate Daoud and other political dissidents from the mainstream politics of Afghanistan.

One of the officials targeted by the new government was Dr. Hassan Sharq, who had served as the special secretary of Daoud during his time as Prime Minister. Though he was dismissed from his post, Dr. Sharq continued earning his livelihood, working with the health insurance department of the Textile Company and Power Corporation on the basis of his previous contract. A few days after his resignation from the Special Secretariat, the government sent a letter to the Textile Company, demanding the immediate dismissal of Dr. Sharq from his position. When I read the letter, I thought what a callous gesture it would be if the company actually implemented the order. I, therefore, thought of ways to approach high-ranking members of the Textile Company to discuss the issue.

One of the directors of the company, who I knew had good ties with Dr. Sharq, was Salih Mohammed Hanifi. I took the letter to Mr. Hanifi, asking him if we could have a few minutes of privacy. When he read the letter, Mr. Hanifi became lost in thought for a moment and then said, "The Textile Company is a national and independent organization which has its own charter, code of regulations, and by-laws. No one has the right to interfere with the internal affairs of the company."

He asked me my opinion, and I told him I agreed. "We cannot fire him without any justifiable reason. That would compromise our company ethics. I think we can announce our disagreement with the letter on these grounds and therefore avoid implementing the order."

Mr. Hanifi instructed me to draft a reply, mentioning all the reasons the company could not fire Dr. Sharq. I returned to my office immediately and began to write an answer to the government. Then, after having the letter signed by Mr. Hanifi, I sent it back to the government.

Some time passed, and we received no response. We were almost sure the authorities were convinced by our reasons and had given up the issue. Alas, the silence did not last. Soon enough, the correspondence between the government and the Textile Company began anew. Every couple of months, the government would send a letter to the company, demanding the dismissal of Dr. Sharq, and it was always me who drafted the reply, trying to carve out excuses, mentioning that the company rules and regulations would not allow us to carry out the order.

This was the state of things when the Textile Company decided to shift its head office from Kabul to Gulbahar. As a consequence, a large amount of staff working in the head office moved to Gulbahar. Since my children had already been admitted to schools in Kabul, I was among those who chose not to continue their services with the Textile Company.

Instead, I began my own business, and as a consequence, I never learned what happened to Dr. Sharq nor did I discover where the correspondence had led to between the company and the government.

THIRTY-EIGHT

My father and uncle were not the only ones left in exile during our years in captivity. My cousins, Hassan and Usman, had left to study in France and Germany before our family had been engulfed by the gruesome events of 1932, and over the last year, the two of them had made frequent requests to the Afghan Embassy in Berlin for a visa. After a year of correspondence with the Kabul government, the Afghan Embassy finally issued their permission letter. Finally, they were allowed to visit a homeland they had not seen for more than three decades.

The day they arrived in Kabul, there were cries of exultation and joy as our family and all our friends journeyed from Charkh to see their missing relatives. There were hours of hugs and kisses exchanged between the newly arrived guests and the seemingly endless procession of arriving visitors.

One day during their first week back, Shirjan Ulumi, the son of the late Deputy Governor Abdul Karim Khan, came to our house to visit. Mr. Ulumi had once served as Deputy Chief of Royal Guest Relations, and he came to pay his respects because of an old acquaintanceship between his father and our elder family members. "You are most welcome to Afghanistan," he said to my cousins. "I have a suggestion for you. Now that both Hassan *jan* and Usman *jan* are here, I think you should pay a visit to His Majesty. If it is alright with you, I will get you an appointment and confirm the date with you over the phone." Mr. Ulumi added that such a visit could be very beneficial for our future.

My cousins thanked him for his good intent and sincere advice, assuring him they would be honored to meet His Majesty Zahir Shah.

Mr. Ulumi turned to my brothers and me. "I will inform you one day before the appointment is set. I hope all of you will be present on that day," he said

A few days later, he called us saying, "Come tomorrow at 11 a.m. When you reach the palace gate, introduce yourselves to the guards and say that you would like to meet with the Deputy Chief of Royal Guest Relations. They will phone me and I will instruct them to let you into Dilkusha Palace."

As we left for the Royal Palace the next morning, I wondered how Zahir Shah would treat us. After all the years we'd suffered at his hand, maybe this meeting would finally create some space for kindness on his part. Maybe we'd finally get our land and properties returned to us.

At last, we arrived at the palace, and Mr. Ulumi escorted us to the office of the Chief of Royal Guest Relations, Mr. Kohgadai.

"Your father and I used to work together during the era of Amanullah Khan," Mr. Kohgadai said, recognizing the friendship he shared with our elderly family members. "He was the Chief Secretary and I was a scribe. He was a very kind man, always respectful to his subordinates. As soon as the others leave, I will take you to His Majesty."

We waited for hours, long enough that I wished I had eaten a full breakfast. The time crawled, and I began to reflect on the reality of the man I was about to meet.

Zahir Shah had been the King when Mustafa, Rabbani, Abdul-Latif, Abdul-Khaliq, and Khuddadad were executed. He was the ruling sovereign during my fifteen years of prison—through Sarai Badam, Sarai Ali Khan, and Dehmazang. This was the King who kept me from seeing my father for so many years and threatened my father with death if he entered Afghanistan. This King and his family have caused nothing but suffering for my family. My appetite vanished. I took a deep breath to clear my mind. Dastgir put his hand on my shoulder and gave me a look of reassurance.

The clock struck three, and an office clerk came down the hall and informed Mr. Kohgadai that His Majesty had just finished his meeting. I dried my sweaty palms on my pants. Mr. Kohgadai stood up and led us into the office of the King.

We entered a spacious, luxurious room with a desk in the middle surrounded by five chairs and one chair occupied by His Majesty, Zahir Shah. As we approached the chairs, Mr. Kohgadai left the room, walking backwards with his face to His Majesty and his hands held to his chest in a gesture of homage.

Standing halfway up, Zahir Shah shook hands with us, holding his hand out for us to kiss it. It was traditional in Afghanistan to kiss the hands of men of high power. The idea of showing this man such reverence repulsed us, but we didn't want to make any trouble, so we complied appropriately. One by one, we all kissed the King's hand. When it was my turn, I kissed it lightly and quickly, just to get it over with.

Zahir Shah seated himself, gesturing for us to be seated as well. He immediately began talking with pride about the improvements his government had brought to Afghanistan despite its extremely low budget. He boasted about completed projects and the upcoming projects for over an hour, while we listened passively, wondering when he'd speak about restoring our properties. Looking at my cousins, he said, "Go and have a look at our military cantonment in Pul-i-Charkhi and Rishkhoor. You will come to know the volume of developments occurring in Afghanistan."

Zahir Shah wrapped up his self-aggrandizing diatribe with a familiar cliché, "Afghanistan is yours, and you are Afghanistan's," he said. Then, he added, "Though there have been some disagreeable incidents in the past, I have forgotten them. You should also try to forget them." With that, he grew coldly silent, indicating the meeting was over.

We stood up and out of traditional courtesy, thanked him for the honor of having the chance to meet him.

Unfortunately, Zahir Shah did not grant us our properties back. The way he looked at us and spoke to us was as if we were foreigners, as if he didn't even know who we were. But of course, he knew. He knew that we'd all languished in different prisons for years, deprived of our basic human rights.

The least he could have done was make a small gesture of kindness and sympathy by returning our estates. But he did nothing. He lacked the moral courage to do so. His grudge against us was so deep he couldn't even acknowledge us as human beings. This was a great disappointment, but then again, when had the ruling regime not disappointed us? We left the palace bitterly reminded that, no matter how much time had passed, the royal family had not changed their stance towards our family.

A few days later, we were sitting down for lunch when my cousin Hassan suggested we meet with former Prime Minister Daoud. "My friendship with Daoud Khan was great back in France," he said. "Even when he was in office, he visited Hamburg once and met with me, speaking at length about our good old days in France. I'm sure there can be some benefit to us all in meeting with him. Khaled *jan*, let's both go together," he suggested.

So the next day at 11 a.m., Hassan and I went to *Sardar* Daoud's house to request a meeting. At the gate, I gave my visiting card to *Sardar* Daoud's special attendant. It read:

> My cousin, Hassan, the son of Ghulam Nabi Khan Charkhi, has come from Europe wishing to meet Your Highness.

The attendant told us to wait, and then bearing the card, he made his way across the courtyard and into the house. He came out a minute later. "I presented your card to His Highness," he said. "He said he was extremely happy to meet with you, but he has a meeting with the U.S. ambassador today. He asked if you could come back tomorrow at this time."

When we came back the following day, Daoud Khan was waiting on his terrace to welcome Hassan. He greeted my cousin very warmly, giving him a big hug, and shook hands with me before we entered his living room. When we took our seats, Daoud turned to Hassan. "Ok, tell me if you are married or not," he said. "And if yes, how many children have you got?"

"Not married and no children," said Hassan.

Daoud smiled, "You are still the most intelligent person among us." By "us," he meant their mutual school friends back in France. His Highness and my cousin exchanged more friendly small talk before Daoud turned the conversation to me.

"Are you still working with the Textile Company?"

I was shocked. It didn't occur to me that Daoud Khan knew anything about my career or me.

"No sir, I am running a personal business now."

"Why?" he said slightly taken aback. "The Textile Company has very good prospects for the future."

"Well, you are right, sir, but the headquarters moved to Gulbahar, and my children are studying here in Kabul. I thought any change in their schooling might disturb their learning progress."

Daoud was not satisfied with my answer. He persisted in talking with Hassan *jan* about the Gulbahar factory, its development, and the existence of a good school in the area. At this point, my cousin shifted the conversation to the remarkable developments in Afghanistan during Daoud's time in office, mentioning, in particular, the paving of the city streets, an obvious sign of progress.

Daoud lit a cigarette and responded, "Hassan *Agha*[103], it's not the job of a single person to make a country. It requires the concerted efforts of a whole nation—a nation like Israel. We have many slots in Afghanistan and to fill them, we need to make tireless efforts," he said.

Daoud then went on to talk about a series of development programs. However, my cousin was now anxious to end the meeting and asked His Highness for permission to leave. Daoud accompanied us to the terrace of his house and shared a firm goodbye handshake with my cousin. He didn't shake my hand. His disdain for me was clear.

Surprisingly, although Hassan was my cousin and the son of Ghulam Nabi Khan, Daoud saw him differently. Hassan was even in exile, like my father and the rest of my family in Berlin. Had he come to Afghanistan anytime during our imprisonment, he would've surely been imprisoned or executed. But Daoud didn't give the slightest acknowledgment of any of his family's inhumane acts towards us. It was as if Hassan just was an old friend, completely unrelated to any of this.

After a few months, my cousins had to return to Germany. We hosted an emotional farewell party the day before their departure. People came in droves to eat, sing, dance, and pay their respects.

---

[103] Sir or mister; term of respect towards a man.

A week later, I received a message from the new Prime Minister, Nur Ahmad Khan Etimadi. Mr. Etimadi was married to a niece of my aunt Shah Bi Bi, the wife of Ghulam Jailani Khan. As such, he respected my aunt greatly and would always visit her. During one of his visits, Mr. Etimadi asked my aunt if my brother Zaid and I could pay him a visit at his house one morning during the week.

Zaid and I went to His Excellency's house the next day at seven a.m. and shared breakfast and *chai* with him. Mr. Etimadi spoke of his love and respect for our family, adding that he had always wanted to do us a favor if possible. "Now, I think it is the right time to fulfill this wish. You should prepare a list of any of your properties still held by the government and write a petition to His Majesty. Bring me both documents, but please overlook those estates the government has donated to other people and entities, for it will be nearly impossible to have them reinstated. I strongly hope we will be able to restore some of your estates, *inshallah*," he said.

We were overjoyed at his offer and moved quickly to attain what records we could. From official government records, we learned those of our properties still held by the government consisted of a few residential houses, belonging to my father and uncles, as well as a few acres of agricultural land. The rest of the properties in the south, which belonged to my grandfather, had been given to locals and honorary generals as gifts, including one of Zahir Shah's uncles, Shah-Wali.

Nevertheless, we prepared the list of our remaining properties and presented it to the Prime Minister. He told me to call him in a week for a progress update. The week ended with an update that was all too familiar, given our history: the ruling family still bore resentment towards us. The gesture of goodwill on the part of the Prime Minister had been completely ignored by the King.

THIRTY-NINE

My daughter Bereshkai was now starting high school, but during her first week, I was notified she'd been sent to the principal's office. When I returned home that afternoon, I asked her why.

"I was filling out the school form, and I put our family name. They said I couldn't use or even speak of the word Charkhi," she explained. "Why, Father?" She was distraught by the situation.

"Bereskhai *jan*, it's not safe to use our family name. Just say your last name is Siddiq," I said.

"But why, Father? Why can't we use our last name? It's our last name! Everyone else can use their family name, why not us?" she persisted.

"Because we can't, Bershkai *jan*."

It broke my heart to have to tell my daughter to weather this indignity, but the ruling family was still obviously sensitive about our family name, and we had to adjust.

As the years wore on, we still heard nothing about our land. My businesses expanded as I imported medicine, cars, and other goods from Germany. Aside from the unfulfilled promises from the ruling family, life was progressing just fine, until another tragedy struck. This time it was my dear mother.

My mother had been sick for some time, transitioning between living at home and staying in the hospital. During her last stay in the hospital, her doctor told me that while she didn't have any particular illness, her organs were no longer functioning properly. Her kidneys and liver had all but shut down, and her lungs were weak, filling up with fluid. Her heart wasn't operating at full capacity either. The doctor told me three days before I brought her home that she didn't have much time and that it was better we spent time with her during her last days. So on a weekend afternoon, we all gathered together at the house to share a meal and spend time together. I read verses from the Qur'an at my mother's bedside along with my brother Ghaffar. She died peacefully with her children beside her.

I prayed my mother's death would be the last one our family would experience for a long time. My siblings and I had all suffered greatly and seen so much loss as young children. Now, my children were experiencing that loss as well.

My mom, 1954.

At the time of her passing, I was still having night terrors, and with her loss, these nightmares only intensified. My mother's death cracked my heart wide open as I relived all the pain I'd felt before—my father's death, the deaths of my uncles, cousins, and my brother Samad, and the executions of my other extended family members. All of it broke loose, and I prayed we all could just have some peace.

Our resilience was strong. After a funeral ceremony, we had weeks and months of continued grief. Still, we did our best to continue growing in our lives and raising our families, and we persisted in meeting with officials about the restoration of our land.

Nothing new changed with the ruling regime until 1973. One day while Zahir Shah was in Europe, Daoud Khan put an underground movement into action and overthrew Zahir Shah's monarchy. It was a bloodless coup backed by the People's Democratic Party of Afghanistan (PDPA), a Marxist-Leninist group. Afghanistan quietly accepted the coup, mainly because many people perceived it as a pre-arranged transfer of power with Zahir Shah's agreement. Since Daoud was a well-known senior member of the royal family, the change was quite natural for many people. The Afghan people were also tired of Zahir Shah's forty-year-old monarchy and took it as a good omen when Daoud Khan addressed Afghanistan as a "republic" in his first radio address. They hoped he would live up to that word and institute a democratic government.

Unfortunately, their hopes were in vain. As time went on, it became increasingly evident that Daoud was not in tune with the principles of democracy. He did not let his people elect their President, and he created a puppet National Assembly consisting of a handful of his supporters. Terrified after forty years of tyranny, no other Afghan dared nominate himself to run against Daoud in a presidential election. As a result, the appointed representatives elected Daoud as President, giving him one hundred percent of the vote.

Aside from hope-inducing slogans carved on placards and billboards promising a new era in Afghanistan, there was not much difference between the new Republic and the previous Kingdom. Over time, all these slogans proved to be no more than deceptive propaganda used by the government to keep the people "happy."

Despite Afghanistan's political disappointments, I was enjoying life, proudly watching my kids enter adulthood. My youngest son Siddiq was now in high school, my oldest daughter Bereshkai was engaged, Farid was studying in Germany, and Homa was taking college courses in Kabul.

There was much to be cheerful about, and then, in 1975, I experienced one of the worst days of my life.

My brother Dastgir was in a large movie theatre when he fell from the top of the stairwell and landed on his head at the bottom. He was immediately sent to the Ali Abad hospital. My sister Siddiqa told me the news as soon as she heard it. I quickly rushed to the hospital and found my brother in a coma. I asked my doctor friends at the hospital if there was anything they could do. They explained that Dastgir was in a very bad state and there was nothing that could be done.

"Can you send him to Germany to receive medical treatment there?" I asked desperately.

"Sorry, Khaled *jan*. Unfortunately, there's nothing anyone can do for him." They told me what had happened with the trauma to his brain. His skull was cracked. There would be no recovery. Dastgir was dead the next morning.

When Siddiqa heard the news of his death, she collapsed of a heart attack. She was then rushed to a hospital, but unfortunately, she couldn't be revived. I was in the throes of grief from losing my brother, and now I had lost my sister. Two siblings on the same day. I thought my heart had borne enough scars, but this one was unbearable. I felt it would be impossible to move on. I thought of my brother and sister every night, just as I thought of my mother and father.

Losing my beloved siblings was difficult, but to make matters worse, my sister Mastoora was becoming more ill as well. Her kidneys weren't functioning properly, and she was spending a lot of time going between our home and Ali Abad. One day I received the devastating news that she too had passed away in her hospital bed at Ali Abad.

I had been broken down by life many times, and I had learned to be resilient, but to lose three siblings in one year was heartbreaking. Still, I lived on, honoring them and all those who had passed before me. I'd think, *they'd want me to make the most of my life, not squander it in misery. We've all suffered enough in our life. Joy is our medicine.*

I thought about Mastoora, Siddiqa, and Dastgir every day. I thought of all the time we had shared together in prison as children and the decades since our release. I remembered the notes Siddiqa had sewn into our laundry, and the encouragement Dastgir had given me upon my arrival in Dehmazang. My children dearly missed their aunts and uncle as well and grieved them long after they were gone.

FORTY

On March 3rd, 1976, I was invited to a party arranged by the German Embassy of Afghanistan and hosted at the Consulate building. It was an evening gathering, and there were high-ranking Afghan authorities, some political representatives of other embassies in Kabul and some friends and acquaintances. The party was to mark the fiftieth anniversary of the Afghan-German friendship treaty of 1926—the treaty signed by Mr. Streseman, the German Minister of State and my father, Ghulam Siddiq Khan Charkhi, when he was the Afghan Ambassador to Berlin.

The treaty contained various aid packages to be delivered to Afghanistan by the German government over the span of fifty years. His Majesty King Amanullah Khan had approved the treaty in Paghman, a district in western Kabul. At the party that night, a three-page journal in English and German was distributed to the participants by the embassy staff. The journal explained the contents and purpose of the treaty and who had signed it. I still keep a copy of that journal with me today.

DEUTSCHES NACHRICHTENBLATT

Herausgegeben von der Botschaft
der Bundesrepublik Deutschland

Kabul

Nr. 60   Kabul, den 3. März 1976

Telegrammwechsel der Staatsoberhäupter anläßlich des
50. Jahrestages der Unterzeichnung des deutsch-afghanischen
Freundschaftsvertrags vom 3. 3. 1926

Der Präsident der Republik Afghanistan richtete an den
Präsidenten der Bundesrepublik Deutschland heute folgendes
Telegramm:

Exzellenz!
Unsere beiden Völker feiern heute den 50. Jahrestag des
afghanisch-deutschen Freundschaftsvertrages. Wir sehen
mit Freude und Genugtuung, daß dieser Vertrag auf der
festen Basis der Beziehungen und erfolgreichen Zusammenarbeit beruht und nicht nur allen Belastungen in den vergangenen
Jahren erfolgreich standgehalten hat, sondern zu einer
stetigen Ausbreitung und Vertiefung der Freundschaft und
Zusammenarbeit zwischen Afghanistan und der Bundesrepublik
Deutschland zum Wohle unserer beiden Völker geführt hat.

Ich bin sicher, daß die Freundschaft und die dauerhafte und
fruchtbringende Zusammenarbeit zwischen Afghanistan und der
Bundesrepublik Deutschland auch in Zukunft auf der Basis des
fest gegründeten Freundschaftsvertrags von 1926 sich weiter
erweitern und vertiefen wird.

Aus diesem Anlaß wünsche ich Eurer Exzellenz und dem
deutschen Volke Wohlergehen.

Gleichzeitig erhielt der Präsident der Republik
Afghanistan die folgende deutsche Gegenadresse:

Exzellenz!

Mit Freude und Genugtuung gedenkt das deutsche Volk
des Tages, an dem vor 5o Jahren der deutsch-afghanische
Freundschaftsvertrag unterzeichnet wurde. Dieser Vertrag
begründete eine vertrauensvolle Zusammenarbeit zwischen
unseren Ländern zum Wohle unserer beiden Völker. Die
Erwartungen, die die Regierungen mit der Unterzeichnung
an den Vertrag geknüpft hatten, sind in Erfüllung gegangen.
Unsere Freundschaft hat sich in den vergangenen 5o Jahren als
dauerhaft erwiesen, und ich bin zuversichtlich, daß die
Zukunft eine weitere engere Ausgestaltung der deutsch-
afghanischen Beziehungen bringen wird.

Erlauben Sie mir, Exzellenz, Ihnen bei dieser Gelegenheit
die besten Wünsche für Ihr persönliches Wohlergehen und
für eine friedliche und glückliche Zukunft des befreun-
deten afghanischen Volkes auszusprechen.

Zum 50. Jahrestag des deutsch-afghanischen Freundschaftsvertrages vom 3. 3. 1926

Am 3. März jährt sich zum 50. Mal der Tag, an dem in Berlin
der deutsch-afghanische Freundschaftsvertrag von dem afghanischen Gesandten Gholam Siddiq Khan und Reichsminister Dr.
Gustav Stresemann unterzeichnet wurde. Die Ratifikations-
urkunden wurden am 14. 9. 1926 in Paghman bei Kabul ausge-
tauscht. Dieser Vertrag war der Ausdruck freundschaftlicher
Beziehungen, die offiziell zwischen den beiden Ländern bereits
1915/16 aufgenommen worden waren. Sie führten im Laufe der
folgenden Jahre zu einer stetigen Vertiefung der gemeinsamen
Bemühungen um den Fortschritt und die technische Entwicklung
Afghanistans. In diese Jahre fällt auch die Aufnahme der
diplomatischen Beziehungen. 1921 wurde eine afghanische Ge-
sandschaft in Berlin und 1923 eine deutsche in Kabul eröffnet.
Besonderen Ausdruck fand die Gemeinsamkeit zwischen den beiden
Völkern in der Begründung der Amani-Oberrealschule im Jahr 1924.

In der Folgezeit trug eine Reihe von Abkommen wirtschaftlicher
und kultureller Art zu weiterer Festigung der deutsch-afghanischen
Freundschaft bei. 1936 wurde die erste gemeinsame Gewerbeschule in
Kabul eröffnet.

On the Occasion of the 50th Anniversary of the
German - Afghan Treaty of Friendship

March 3rd will be the 50th anniversary of the day on which the
Afghan-German treaty of friedship was signed in Berlin by the
Afghan Ambassador Gholam Siddiq Khan and Reichsminister Dr.
Gustav Stresemann. The instruments of ratification were
exchanged in Paghman on September 14th, 1926. This treaty
was the expression of the friendly relations which officially
had been initiated already in 1915/16 between the two countries.
During the following years the joint efforts for the progress
and technical development of Afghanistan were continuously
intensified. In these years also diplomatic relations were
established. An Afghan Diplomatic Mission was set up in Berlin
in 1921 and a German Legation in Kabul in 1923. A special
evidence of the common aspirations of the two peoples has been
the foundation of the Amani Highschool in 1924.

Subsequently a series of economic and cultural agreements
contributed to further strengthening the Afghan-German
friendship. In 1936 the first joint technical school was
opened in Kabul.

On this solid basis the friendly relations between the two countries
and the cultural, technical and economic co-operation could further
be developed.

In January 31st, 1958, an agreement on economic and technical
co-operation was signed which laid the foundation for more than
50 important Afghan-German projects for the economic and technical
development of Afghanistan with a total financial volume of ca. Afs.
10 Milliards. Most of these projects have already been finalized.

-2-

to the benefit of Afghanistan. The main principles of this agreement have proved so effective, that only once, on July 21st, 1965, the agreement had to be modified to adapt it to the development and the progress of Afghanistan. Further co-operation in the economic and technical fields is envisaged.

On April 18, 1961, an Afghan-German cultural agreement has been concluded which formed the basis for further fostering the Amani Highschool, the affiliation between the Universities of Kabul on the one hand and of those of Bonn, Bochum and Cologne on the other, as well as the co-operation of the two countries in other academic fields. Towards the end of 1975 the partnership agreements between the Universities were adapted to new circumstances by initialling a new arrangement on Afghan-German academic co-operation.

During the past 50 years the Afghan-German friendship has withstood all the encumbrances of political changes, because it is not based on expediency, but on mutual respect and bonds of affection.

Surprisingly, I did not see any of the Afghan authorities at that party, except for Syed-Wahidullah, the Deputy Minister of Foreign Affairs, who arrived later that night. He stood on the terrace of the embassy building for a few minutes, doing the formal greeting with the ambassador, consul, and other embassy staff members and then left shortly after. Observing this scene,

I understood that Daoud's government was no longer willing to maintain its friendly relations with the west. And it was obvious why: They didn't want to inconvenience the USSR.

At the time, one of my relatives was serving as a high government official and was also supposed to take part in that party. The following night, when I saw him in a private family gathering, I asked him why he had missed the event.

"No reason in particular," he replied. Then, in confidence, he said, "To be honest Khaled *jan*, I had fully prepared to take part in the party until I learned later that I was not allowed to participate in any party held by a western embassy."

Interestingly, this ceremony, arranged by the German Embassy, coincided with the replacement of the former consul, Mr. Kanzy, by the new consul, Mr. Jeske (pronounced Yeske). At the party, Mr. Kanzy introduced me to Mr. Jeske, saying, "The Afghan Ambassador who signed this treaty fifty years ago is this gentleman's father."

Mr. Jeske greeted me enthusiastically and said, "I have a group photo from when this treaty was approved by King Amanullah Khan. The photo shows Amanullah Khan sitting on his chair and a number of people standing behind him. I wish I could meet some of these men or at least one of them. I would be extremely grateful if you could arrange it."

Sadly, I had to explain to Mr. Jeske and Mr. Kanzy that none of the people in the photo, including my father and King Amanullah Khan, were still alive.

As we spoke, two other acquaintances joined our circle. One of them who did not speak German asked me to ask Mr. Jeske if the government of Germany was willing to extend the treaty with the Afghan government.

After I interpreted the question, Mr. Jeske said without hesitation, "No."

"Why?" the man asked.

At this, I asked Mr. Jeske if he could speak English so that the man could understand. Mr. Jeske replied in English by stating quite frankly, "Because Afghanistan is under the influence of a Communist government. We cannot enter into a treaty of friendship and cooperation with any Communist state."

Mr. Jeske's candid answer did not sit well with the man, and the man apologized and walked away with his companion to join another circle of guests.

What was surprising and even ironic was that even though the Afghan government did not support this event, the following day's news bulletin from Radio Afghanistan fully covered the ceremony, both in Farsi and Pashto. Full of bombast and unfamiliar vocabulary, the announcer spoke about the fifty-year-friendship treaty between Afghanistan and Germany. However, due to the government's personal grudge, the news bulletin left out who had signed the treaty and who had approved it. Even after fifty years, the ruling family could not tolerate hearing the names of my family nor King Amanullah.

Meanwhile, the Soviet Union was silently lurking in the background. Since Peter the Great, the Russians had always dreamed of gaining access to Afghanistan due to its strategic location, and during Zahir Shah's rule, the Soviet Union had laid the foundation for such a plan, particularly during Daoud's time in office. As a result, the Soviet Union had been awarded important development contracts throughout Afghanistan, such as gas extraction in Sheberghan and the construction of the Salaang Highway. These projects led to a huge number of Soviet specialists and advisers entering Afghanistan to train the pro-Soviet military and civil personnel.

The Soviet Union knew it would be a very difficult task for ordinary Afghan citizens to overthrow a firmly established monarchy, especially one that had suppressed its people for forty years. So, they were very happy that a member of the royal family had toppled the dictatorial regime, and they made the most of the opportunity. When the PDPA members obtained a good number of high-ranking posts in Daoud's cabinet, the Soviet Union felt it was a better time than any to implement their hidden agenda.

The PDPA members did their best to persuade Daoud to build good relations with the Soviets, and as a result, the Soviet Union was able to directly interfere in the internal affairs of the government. Later, Daoud came to realize his mistake as he noticed Afghanistan slipping closer to becoming a Soviet satellite.

This awakened his pride. Deciding to rid himself of the yoke of Russian colonization, Daoud dismissed a number of key PDPA members from their government positions, by deploying them abroad as ambassadors, and filled the space with some of his own trusted men. Daoud then went to Moscow to attend a meeting with the Communist Party, including the Soviet Union's General Secretary, Leonid Brezhnev. During the negotiation, Daoud had a row with Brezhnev and left the meeting in protest, making it clear that Afghanistan was not under Soviet rule. In response, the PDPA intensified its political activities against Daoud's government, looking for an opportunity to take power.

That opportunity came in April 1978, when the political activities of both of the PDPA factions (the Khalq and Parcham parties) were at their peak, triggering a massive response from the government. In the midst of this turmoil, one of the most important Parcham figures, Mir Akbar Khyber, was mysteriously assassinated while walking home near the Mikrorayan neighborhood in Kabul. Some reports said he was dragged out of his house and killed.

This incident triggered a wave of rioting among the Khalqites and Parchamites. A large number of Mir Khyber's following attended his funeral ceremony. They were mainly the youth of Kabul, high school boys and girls, holding red banners and shouting revolutionary slogans. The government security forces and Intelligence Office kept these moves under scrutiny by escorting the mourning procession from Mir Akbar's home to his gravesite, but the huge procession was unbearable for Daoud. He responded by arresting most of the PDPA leaders, including Nur Mohammed Taraki and Babrak Karmal, and putting them in separate cells.

A few days later, *Sardar* Daoud held a cabinet meeting to discuss what to do with the arrested PDPA leaders. But it was too late. Hafizullah Amin, PDPA members, and Soviets within the Afghan army and police staged a coup, and due to the inadequacy of Daoud's security forces, the coup was a success.

Defection within the military against Daoud occurred as a result of his actions. Ever since King Amanullah ruled Afghanistan, Afghan army and police officers had been sent to western countries, such as Turkey, Germany and England for training and higher education. However, in 1954, when as

Daoud claimed, the U.S. Vice President Richard Nixon stated, "The U.S. does not cover Afghanistan in its defense strategy," a disappointed Daoud opened Afghanistan's gates of friendship to Russia.

Grasping the opportunity, Russia promised full cooperation with Afghanistan in various economic and military areas. That same year, Khrushchev and Bulganin (the head and secretary of the Soviet Communist Party) came to Afghanistan and granted one hundred million dollars in aid to the country, pledging much more help in the years to come. In turn, *Sardar* Daoud not only awarded the rest of the construction projects to Russia, but he also altered the course of the training program for the Afghan army and police. Now, instead of sending Afghan officers to western countries, he sent most of them to Russia for their higher education. As a result, many of these officers were brainwashed, heavily affected by an ideology that prompted them to later follow the Soviet's interventionist instructions and policies blindly.

That is how members of the PDPA, such as Hafizullah Amin and Abdul Qadir Farahi, an officer in the Afghan Air Force, were infected with pro-Soviet ideology. Backed by the Afghan police and army forces, the PDPA finally staged their coup, and in the ensuing fray, Daoud, his brother Naim, and approximately 18 members of his family, including women and children, were killed in a barrage of bombs and artillery fire. Daoud's government collapsed at last, and the PDPA took office.

On this night, I was in Iran visiting my daughters Berekshai and Homa. Homa was living here with her husband at the time. My son, Siddiq, a young adult now, was the only one still in Kabul at the time. As soon as I heard the news of the revolution, I phoned him.

"*Baba*[104]," it's dangerous here," he told me.

"Be safe, and stay indoors," I told him. "I'm coming home."

The next day, when I had returned to Kabul, Siddiq told me a horrific story. He was about to drive with his friend, Najib, to pick up two girls for a date when the girls called and said something serious had happened at Daoud

---

[104] Father.

Khan's home. They said there were loud noises, planes flying, bombs dropping, and people shooting each other in the street.

Instead of taking this as a warning, Siddiq and Najib decided to discover what was happening and drove by Daoud's estate. They were at a traffic light, nearby Daoud's home, when they heard gunshots. They didn't know exactly where they were coming from, until Najib pointed out the troops lying beside them in the gutter. The forces were firing their rifles at a tank only 200 meters away with a large number of soldiers walking behind it.

Siddiq quickly sped through the traffic light, driving as fast as he could to Najib's home. Just as they passed a movie theater, he saw rockets flying right above him and heard a huge explosion. The theater was falling down behind them, and people were running all over, seeking cover. The few other drivers on the road sped through the intersections, swerving for cover. Fortunately, they weren't hit by the rockets or the debris.

Siddiq dropped Najib off and went home, arriving just in time to receive my phone call. I was upset with Siddiq for acting carelessly with his life, but I was grateful he wasn't harmed. Ultimately, I knew our home wasn't safe anymore. It was time for all of us to leave Afghanistan.

FORTY-ONE

Soon after the Saur[105] Revolution, scores of people who were followers of Zahir Shah and *Sardar* Daoud were arrested, and some of them were secretly executed. One of these groups who mysteriously disappeared was the Mojaddedi family. The PDPA targeted this family because Professor Sibghatullah Mojaddedi was the founder of an Islamist movement opposing the PDPA.

Later, I discovered that many of the Mojaddedis, including Shir-Padshah, the son of Saint Nur-ul-Mashayekh, and the sons of Saint Shams-ul-Mashayekh had also been executed, and the women and young girls of the family had been thrown into jail. Twenty-five of the Mojaddedi women and girls were imprisoned; 57 men and boys went missing, and another 27 men, who were friends of the family, also disappeared. Hearing about these events reminded me of my experiences with the family of Nadir Shah. It was disheartening to witness this familiar struggle for power, and to witness innocent children once again suffering unfortunate fates.

Unlike Zahir Shah's government, where many of the key posts were occupied by the Mohammed Zai tribe, the PDPA, headed by Nur Mohammed Taraki, was comprised of people from various nationalities and ethnic groups. The PDPA, which chanted glittering slogans like "food and shelter for all," made some of the Afghan people naively accept it as a populist movement promoting social justice, equality, and non-discrimination. Even some of the

---

105 Saur is the second month of the Afghan calendar.

Afghan intellectuals and writers, who were not previously associated with the PDPA, came to trust the party's ideology, considering it better than the previous government systems. They believed the movement would bring tremendous change to the life of the poverty-stricken people in the country, which was, unfortunately, the majority of the Afghan population.

At the same time, others understood that the ideology adopted by the PDPA was a foreign ideology, not feasible in Afghanistan. They knew it was not an easy task to simply import an ideology from a foreign country and put it into practice through a handful of emotional people. In their minds, true reform required a thorough knowledge of the country's citizens, their beliefs, traditions, customs, religion and lifestyle. Those who impose such an ideology should be well aware of the religious and traditional sensitivities both in the urban and rural areas of the country as they extensively study the cultural implications of change. Sadly, the PDPA lacked such essential knowledge. By staging their military coup, without considering the consequences, they created endless problems for themselves as well as their ideological sponsor, the Soviet Union.

FORTY-TWO

After the PDPA came to power, the new Ministry of Defense imposed a curfew and began conducting night searches to hunt down those closely associated or sympathized with the royal family. Every night, the Defense Ministry would carry the detained families to the Pul-i-Charkhi prison, located in an eastern suburb of Kabul. Among these families were elderly women and young children who had been arrested in the name of "national security." At night, dignitaries waited anxiously for what fate would befall them the following day. Residents of Kabul who looked suspicious or acted coldly to a government official would soon find themselves arrested and put behind bars. The city became a hotbed of terror and uncertainty.

One early morning, my brother Zaid rushed to me, looking as if he hadn't slept. "Do you know anybody in the PDPA government?" he asked frantically.

"What happened?" I asked. "What's the matter?"

"Last night, the men from the Ministry of Defense detained Mahboob *jan* and her husband, Abdullah Rafiq."

Mahboob was the daughter of Dr. Abdul Sattar Siraj, and Zaid's sister-in-law, but Dr. Abdul Sattar Siraj was not in Kabul at the time; he was in Iran. Zaid added that his wife, Alia, and her mother, Jamila Tarzai, had cried throughout the night.

When I heard the whole story from Zaid, I said, "The only person I know in the government is Babrak Karmal, whose house is situated adjacent to ours in Deh-bori area. We'd better meet him at his home before he leaves for his office. He may be of some help."

Babrak Karmal was the Deputy Prime Minister and PDPA Secretary. I knew him through Farooq *Telegrafi*, his uncle, who had been a political prisoner in Dehmazang. As a young schoolboy, Babrak used to visit his uncle Farooq in Dehmazang during *mulaqat* every week. Farooq was always proud of his nephew and loved him. He claimed Babrak was very clever and spoke well compared to others his age. Whenever the young Babrak came to visit him, Farooq would bring the boy into our cell since my brothers, Azim and I were the closest to his age, and he would stay and chat with us for a couple of hours. The young boy was indeed bright, able to answer any questions directed at him. His uncle thought the world of him. Later, when my family was set free, I used to see Mr. Karmal at wedding parties and other social gatherings, and he always treated me with respect. Other than that, there were no ideological or political commonalities between us.

During the early days of the coup, Mr. Karmal was still residing in his house in Deh-bori. He had not moved to the *Arg* or any of the state buildings yet. Zaid and I rushed to his home as quickly as possible. Outside Mr. Karmal's house, a group of people had lined up with their petitions, waiting for him to come out. We stood in line with the rest of the applicants, and I handed my visiting card to a soldier guarding the door with his Kalashnikov. He brought it inside, and Mr. Karmal came out of the house a few minutes later with my card in hand. After the traditional greetings, I introduced him to my brother.

As I began to tell him about Mahboob *jan*'s detention and imprisonment, he interrupted me. He had been under the impression that I had come to ask him about my properties which had been confiscated at the time of Nadir Shah. "Give me a few days' time," he said, "everything will be alright."

"Karmal *Sahib*!" I insisted, "It's a pressing issue."

When he heard the word "pressing," Mr. Karmal responded, "Please wait in my car. I am going to see to the applications of these people now. We can talk together on the way to *Sadarat*." He then told an officer who appeared to be his bodyguard to join us.

The officer, Zaid and I sat in the backseat of a Russian jeep, waiting for Mr. Karmal. We watched him greet everyone warmly and read their applications, issuing instructions to a clerk from *Sadarat*. It did not last too long, and in a short while, Mr. Karmal said goodbye to everyone and entered the jeep, telling the driver to drive towards *Sadarat*.

On the way, he did not let us talk about our problem. Rather, he began telling us the story of the PDPA coup. It was so long and captivating that we did not even notice the length of the drive. When we approached *Sadarat*, Mr. Karmal saw Hafizullah Amin heading into his ministerial meeting at the Ministry of Foreign Affairs. He instructed his driver, "Go and tell Mr. Amin to begin the meeting. I will come in a few minutes." After the driver left, Mr. Karmal turned to my brother and me. "Now, tell me. What is the pressing matter?"

I told him every detail, explaining how the Ministry of Defense had been arresting people arbitrarily during the night and had been putting them in the Pul-i-Charkhi prison, and that such action, taken by the government, would scare the people and render them in a state of insecurity. Zaid also explained about the arrest of his sister-in-law, Mahboob *jan*, and her family. Mr. Karmal listened, and at the end of our story, he said, "It is *Rahbar*[106] Sahib Taraki[107] who deals with the Ministry of Defense issues. I think I'd better introduce you to him."

He told his driver to head towards the palace, where *Rahbar Sahib* was residing. The car stopped before the gate of the palace, and we started to follow Mr. Karmal out of the car before he stopped us. "Wait a few minutes," he said. "I'm going to see His Excellency first, and then, I'll invite you in."

Mr. Karmal entered the palace while we sat in the car with his driver. After 15 minutes, Mr. Karmal came out, accompanied by Daoud Taroon, the Head of the Police Department. "I have explained the whole story to *Rahbar Sahib* Taraki," he said. "However, Mr. Taraki wants to meet you in person. Mr. Taroon here is going to take you to His Excellency."

Mr. Taroon led us into a spacious room we assumed to be the reception room of *Rahbar Sahib*. But apart from Mr. Taroon and us, no one else was there. A few minutes later, Mr. Taraki came down from the upper story and welcomed us warmly, giving us a tight hug.

---

[106] Leader.
[107] Taraki was often referred to as *Rahbar Sahib*.

As soon as we took our chairs, *Rahbar Sahib* Taraki began complimenting our family. "The Charkhis are the *nur*[108] of our eyes," he said. "The Afghan nation will never forget their invaluable sacrifices and service. The Charkhis rest in the hearts of the people forever."

Rahbar Sahib was still complimenting our elderly family members when a waiter came in with a tray of *chai* and *shirni*. Offering us *chai*, *Rahbar Sahib* asked, "By the way, you had another brother. His name has slipped my memory at the moment, but I remember he had a fair complexion and medium height. Where is he now and what is he doing?"

I had never seen Mr. Taraki before, but I guessed he meant Dastgir. "Do you mean Dastgir, sir?"

"Yes, exactly, Dastgir *jan*. I know him."

"Well," I said, dredging up the sad memory, "he passed away due to an accident last year."

Mr. Taraki said he was unaware of the tragic incident and expressed his condolences. Then he turned to our business. "Karmal *Sahib* has told me about your problem, but I would rather hear your story in person."

So I explained to *Rahbar Sahib* the whole story as I had told it to Mr. Karmal, reminding him that my brother's sister-in-law, Mahboob *jan*, had been picked up by the Ministry of Defense the night before and put in the Pul-i-Charkhi prison.

Having heard all this, *Rahbar Sahib* turned to Mr. Taroon and asked him in Pashto, "Did you know these gentlemen before?"

"No sir," replied Mr. Taroon. "I have received the honor of their acquaintanceship today."

"Very well," said *Rahbar Sahib*. "Go with them and do what they ask."

"*Ba cheshm*[109], I will," said Mr. Taroon.

We thanked *Rahbar Sahib* for issuing such a straightforward instruction and asked for his permission to leave. When we left the palace, Mr. Taroon offered us a ride home in his car. On the way home, Mr. Taroon spoke about the coup and how the Mercedes limousine he was driving belonged to Qadeer

---

[108] Light.
[109] I swear.

Nuristani, the Minister of the Interior in *Sardar* Daoud's cabinet. Qadeer Nuristani had been in the Presidential Palace when the coup began. He was severely injured and later died in the hospital.

"Where should I bring you?" he asked.

"If you could, please drop us off at my house in Wazir Akbar Khan," replied my brother. "It is closer."

On our way to Zaid's house, some of our friends and acquaintances saw us driving with Mr. Taroon in his official car. Kabul was a small city at the time, less than a million people, so us being recognized by someone was inevitable, especially when we were traveling with someone as well known as Mr. Taroon.

We got out of the car and went into Zaid's house. When we went inside, Mr. Taroon turned to Zaid. "Do you have a phone here," he asked. Zaid did. Mr. Taroon inquired about Mahboob *jan*'s full identity and then phoned the chief of the Pul-i-Charkhi prison, telling him to release Mahboob, the daughter of Dr. Siraj, as per the instructions of *Rahbar Sahib*. "Tell her to get ready, for we will come to take her home. Let me know when you do this," he added, giving Zaid's telephone number to the chief of the prison.

A few minutes later, the phone rang. It was the chief of the prison asking to speak with Mr. Taroon. After a few minutes, Mr. Taroon put down the receiver and turned to us. "The order has been implemented. However, Mahboob refused to leave prison unless her husband, Abdullah Rafiq, is also set free."

"Can you kindly have her husband released as well?" I asked Mr. Taroon. "He is a good young man."

"I have to inform *Rahbar Sahib* about it first and ask for instruction," he responded.

Mr. Taroon then picked up the receiver again and called *Rahbar Sahib*'s office, explaining everything in detail to the office manager at the Presidential Palace. About half an hour later, while Mr. Taroon was heroically talking about the coup d'état or "the revolution report" as he put it, the head of the Presidential Palace phoned back, ensuring Mr. Taroon that *Rahbar Sahib* had no objection to the release of Abdullah Rafiq, Mahboob *jan*'s husband. Mr. Taroon phoned the chief of the prison once again and communicated *Rahbar Sahib's* instructions for Abdullah Rafiq to be released along with his wife, Mahboob.

"Tell him to pack up," Mr. Taroon said. "We are coming to take him and his wife home."

But a few minutes later, the chief of the prison called Mr. Taroon to tell him that Abdullah Rafiq had also refused to leave prison unless his son and mother were also released. When Mr. Taroon told us about the demand, he added, "I will have to ask for instruction from *Rahbar Sahib* once again."

Mr. Taroon called the head of the presidential office for the second time, however, this time, Mr. Taroon could not get an immediate response from the office of the president. *Rahbar Sahib* was busy, tending to some other work at the time. So, we had to wait. An hour had passed, and now it was almost time for the government offices to close. Mr. Taroon made a final call and found out *Rahbar Sahib* was no longer around.

We were running out of time. If the release order became postponed for the next day, nobody could predict what would happen then.

"Taroon *Sahib*!" I pleaded, "I'm sure *Rahbar Sahib* wouldn't have any objection to the release of Abdullah Rafiq's mother[110] and young son. Could you use a bit of your *mardanagi*[111] and have these two people set free as well?"

Hearing the word "*mardanagi*," a large smile formed on Mr. Taroon's face. "I think you're right, Khaled *Sahib*," he said, still smiling. Then he picked up the phone and called the chief of the prison and said, "In addition to Mahboob and her husband, let her mother-in-law and son be free as well. Tell them all to get ready. We are coming now to take them home."

Zaid and Mr. Taroon left for the Pul-i-Charkhi prison to bring the four people to Zaid's home. As I had to tend to another piece of work that afternoon, I apologized for being unable to accompany them on their way to the prison. However, I promised that I'd visit the released detainees at my brother's home later on.

---

[110] Abdullah Rafiq's mother was Maimoona. She was the wife of *Sardar* Atiqullah Khan Rafiq and the sister of Humaira *Khanum*, the Queen of Afghanistan and wife of Zahir Shah.

[111] Generosity.

In the evening, I went to Zaid's house to visit his sister-in-law and her family. Fortunately, I found all of them in good health and sat with them for an hour before I left them to rest. After my own experience in prison, I knew how exhausted they must have been.

The next day after conducting my daily business, I stopped to see my cousin Najia *jan*—a granddaughter of Ghulam Nabi Khan. She was living in an apartment in the Mikrorayan neighborhood of Kabul at the time. When I called my wife to tell her I was with Najia, she picked up the receiver and asked anxiously, "Where have you been? Zaid *jan* has been looking for you all day. He called several times, asking about you. You should call him as soon as you can."

I dialed Zaid's number right away, and he also asked where I was. "I've looked for you everywhere, but I couldn't find you," he said. "Mr. Watanjar and Mr. Taroon are at my house. They say *Rahbar Sahib* wants us to pay him a visit with Mahboob *jan*. So, please hurry so we can visit His Excellency as soon as possible."

I apologized to Najia *jan* for leaving her house so urgently, and I hurriedly made my way to Zaid's place. When I entered the house, I saw a man staring and paying tribute to the pictures hanging on the walls of my brother's living room. The pictures were of my grandfather, *Sepah-Salar* Ghulam Haidar Khan, and my uncle, *Nayeb-Salar* Ghulam Nabi Khan. In the other corner of the room, Mr. Taroon was leaning against an armchair, chatting with Mahboob *jan* and the rest of the family.

As soon as the man's eyes fell on me, he spoke to me as if he knew me. "Khaled *jan,* where have you been, brother? It has been a long time that we have been looking for you, but you are nowhere to be found!"

"My sincere apologies, sir. Is there anything I can help you with?" I asked.

"*Rahbar Sahib* wants to see you two brothers along with Mahboob *jan* today," he said.

I was certain this man was high in Taraki's organization because of how he referred to him. I addressed the man as "sir" at every chance, so that it came across as if I knew him and respected him, even though I had no idea who he was.

The man continued speaking, "Unfortunately, it is too late now. Let me phone the Head of the Presidential office to confirm the meeting schedule." With that, he picked up the receiver and called the office of the President.

A few minutes later, the telephone rang. It was the Head of the President's office. "Unfortunately," he said, "*Rahbar Sahib* is busy now. But he instructed me to invite you for breakfast tomorrow morning."

"Very well," the man said. "All of us will meet here early tomorrow morning and then go to *Rahbar Sahib* together."

After they all left, I asked Zaid who he was.

"His name is Mr. Watanjar. He's the Minister of Communication," Zaid explained. "Where were you earlier?"

I told Zaid that I went to visit a cousin.

"I was worried I wouldn't be able to get a hold of you. This is a very important matter, Khaled *jan*," he said. "I'm glad you came, though."

As scheduled, I went to Zaid's place the following morning. However, Mr. Watanjar did not show up. Mr. Taroon said he had urgent business and had apologized for not being able to attend. Zaid, Mahboob, Alia, Mr. Taroon and I made our way towards *Rahbar Sahib's* place. After some time, Mr. Taraki arrived and welcomed us all warmly.

Over breakfast, *Rahbar Sahib* began praising and paying tribute to our elderly family members and ancestors. Meanwhile, he mentioned that his government had to take strict measures to maintain national security. He said that such measures were likely to create an inconvenience for some citizens, but it would ultimately prove very useful for the general public. To conclude, he addressed Mahboob *jan* directly. "I am of the opinion that you and your family should be away from the country for a while. You can return home when the security situation improves a little." He then turned to Mr. Taroon and asked him in Pashto, "How many people are they?"

"Four people, *Sahib*."

"Okay," said Mr. Taraki, "try to issue them passports and make the necessary arrangements for their departure as quickly as you can."

Zaid and I thanked His Excellency profusely for such a favor. After an hour or so, we said adieu and left for Zaid's home along with Mr. Taroon.

With Mr. Taroon's help, the passport procedures were completed for the four people with ease, and Mahboob, Maimoona, Abdullah, and his son prepared themselves to take the first flight to Tehran.

On the day of their departure, Zaid and I accompanied the family to the Kabul airport. As promised, Mr. Taroon also came to see them off. Before they left, Abdullah came to me and said, "Khaled *jan*, I owe you greatly."

At first, I didn't understand the depth of emotion in his voice, but then I thought about all the years I had languished in prison and afterward struggled to get my passport. In a flash, I remembered how it felt to suffer in that way, and I realized how great it was to relieve someone, a small family, from having to endure such a burden. It was a gift—to spare someone such misery.

"You owe me nothing, Abdullah *jan*. Go. Be free. Take care of your family and create a brighter future for them," I said. He grabbed my right hand with both of his hands, and I could see his soul speaking to me as he said, "Thank you, Khaled *jan*."

They all bade their farewells with sincere gratitude. As Abdullah's family walked to board the plane, my attention went to his young son. Only days before, he had been imprisoned unjustly, his whole world taken away from him, and now he was free. Looking at the boy, I felt like a part of me had been liberated. I left the airport with a smile on my heart.

FORTY-THREE

Although I had no relationship with any of the existing political factions and avoided talk of politics or revolution, I was acquainted with many members of the PDPA, and they trusted and respected me. Family and friends would often come to me when their loved ones were jailed during this time. Hearing of innocent men, women and children being wrongfully imprisoned deeply disturbed me, so I did what I could to leverage my associations to free the innocent.

As I received more requests from family and friends to free their loved ones, I became more acquainted with Mr. Taroon. He'd phone me often, asking how I was, and I used these phone calls as opportunities to strengthen our relationship so that I could seek his assistance later. Most often, I was able to get passports for my friends and acquaintances that, due to the growing danger, were desperate to leave Afghanistan. Mr. Taroon was warm and welcoming about my requests for my friends, instructing the passport office to issue whatever passports I asked for. He had that kind of power.

One of these friends who came to me for help with a passport was Abdul Ali Siraj, the son of *Sardar* Abdul Ghafoor Siraj. He was on the PDPA government's blacklist, both because he was from the Mohammed Zai tribe and because he had married an American woman. Doing so had automatically put him under suspicion for fraternizing with the West. With my help using Mr. Taroon's power, he was able to leave the country.

Due to the extreme governmental deterioration in Afghanistan at the time, scores of defenseless people were arbitrarily arrested and put behind bars without any trial or investigation. They languished in prisons indefinitely, treated mercilessly by the brutal prison guards.

It was a trying time for the country, but fortunately, there were moments when I could intercede on a prisoner's behalf. Two of these incidents stood out to me most.

On one Friday in 1978, Hamidullah *jan* Tarzi, the son of Habibullah Khan Tarzi went to the Pul-i-Charkhi prison with his sister Jamila *jan* Tarzi, the wife of Dr. Abdul Sattar Siraj, to visit some of their relatives in jail. Their family had close relations with *Sardar* Mohammed Wali *jan*, Daoud Khan's cousin. *Sardar* Mohammed Wali had been arrested with the rest of the surviving members of the royal family soon after the PDPA takeover.

Hamidullah and Jamila went to the prison that day as *paiwazes*, taking with them some food and clothes for their arrested relatives. However, while they were there, a riot erupted within the prison, and to bring the situation under control, the warden commanded his soldiers to move everyone into the prison cells at gunpoint, both prisoners and *paiwazes*. Hamidullah and his sister, Jamila, were among those *paiwazes* forced behind bars. Fortunately, they were able to inform Alia, Zaid's wife, about their predicament.

Alia was the second daughter of Jamila Tarzi and Dr. Abdul Sattar Siraj. As soon as she found out about the arrest of her mother and uncle, she rushed to inform me of the incident. I immediately called Mr. Taroon. The telephone operator told me he had gone to the Police Academy, so I asked him if he could have Mr. Taroon call me when he returned. I hung up and told Alia to go home to her children and that I would let her know as soon as there was any good news.

Late in the afternoon, the telephone rang. It was Mr. Taroon. "How are you Khaled *jan*?" he said, "What is the matter?"

I told him the whole story, mentioning Jamila Tarzi and her brother, Hamidullah Tarzi, and asked for his assistance.

"Give me some time," he said. "I will study the case and then let you know." He then called me after twenty minutes, saying, "I have given the names of Jamila *jan* and Hamidullah *jan* to the chief of the Pul-i-Charkhi prison and issued their release order. You needn't worry. They will be released and sent home very soon."

I called Alia *jan* immediately and gave her the good news. "They will soon be released and sent home," I assured her, quoting Mr. Taroon. I told her to relax and let me know when they arrived. It was about 10:00 p.m. when Alia called me, saying her mother and uncle to her great relief had finally arrived home.

The other incident involved the sons of La La Lakmi Chand. I had known this family for many years. They were my Hindu friends, and when their father had passed away, the sons had opened a currency exchange in Sarai Shahzada. Most of the embassies, consulates and the people of Kabul knew the sons of La La Lakmi and went to them to exchange their money. They were kind people, known by everyone for their honesty and decency.

Once, one of the sons came to me and informed me that, the week prior, his elder brother had been arrested by the government under the accusation of spying on behalf of U.S. Imperialism. "We have tried our best to find out if he is alive or dead, but we couldn't get any information. Now, I've come to ask for your help."

By now, I knew my network very well, so, I called Mr. Taroon and got an appointment for the next day at one p.m. to bring one of La La Lakmi's sons to his office, adding that I had known these men for many years and respected them as fellow businessmen.

Mr. Taroon asked the man his brother's name and said he would investigate his case. "Give me two days' time. I will look into the case to see what I can do for you." Exactly, two days later, one of La La Lakmi's sons called me, saying that his brother had been released from the prison and sent home.

In all this time, I observed that so long as Mr. Taroon was on good terms with Nur Mohammed Taraki (the head of the Khalq branch of the PDPA), he would always treat me decently, for he had seen how Mr. Taraki had welcomed me the day Babrak Karmal took me to the Palace. Because of this connection, Mr. Taroon would always help my friends and I; however, when he parted from Mr. Taraki and joined Hafizullah Amin, the then Foreign Minister, his behavior and treatment towards me drastically changed.

On a blazing summer day in 1978, Qudsia and Mahjooba, the young girls of Mr. Kareemi, came to my house quite unexpectedly. They told me of the recent arrest of their father due to a cleared murder case from five years before. I knew the case they were speaking of as Mr. Kareemi had already told me about it, when it had happened.

A young boy of family friends had come to Mr. Kareemi's house for a visit. While there, the young boy started playing with a revolver, unaware that it was loaded. The gun suddenly fired and killed the boy. However, because it was an accident, the then government had acquitted Mr. Kareemi of the matter. "Apparently," the girls told me, "a relative of the victim, who is linked with Mr. Jalalar, the Minister of Commerce—an important PDPA member—has filed a new complaint against him. As a result, our father has been thrown in jail."

They added that Mr. Taroon not only did not listen to their complaints, but he also forced them out of his office, calling them bad names. These girls were shocked by his treatment towards them and asked for my help.

I was also shocked by the description of Mr. Taroon's behavior and agreed to help. I phoned Mr. Taroon right away and told him I wanted to meet him if he had time. He accepted my request on the spot.

"What time would be fine, sir?" I asked.

"Right now, Khaled *Sahib*."

I tried to calm Qudsia and Mahjooba a little and told them not to worry.

Alas, I was utterly disappointed by Mr. Taroon this time. He was not the same man I knew. When I entered his office, he treated me very formally, sitting on his revolving chair and turning from side to side, talking arrogantly to the police officers and other applicants. At last, he turned to me and asked, "What do you want?"

I mentioned Mohammed Hassan Kareemi and began talking about his innocence. He interrupted me. "I wonder how well-connected he is!" he said. He then asked me very formally not to interfere in such matters anymore.

When I heard these words from him, I did not insist, for I feared he would dishonor me the way I heard he had done to others. "Please, excuse me," I left without saying goodbye and walked out of Mr. Taroon's office and never phoned him again. He did not contact me again either.

FORTY-FOUR

Throughout the time I helped free innocent people from unjust imprisonment, I was focused on a plan to get my own family out of Afghanistan. Times in Afghanistan were getting more dangerous. People were "mysteriously disappearing" by the hundreds, probably thousands. The country lost some of its best and brightest during that time. One of my best friends, Nainawaz, a talented singer and composer, was one of them. The widely popular and talented Ahmad Zahir was another victim. His mysterious assassination, called a "traffic accident" by Radio Afghanistan, shocked the nation with grief. With secret service eavesdropping in conversations and more mysterious deaths, I knew we had to leave as soon as possible.

Fortunately, Bereshkai was already living in New York with her husband, and Farid and Homa were taking college courses in Germany. Farid was in Krefeld, and Homa was studying in Berlin, where she stayed with Parwin. They were all safe. That left my wife, Siddiq, and myself in Kabul.

I devised a plan whereby Parwin's husband, Mr. Ansari, would accompany my wife to Saudi Arabia. She had always wanted to go to *hajj*, so I got her a passport for that purpose and told her, when she completed her pilgrimage, to go from Saudi Arabia directly to Germany to stay with Farid. Now, it came down to Siddiq and me.

It was now September of 1979. Mr. Amin was the Minister of Foreign Affairs and the only person who could approve passports. Anyone wishing to get one would have to write an application to him and await a positive response. Therefore, any individual or family member who wanted to go abroad had to carve out a reason (whether true or false) to convince the minister that their leaving Afghanistan was justified.

In my case, I wrote an application to the Minister of Foreign Affairs, attaching my brother Dastgir's documents, consisting of his will and a power of attorney. I explained that the reason for my trip to Germany was to sort out some of the inheritance issues of my late brother. On the scheduled date, I submitted my application along with the relevant attachments to Mr. Amin's office. I thought my result would be positive for sure. However, when I got my papers back the next day, I saw a line at the end of my application, written by the Foreign Minister. It read:

> Directorate of Foreign Affairs shall process the inheritance issues through the Afghan embassy in Bonn, Germany.

No...I need to find another way, I thought. Nevertheless, according to the instruction, I was forced to submit my brother's documents to the Directorate of Foreign Affairs and wait for word from the Afghan Embassy in Bonn. So, a few days later, I returned to the Directorate of Foreign Affairs to see what had happened to my documents. In response to the letter from the Directorate of Foreign Affairs, the Afghan Embassy in Bonn sent a two-page form for me to fill out and sign. However, I did not sign the form immediately. Instead, I asked the director if I could take it home to study it and fill it out more thoroughly.

He said he had no objection. "Yes, it's yours."

I took my papers and left the department, deciding never to return them. Instead, I thought of another solution. Of late, a friend of mine had introduced me to Mr. Hadi Mukammil, the Administrative Deputy of the Ministry of Foreign Affairs. He would come to my place once every fortnight. He was very kind to me. I also respected him dearly.

During one of his visits, Mr. Mukammil had brought his son and two young nephews with him, further showing his sincerity. That evening, Mr. Mukammil told the young boys, "Tonight, I have brought you to the house of a person whose fathers and ancestors have shaped a major part of Afghan history. Try to be close to them to know more about their family." Then, he stood up and showed them the pictures of my grandfather and uncles hanging on the wall, introducing the men in the photos to the boys and speaking of my ancestors with reverence.

As far as I knew, Mr. Mukammil was a kind-hearted man with a laudable character. I could feel his affection and kindness was sincere. So one day, I shared my thought with him, saying, "In order to get around to a bit of my personal business, I would like to travel to Germany, but for this, I need a passport." I did not tell him anything about my first attempt at the Ministry of Foreign Affairs.

Mr. Mukammil laughed saying, "Looks like you are leaving us."

"No, sir! I will return once I am done with my work."

"Very well," said Mr. Mukammil in a more serious tone. "You should write an application to the Ministry of Foreign Affairs and bring it to me tomorrow. I promise I will get your application signed by His Excellency. But you must commit that you will return home when your work is finished."

The following day, I went to the office of the administrative deputy and presented my application. Having reviewed it thoroughly, Mr. Mukammil said, "I will phone you this afternoon."

Holding to his word, he called me later that day and told me to pay him a visit if I had time, for he had gotten my application approved by the Minister of Foreign Affairs. When I saw him that same afternoon, Mr. Mukammil stood up and handed me my application, at the bottom of which Mr. Amin, the Minister of Foreign Affairs, had signed and written a single Farsi word, *berawad*[112].

I finally had my passport. Now I needed to find a solution for my son, Siddiq. The Afghan army was drafting any man 21 years or older into the military, and Siddiq was 21. I knew this would be an obstacle. I decided not to ask for my son Siddiq to be granted a passport. Surely, the officials would know that we were planning to escape. We had to be very careful about these matters and not complicate matters for both us. Fortunately, Zaid was still in Kabul at the time, staying with me. I asked him to devise a plan for Siddiq's departure, and he agreed.

With that, I packed a suitcase, two suits, and two books and left for Germany.

---

[112] He can go.

FORTY-FIVE

I arrived in Germany in 1979 to cheerful embraces from my wife, Habiba, and my children, Homa, Farid and his fiancée, Petra. We stayed with Petra as we waited for Siddiq to join us. During those weeks, Siddiq wrote me letters without giving me too many details. With the PDPA likely going through correspondence, it was safer to keep conversations simple. Still, by receiving his letters, I knew he was alive. Unfortunately, I knew he was still in Kabul, and that concerned me.

During that time, I learned that Mr. Taraki had been abroad to participate in a conference for communist countries in Cuba. On his way back home, he visited Leonid Brezhnev in Moscow. When Mr. Taraki returned to Afghanistan, Hafizullah Amin immediately killed him and proclaimed himself Head of the PDPA government. As I expected, it wasn't long before the Soviet Army marched into Afghanistan. Mr. Amin was then killed and succeeded by Babrak Karmal, who became the General Secretary and Head of the PDPA government. From then on, the atrocities against the Afghan people by the government only worsened.

Fortunately, my son Siddiq made it to Berlin, just as the war in Afghanistan was getting started. The night he arrived, my wife prepared a feast for us all. Together, we enjoyed a family reunion with aushak[113], kabuli

---

[113] Afghan dish made of pasta dumplings filled with scallion, with a (frequently meaty) tomato sauce, topped with yogurt and dried mint.

palaw[114], borani banjan[115] and other traditional Afghan food. "This was exactly what I needed after all the stress and travel to get here," said Siddiq. "Mother's cooking."

We laughed, grateful to be safe together again. The following morning after breakfast, I took Siddiq on a walk around Thielpark. As we walked down the same road I used to walk with my father, I asked Siddiq if anybody bothered him while he was still in Kabul.

"No, father. I was able to escape with the help of uncle Zaid and Ahmad Wali. Since the government wanted to draft all men 21 or older, I had to get a fake I.D. We tried other options for a few months, but none of them worked. Some of my friends escaped through Pakistan, but that was very risky. I heard many stories of people being caught and imprisoned or killed, so I didn't want to take that chance, and neither did uncle Zaid. So, uncle Zaid bought me a fake I.D. for 20,000 Afghani," said Siddiq.

"What happened while you were still there?" I asked.

"It's very terrible, father. Many people are dying or 'disappearing.' There were tanks in every intersection and jeeps filled with Soviet soldiers and more soldiers standing guard beside them. There's no safety. There's no privacy. The sounds of gunfire and bombs can be heard throughout the day. It's a terrible mess, father."

I felt disheartened. *How could a country with so much potential crumble like that?* I thought about all the things my father would tell me when we would take this same walk—all the stories of what he and his brother had accomplished with King Amanullah and their vision for where the country was headed. *What a shame*, I thought. I looked over to see Siddiq staring out at the pond. We took a seat on the bench, and I put my arm around him. "I'm thankful to God that you're safe and that you're here."

"Me too, Father," he replied.

As we looked out at the pond, we got lost in a random conversation about life, filled with laughter and fun reminiscence. Next thing we knew, two hours

---

[114] An Afghan dish consisting of steamed rice mixed with raisins, carrots, and lamb.
[115] An Afghan dish consisting of cooked eggplant with yogurt, tomato sauce, and spices.

had passed. As we began to make our way back to the apartment, I felt as if my father was beside me, watching my son and I bond together. I walked on the left side of Siddiq, just as my father did with me, and got lost for a moment, thinking about the circle of life.

We had returned to the place where my father had made a new life for himself. For the first time in our lives, we were living in a country that didn't oppress us or hold an inexplicable grudge against us. The Charkhi name was no longer something we had to fear of speaking in public, but rather a source of pride. I looked up to the sky knowing a brighter future lay ahead for my family. After 47 years, we were finally free.

EPILOGUE

During the time I was in Berlin, I still had some family members in Kabul. My cousin, Azim, was there. He died in 1982 during one of his seizure episodes. My brother, Ghaffar, was there as well. With the war going on, it was impossible to communicate with him. I didn't see or hear from him for years until we finally reunited in San Francisco in 1985. By then, I had started a new life in Hamburg, running an import/export business and the Hotel Phoenix.

Ever since I left Afghanistan, I thought about when I'd move back there. I waited for the opportunity when things would turn around. Unfortunately, they never did. Over the decades, I watched and listened as Afghanistan crumbled from the destruction wrought by the Soviet Union and later the Taliban.

Disappointed, I often pondered how life in Afghanistan would've turned out if King Amanullah's plan had been allowed to go through…if Nadir Shah had never betrayed him and my family. Remembering the conversations I had with my father around Thielpark, I envisioned an Afghanistan that was thriving and collaborating with the world. Unfortunately, this was far from the reality.

Eventually, in the spring of 2000, I left Hamburg for California to be closer to my son, Siddiq, and my grandchildren—Adam, Abeal, and Eve. In 2002, I suffered a stroke and a heart attack. I made a strong recovery, and afterward, made a few trips to Afghanistan. I visited Charkh and paid respects at the grave of my grandfather, Ghulam Haidar Khan Charkhi. Ghaffar and

I were attempting to restore our properties, hopeful that with a change in government we'd finally see progress. The new regime repetitively said they were working on it, but unfortunately, it was more empty promises. To this day, it's been 85 years and my family has still not had our properties reinstated.

In October of 2009, my beloved wife Habiba died. She had Alzheimer's, and her organs weren't functioning well. She had been with me through it all, from the first day we were imprisoned when Ghulam Nabi Khan's body was brought to our home, through the tough times in Sarai Badam and Sarai Ali Khan, through the house imprisonment in Qala-e-Futuh, through starting a family and building a life, through escaping the country and starting a new life in Germany, and through raising our grandchildren. Habiba was an angel. It's no wonder she was the daughter of Ku Ku *jan*, for she too approached life with perseverance and optimism.

Shortly after my wife's death, my grandson Adam approached me. He was curious to learn more about my life story. He wanted to know all that had happened. I had written a memoir about my life in Farsi, covering these stories and the history, titled "From My Memories." I told Adam to wait until I had it translated into English. When that day finally came, he was disappointed. "In the translation from Farsi to English, all the emotion and life has left the story," he told me. "I want to write your story in English." I agreed to let him.

Although this book only contains a fraction of my memories, it carries the spirit of my family. I hope that through reading our journey, you've gained more faith in the resilience of your soul.

The women and children of our family who languished in Sarai Badam, Sarai Ali Khan and Qala Cha prisons:

1. Wazir Begum, nicknamed Shirin Bi Bi (Ghulam Nabi Khan's wife)
2. Mariam, nicknamed as Ku Ku *jan* (Ghulam Nabi Khan's wife)
3. Bi Bi *jan* (Padsha Khan's sister and Ghulam Nabi Khan's wife)
4. Shah Bi Bi (Asil Khan's sister and Ghulam Nabi Khan's wife)
5. Mah Parwar, nicknamed Shah Bi Bi (Ghulam Jailani Khan's wife)
6. Gulshah, nicknamed Shirin Bu Bu (Abdul Aziz Khan's wife)
7. Hajira, nicknamed Shirin Gul (Abdul Aziz Khan's wife)
8. Mirman, nicknamed Ku Ku Gul (Ghulam Siddiq Khan's wife)
9. Shah Gul, nicknamed Bi Bi Gul (Ghulam Siddiq Khan's wife)
10. Ayesha (Ghulam Nabi Khan's daughter and Ghulam Safdar Khan's wife)
11. Khadija (Ghulam Nabi Khan's daughter)
12. Azra (Ghulam Nabi Khan's daughter)
13. Habiba (Ghulam Nabi Khan's daughter)
14. Najia (Ghulam Nabi Khan's granddaughter)
15. Kubra (Ghulam Jailani Khan's daughter)
16. Zubaida (Ghulam Jailani Khan's daughter)
17. Saliha (Ghulam Jailani Khan's daughter)
18. Razia (Ghulam Jailani Khan's daughter)
19. Maliha (Ghulam Jailani Khan's daughter)
20. Rabia (Ghulam Jailani Khan's daughter)
21. Abdul Hamid (Abdul Aziz Khan's son)
22. Abdul Habib (Abdul Aziz Khan's son)
23. Aziza (Abdul Aziz Khan's daughter)
24. Abdul Azim (Abdul Aziz Khan's son)
25. Siddiqa (Ghulam Siddiq Khan's daughter)
26. Mastoora (Ghulam Siddiq Khan's daughter)
27. Abdul Samad (Ghulam Siddiq Khan's son)
28. Abdul Ghaffar (Ghulam Siddiq Khan's son)
29. Ghulam Dastgir (Ghulam Siddiq Khan's son)
30. Khaled (Ghulam Siddiq Khan's son)

31. Bigum (Ghulam Anwar Khan's wife)

32. Guhar, nicknamed Shirin *jan* (Mir Enyatullah Khan's wife)

33. Mamy (Mir Enyatullah Khan's mother-in-law)

34. Bahrawar (Ghulam Anwar Khan's daughter)

35. Ubaidullah (Ghulam Anwar Khan's son)

36. Sharifa (Ghulam Anwar Khan's daughter)

37. Tahira (Ghulam Anwar Khan's daughter)

38. Apa Gul (housemaid)

39. Ju Ju (housemaid)

40. Riza Gol (housemaid)

41. Janu (attendant)

42. Zan-e-Malang (housemaid)

43. Khanum (housemaid)

44. Gul Shirin (Janbaz Khan's wife)

45. Hawa (Janbaz Khan's wife)

46. Khadija (Janbaz Khan's daughter)

47. Amina (Janbaz Khan's daughter)

48. Yahya (Janbaz Khan's son)

49. Abdul Rahman (Janbaz Khan's son)

50. Abdul Qadir (Janbaz Khan's son)

51. Janatoo (Mohammad Alam Khan's wife, the son of Janbaz Khan)

52. Mohammad Aman (Mohammad Alam Khan's son)

53. Bu Bu (Janbaz Khan's mother)

54. Gulnaz (Abdul Khaliq's aunt in Qala Cha prison)

55. Haifza (Abdul Khaliq's sister in Qala Cha prison)

Our male family members who languished in various prisons across Afghanistan:

1. *Nayeb-Salar* Janbaz Khan Charkhi (passed away in the hospital of Dehmazang after languishing for 14 years in the Arg)
2. Mohammad Omar Khan Charkhi, brother of Janbaz Khan (imprisoned for 14 years in the Arg)
3. Mohammad Usman Khan Charkhi, brother of Janbaz Khan (imprisoned for 14 years in the Arg)
4. Peer Mohammad Khan, Janbaz Khan's son (imprisoned for 14 years in the Arg)
5. Mohammed Alam Khan, Janbaz Khan's son (imprisoned for 14 years in the Arg)
6. Abdul Rahman, Janbaz Khan's son (imprisoned for 14 years between Sarai Badam, Sarai Ali Jhan, and the Arg)
7. Yahya, Janbaz Khan's son (passed away in the hospital of Dehmazang after being imprisoned for 14 years in the Arg)
8. Abdussalam Khan, cousin of Ghulam Nabi Khan (passed away in the Arg)
9. Ziauddin Khan (passed away in the Arg)
10. Khalifa Naseem Khan (passed away in the Arg)
11. Din Mohammed Khan (passed away in the Arg)
12. Ghulam Siddiq Khan, my father's cousin (imprisoned for 14 years in Tawqif Khana prison)
13. Ghulam Ghaws Khan, my father's cousin (imprisoned for 14 years in Tawqif Khana prison)
14. Engineer Shir Mohammed Khan, graduate from Germany and my aunt's husband (passed away in Sarai Moti prison)
15. Mirza Noor Mohammed Khan, Shir Mohammed Khan's brother
16. Mohammed Omar Khan, known as Tata, my mother's cousin (imprisoned for 14 years in the Arg)
17. Mohammed Amin Khan, my mother's cousin (imprisoned for 14 years in the Arg)

18. Ghulam Anwar Khan, my father's cousin (imprisoned for 14 years in the Arg and Dehmazang)

19. Ghulam Mahboob Khan, my father's cousin (imprisoned for 14 years in the Arg and Dehmazang)

20. Ubaidullah, son of Ghulam Anwar Khan (imprisoned for 14 years between the Arg, Sarai Badam, Sarai Ali Khan, and Dehmazang)

21. Mir Enyatullah Khan (imprisoned for 14 years in the Arg and Dehmazang)

22. Abdullah, son of Mawladad Khan who was the uncle of Abdul Khaliq (passed away in Dehmazang)

23. Abdurrahman, son of Abdul Khaliq's uncle (passed away in Dehmazang)

24. Ata Mohammed, son of Abdul Khaliq's maternal aunt (imprisoned for 14 years in Dehmazang)

25. Khaja Mohammed, our former attendant (imprisoned for 14 years in Dehmazang)

26. Mohammed Ayub Khan, my uncle (imprisoned for 14 years in the Arg and Dehmazang)

27. Mohammed Ismael, son of Khalifa Naseem Khan (imprisoned for 14 years in Dehmazang)

28. Mohammed Yaqoob Khan, Minister of the Royal Court under King Amanullah Khan and my uncle (imprisoned in the Arg for one year and then exiled along with his family from Afghanistan)

29. Mohammed Sami Khan, Governor and Security Commander of Kabul under King Amanullah Khan (imprisoned in the Arg for one year and then exiled along with his family from Afghanistan)

30. Abdul Samad, my brother (imprisoned in Sarai Badam, Sarai Ali Khan, and later passed away in Dehmazang)

31. Abdul Ghaffar, my brother (imprisoned for 14 years in Sarai Badam, Sarai Ali Khan, and Dehmazang)

32. Ghulam Dastgir, my brother (imprisoned for 14 years in Sarai Badam, Sarai Ali Khan, and Dehmazang)

33. Abdul Azim, my cousin (imprisoned for 14 years in Sarai Badam, Sarai Ali Khan and Dehmazang)

34. Khaled, myself (imprisoned for 14 years in Sarai Badam, Sarai Ali Khan and Dehmazang)

GRATITUDE

I'd like to thank everybody who supported me throughout this journey. Writing *Shackled* was an intensely emotional process full of frustration, heartbreak, and ultimately, honor, and I could not have done it alone.

First and foremost, I want to thank my hero – my grandfather. Baba *jan*, you have taught me so much. Just from observing your life, I've learned optimism, enthusiasm, love, kindness, and gratitude. I'm beyond honored to have had the privilege to write your story. The time we spent bonding while drafting the manuscript was a priceless experience I will forever hold dear to my heart.

Secondly, I want to thank my family, especially my father Siddiq, my cousin Nadia, and my aunt Bereshkai (or Ama B). Dad, thank you for supporting me from the very beginning of this process, and throughout my life. Nadia, thank you for all the hours of proofreading that you managed to squeeze into your free time. Your support and encouragement were fundamental in bringing this book to life. Ama B, thank you for helping me locate many of the technical details so crucial to this story, and for being a huge support.

Thirdly, I want to thank Donny and Jackie Epstein. Your love, support, and care for my family supported my grandpa and me throughout this process. Donny, thank you for your teachings on epi-energetics and for the transformational experiences my family and I have been able to experience at your programs. They've played a significant role in the sacred nature of this book.

Fourthly, I want to thank my editor, Dustin Schwindt. Dustin, your edits helped me bring more life to this book, along with a clean and necessary polish. Your support and willingness to go the extra mile is greatly appreciated.

Fifthly, I want to thank my book interior designer, Jason Anderson, and my book cover designer, Anne Laborde. Jason, you did an amazing job. Anne, you designed a beautiful cover. Thank you both for your hard work and support.

Lastly, I'd like to thank my ancestors. Although I've never met any of you, I feel a profound connection to you, and I felt your sacred presence throughout the process of writing this book. Thank you and bless you all.